WHY FAMILIES MOVE

PETER H. ROSSI
Preface by W. A.V. CLARK

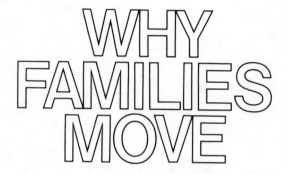

WHY
FAMILIES
MOVE

2nd edition

 SAGE PUBLICATIONS   Beverly Hills   London

For information address:

SAGE Publications, Inc.
275 South Beverly Drive
Beverly Hills, California 90212

SAGE Publications Ltd
28 Banner Street
London EC1Y 8QE, England

Printed in the United States of America

Library of Congress Cataloging in Publication Data

Rossi, Peter Henry, 1921-
   Why families move.

   Bibliography: p.
   1. Residential mobility.   2. Residential mobility
—United States.   I. Title.
HD7287.5.R6   1980   307'.2   79-25370
ISBN 0-8039-1348-6
ISBN 0-8039-1349-4 pbk.

FIRST PRINTING

CONTENTS

PART V: CONCLUSIONS

To Alice, my complement and tender comrade

PREFACE:
LOOKING BACK AT
WHY FAMILIES MOVE

Within the now substantial body of research which is focused on residential mobility and on the housing adjustments of families in cities, there is no work which is more frequently cited than Peter Rossi's study *Why Families Move*. But more significant than the fact that this volume is frequently cited is the wide range of research which can be identified as stemming from this original and seminal work. It is quite possible that when the original study was written and published, the long-term implications of research on mobility were not clear and that its initial publication was perhaps slighted in the changing emphases in social science research in the late 1950s. There is no doubt, however, that as individuals were stimulated to address specific questions concerning the dynamics of the city system, that the Rossi volume was found to provide clues and stimuli for social science investigators. With the publication of this new edition, it is appropriate to ask why the Rossi volume was so important in stimulating research in residential mobility specifically and in the patterns of residential relocation and redistribution generally.

As I have suggested in my introductory comments, the Rossi volume did more than merely bring attention to studies of residential mobility. It combined empirical research with the development of interesting concepts and focused attention on social issues, economic change, and spatial patterns. Moreover, the book successfully integrated two of the three broad traditions which were increasingly important in all social science investigations in the postwar years. The Rossi volume successfully shifted the emphasis from aggregate pattern analysis to a focus on the individual household and an emphasis on explanatory concepts drawn from psychology and social psychology (parenthetically it is useful to reiterate that the full title of the original work is *Why Families Move: A Study in the Social Psychology of Urban Residential Mobility*). It remained for another study (Goldstein, 1954) to take up a third important tradition—the emphasis on dynamic longitudinal studies rather than cross-sectional analyses. The Rossi volume, then, addressed two of the three continuing focuses in studies of residential mobility: individual analyses and the behavioral implications of those analyses. In the sense that the Rossi volume emphasized both individual households and the relationship of those households to their communities, it was truly a transition study from the earlier emphasis on simple analyses of the origins and destinations of migrants.

While these comments set the Rossi volume in the wider social science context, it is the specific contributions of conceptual and empirical analyses which stimulated so much research in residential mobility or intraurban migration. Specifically, the research reported in *Why Families Move* emphasized the interconnection between mobility and neighborhoods and mobility as a specific phenomenon of the housing market. In fact, as Rossi notes in his new introduction to the present edition, it was his attempt to link mobility and housing that sociologists found most objectionable and which was responsible for the original unenthusiastic reception. However, with the passage of years and the mobility and housing research of economists and geographers, the significance of the link between mobility and housing is now taken for granted. Although more recent work has questioned the power of the life-cycle explanation of mobility, there is no doubt that it was a major contribution of *Why Families Move*. The family life cycle further emphasizes the link between housing and mobility.

It is not possible (or necessary) to review the concepts used in *Why Families Move*. It is sufficient to emphasize its contribution to mobility research as a whole and the specific stimulus to research on stress and dissatisfaction which have been extended by Brown and Moore (1970), Speare et al. (1975), and Quigley and Weinberg (1977); neighborhood transition and environmental choice elaborated by Leven et al. (1976), Michelson (1977), and Moore (1978); and to residential choice as in the national survey reported by Butler et al. (1969). In addition, even the research which is focused on the mathematical modeling of mobility and migration partially draws on the concepts outlined in *Why Families Move*. In several cases, the authors support their arguments about family composition with explicit or implicit references to the Rossi volume (Ginsberg, 1972). Also, recent investigations of information and its role in residential mobility have utilized at least elementary observations drawn from *Why Families Move* (Clark and Smith, 1979).

Of course, it is easy to say that almost any research in mobility can be traced to the Rossi volume and that this is nothing more than a comment on the fact that the volume was one of the first in the field of mobility studies. But, at least in my mind, there is no doubt that most research scholars are paying more than lip service to the Rossi volume in their citations. For example, even in the case of the complex modeling of duration of stay in mobility and the interplay of cumulative inertia and dissatisfaction, there is no question but that the life cycle is a critical parameter of these models. Similarly, the work on a family's housing adjustment and the importance of housing space as a motivational force can be traced to comments in the Rossi research. As I have already argued, Rossi emphasized the link between mobility and neighborhoods even though he was not able to formalize the interesting descriptive notions he outlined in the introduction to the book. It is only in the emphasis on longitudinal data and accounting frameworks (Gale and Moore, 1975; Moore and Clatworthy, 1978) that we find research thrusts which cannot be traced directly to the stimulus of the research of the Rossi volume. This, then, is a truly remarkable contribution to the development of a field of study.

Although *Why Families Move* touches upon the policy implications of mobility, this is one topic which was only partially developed in the book and the link between mobility and policy has been only incompletely explored since the book was published. Such a link may be so elusive as to never be established, but recent research on the Housing Allowance Experiments and the Community Block Development Grants has reiterated the need for some understanding of the relationship between programs and outcomes in the urban space. As yet, it is not at all clear in what way mobility is of importance to urban policy. Certainly, the implications of the housing allowance experiment suggests that mobility is not at center stage. We are left with the original Rossi comment:

How do these dramatic changes in residential areas come about? In part, industry and commerce in their expansion encroach upon land used for residences. But, in larger part, the changes are mass movements of families—the end results of countless thousands of residence shifts made by urban Americans every year. Compounded in the mass, the residence shifts of urban households produce most of the change and flux of urban population structures [1955: 1].

This notion of the link between mobility and neighborhood change with wider implications for policy has remained one of the significant reasons cited for studying residential mobility. As Rossi notes in his new introduction to the present volume: "The links between mobility and policy, the links between mobility and neighborhood change, are not spelled out in any of the research on residential mobility." Most research on residential mobility is still divorced from the larger context within which it has taken place. This is obviously a research agenda of some significance.

It is not to say that there have been no critical evaluations of *Why Families Move*. The survey design has been criticized as narrowly focused, as indeed it was on a very selected set of tracts in Philadelphia. The role of the life cycle has been criticized as an excessively general conceptual structure for the explanation of residential mobility and the use of an index of dissatisfaction and its link with mobility has been criticized as a truism. But despite these critical comments, *Why Families Move* can still be identified as one of the major contributions to the study of intraurban migration. It has been and will continue to be basic reading for all students in residential mobility, even though the research thrusts have gone well beyond the initial study. It is a basic resource which summarizes much of the initial thinking in residential mobility and will continue to be studied in the coming years. As a book which was originally designed as a report on an empirical study, it has made a lasting contribution at both the empirical and conceptual levels to the study of intraurban migration.

—W.A.V. Clark
Los Angeles

Los Angeles, California

REFERENCES

BROWN, L. and E. G. MOORE (1970) "The intraurban migration process: a perspective." Geografiska Annaler Series B, 52: 1-13.

BUTLER, E. W., et al. (1969) Moving Behavior and Residential Choice: A National Survey (National Cooperative Highway Research Program, Report 81). Washington, DC: Highway Research Board.

CLARK, W.A.V. and T. R. SMITH (1979) "Modelling information use in a spatial context. Annals of the Association American Geographers 69: 410-420.

GALE, S. and E. G. MOORE (1975) "Urban information systems and the analysis of residential change" (Working Paper 17). Philadelphia: University of Pennsylvania.

GINSBERG, R. (1972) "Critique of probabilistic models: application of the semi-Markov model to migration." Journal of Mathematical Sociology 2: 63-82.

GOLDSTEIN, S. (1954) Patterns of Mobility, 1910-1950: The Norristown Study. Philadelphia: University of Pennsylvania Press.

LEVEN, C., J. LITTLE, H. NOURSE, and R. READ (1976) Neighborhood Change: Lessons in the Dynamics of Urban Decay. Cambridge, MA: Ballinger.

MICHELSON, W. (1977) Environmental Choice, Human Behavior and Residential Satisfaction. New York: Oxford University Press.

MOORE, E. G. (1978) "The impact of residential mobility on population characteristics at the neighborhood level" pp. 151-181 in W.A.V. Clark and E. G. Moore (eds.), Population Mobility and Residential Change. Evanston, IL: Northwestern University Press.

——— and S. CLATWORTHY (1978) "The role of urban data systems in the analysis of housing issues," in L. S. Bourne and J. Hitchcock (eds.), Urban Housing Markets: Recent Directions in Research and Policy. Toronto: University of Toronto Press.

QUIGLEY, T. and D. WEINBERG (1977) "Intra-metropolitan residential mobility: a review and synthesis." International Regional Science Review 2: 41-66.

ROSSI, P. (1955) Why Families Move: A Study in the Social Psychology of Urban Residential Mobility. New York: Macmillan.

SPEARE, A., S. GOLDSTEIN, and W. FREY (1975) Residential Mobility, Migration and Metropolitan Change. Cambridge, MA: Ballinger.

INTRODUCTION TO
THE SECOND EDITION

Each for its own reasons, the study of residential mobility has been a concern of three disciplines: sociology, economics, and geography. For the economist, residential shifts provide a means for studying the housing and land markets. Geographers study mobility to understand the spatial distributions of population types. For the sociologist, interest in residential mobility has two sources: one stemming from the study of human ecology and the other, from a concern with the peculiar qualities of urban life. Of course, these are clearly overlapping concerns and it is often difficult to discern the disciplinary origins of a researcher by solely examining the kinds of questions he or she raises about mobility although it is usually easier to identify a researcher's discipline by noting the methods used and the concepts employed.

Urban mobility first appears in the sociological literature as a term expressing rather generalized qualities of urban, as opposed to nonurban, life. In his classic essay "The metropolis and mental life," Simmel (1950) refers to the mobility of the city as the considerable sum of myriad and incessant sources of stimulation impinging upon the urban dweller, a sort of sensory overload which produces sophistication, indifference, and a lowered level of affect in urban dwellers. There is simply so much to experience that the urban dweller's capacity is reduced to react in a "spontaneous" and "natural" way to urban existence. This theme is picked up in Wirth's (1964) essay, "Urbanism as a way of life," a statement that is still providing grist for urban sociologists. It is mobility in this sense that produces some of the special qualities of urban life, according to the Simmelian formulation, qualities which, on the one hand, appeal to migrants as an escape from the dullness and oppression of rural existence with its lack of change and stimulation— "Staatsluft mach man frei"—and, on the other hand, produces anomie and alienation in a society where men see each other primarily as means to ends rather than as ends in themselves. Of course, mobility in this larger sense of sensory overload is not a concept which lends itself easily to measurement, especially since it is a macrosystem property.

It is not at all surprising therefore that when American sociologists turned to empirical research under the influence of Park (1967) that the concept of mobility as initially stated by Simmel and adapted by Wirth becomes diluted, turning into residential mobility.[1] Thus, in some of the classical studies of the Chicago "ecological" school, residential mobility expressed as rates of moving within small areas becomes an importnat explanatory variable in analyzing the distribution of small area rates of admissions to mental hospitals (Faris and Dunham, 1939), juvenile delinquency rates (Shaw and McKay, 1942), homicides and suicide rates (Henry and Short, 1954), and other "pathologies." Residential shifting is regarded in the same way as mobility in the larger sense with the same consequences. High residential mobility within an area leads to higher incidences of social pathologies of all sorts.

For individuals and families, excessive residential shifts would also produce untoward effects, at minimum, increasing isolation and loneliness, at maximum, leading to individual pathological conditions.[2]

Another strain in American sociology looked at residential mobility from another perspective, as a process of population redistribution. Thus, Stouffer's (1940) theory of intervening opportunities was first tested using data on intertract movements in Cleveland that Green (1934) collected. Other studies sought the characteristics of small areas that varied in their mobility rates or characteristics of households and individuals who were movers.

The initial impetus for *Why Families Move* came more out of the first than the second strain in the American sociology of the 1940s. The proposal— written by Robert K. Merton and jointly submitted by the Bureau of Applied Social Research and The Institute for Urban Land Use and Housing Studies both of Columbia University—stressed the aim of the study as an understanding of why residential mobility would contribute to efforts to stabilize neighborhoods and to increase the well-being of households (presumably by decreasing their mobility). The original study prospectus stressed such objectives as determining the effects of moving on neighborhood friendship ties and satisfaction with what we would currently call "quality of life." It would seek to meet public policy information needs by providing data on what families sought in their seemingly restless searches for new housing and new neighborhood environments, hopefully presenting to planners and policy makers a recipe for building neighborhoods of stability inhabited by satisfied and integrated households.

For some reason, the research branch of the Housing and Home Finance Agency funded the proposal. Although I was merely a senior graduate student and a research assistant at Columbia's Bureau of Applied Social Research, I was hired (apparently *faute de mieux*) as Project Director. I remember hesitating whether I should accept the offer, since I had yet to finish my dissertation and had tentatively agreed to take an assistant professorship in the then-newly refurbished Berkeley Department of Sociology. I decided in favor of taking up Merton's offer, partly because he was so persuasive but also because I wanted to have an opportunity to run a research project on my own. So I postponed working on my dissertation and plunged into the study of residential mobility.

It is difficult to recall when the themes first arose that eventually dominated the monograph. I am sure that they were not present at the start. The project started out as an investigation of the pathological effects of residential shifting, very much "normal science" of the urban sociology of its day. In the shift to the perspectives that eventually arose, I know I was very much influenced by the housing and land economists at Columbia's Institute for Urban Land Use and Housing Studies, particularly Ernest M. Fisher and Chester Rapkin. With great patience they both stressed that moving was about housing and that residential mobility could be looked upon as a phenomenon of the housing market. Of course, there was another impetus for adopting this viewpoint: A careful examination of the literature indicated there was very little evidence for negative effects of mobility. And, when the data began to be analyzed from our own project, it was also clear that there simply were few signs of stressful negative consequences of residential mobility. Indeed, if anything, the data supported the contrary, since those who moved ended up more content than those who did not, *ceteris paribus.* While there may be "pathological" movers whose excessive residential mobility either expressed or resulted in pathology, it was impossible to discern any such among the 924 families studied in Philadelphia.[3]

The end result of my confrontation with the data and its messages plus the urging of the urban land economists and planners at the institute was to arrive at an interpretation of residential mobility as involving primarily the interplay between a household's housing needs and the physical structure it occupied: Residential mobility was finally interpreted as a phenomenon of the housing market (1) driven by autochthonous changes that take place as families and households form, grow, and decline in size and eventually disolve and (1) conditioned by income and the housing opportunities presented by the local housing markets.

Whether this was a new interpretation for all relevant social science fields at the time is, of course, difficult to tell. What I do know is that the monograph was received with a distressing lack of enthusiasm from my sociological colleagues. One review berated me for turning into the "Kinsey of the moving industry." Another stressed the "fact" that we all "knew" that residential mobility was mainly a manifestation of social mobility and hence that my monograph was simply all wrong. Still another had very strongly negative reactions to the use of complicated statistical presentations. (In fact, there was nothing more complicated than multiway contingency tables with a few simple correlations thrown in here and there.)

I have often been asked why this monograph has been the only item I have ever published on residential mobility. I believe that the reactions on the part of the sociological fraternity, as described above, constituted the reason why I simply left this field of research and moved on to other substantive concerns. From my perspective back in the late 1950s, my colleagues either sneered at the book because of its crass empiricism or simply disputed its findings, and hence further pursuit of an understanding of residential mobility might drive me deep into professional obscurity. I turned my attention at that point to the then much more highly regarded field of political sociology. Indeed, *Why Families Move* only began to filter into the literature after about a decade or so and even then received more attention from geographers and economists than from my own discipline.

More than two decades have passed since *Why Families Move* was first published. In that period, more than a hundred empirical studies of residential mobility have been published. The concept of mobility itself has undergone some detailed examination both in nominal and operational terms. I will examine these considerations in the next section.

We know a great deal more about residential mobility as a consequence of these more recent studies. It seems to me to be only acting responsibly to provide those who might consult this book with an up-to-date summary of what we have learned from these later researches: That is the purpose of the next section. Of course, there are still many gaps in our understanding of residential mobility, particularly those aspects which are most closely related to policy issues in land use management and planning: The final section of this introduction is addressed to the issue of how to make future research more relevant to important policy issues in those fields of public policy.

MOBILITY: CONCEPTUAL AND MEASUREMENT ISSUES

For all practical purposes, every person in the United States has an address designating a place to which he/she returns frequently enough to receive timely messages, a place where he/she sleeps fairly frequently, takes his/her meals, and so on. A shift in address is defined as a move, involving a shift in location through space that can vary from a few feet in the case of a shift from one apartment or room to another within a structure to thousands of miles to another country or from one end of the country to the other.

As defined above, residential shifts may be viewed as important because they stand for associated shifts in other activities besides sleeping arrangements and receiving mail. To the extent that such address arrangements are associated with employment, with the consumption of private and public services and other goods, with expressions of political solidarity, with ethnic and racial antagonisms, and with other important phenomena, residential shifts can be taken as a proxy variable that allows the study of such areas of human behavior. Thus, "white flight" may be studied by the net residential shifts of whites from areas inhabited by blacks to the suburbs, an interest which sees such residential shift patterns as expressing white distaste for close association with blacks.

The use of residential mobility as a proxy for other phenomena depends heavily on the extent to which residential location conditions other behavior. The ties between addresses and employment, or friendships, or consumption, and so on have not been studied definitively. In particular, there is little knowledge of the extent to which the widespread ownership of automobiles and usage of telephone services has loosened the connections that may have existed in the past between residential location and activities that are considered to be associated with address. Indeed, the case may be made that the ease with which residential shifts may be studied has stunted the development of lines of research on changes that are believed to be associated with residential shifts.

For the purposes here, however, the essential point is that a shift in address need not necessarily mean anything more than that fact alone, changing the housing services consumed by the individual and household involved and associated journeys to other places, but not necessarily involving changes in the consumption of other services, the maintenance of relationships with other persons, employment, and so on. Whether a residential change involves other changes is problematic.

Migration and Mobility

Not all moves are counted as residential mobility, usually defined as address shifts that do not involve changes in localities. A customary distinction is between migration (changes in addresses involving distinctly different localities) and residential mobility (address changes within one locality). Of course, at the margins, it is difficult to distinguish between the two since so much depends on what are defined as distinctly different localities. The census distinguishes between moves within or between counties, in or between SMSAs, moves that involve crossing state boundaries, or moves that involve shifts across regions. Some metropolitan areas are so extensive that a move within that area may involve distances that would take one completely out of the area in another metropolitan district. For example, a move with the New York-New Jersey Combined SMSA amy involve an address shift of more than 100 miles, about the distance between Boston and Springfield.

The distinction between migration and residential mobility rests on two lines of reasoning. First, migration is distinguished from residential mobility because it involves a shift from one local labor market to another and hence ordinarily involves employment considerations in the move, while residential mobility includes shifts that could take place without changes in employment. Second, the empirical concomitants of migration are different from those involved in residential mobility: Indeed, some of the factors that predict migration are opposite in sign when applied to residential mobility.

Of course, the difficulty of defining a labor market means that, in the end, arbitrary geographical definitions have to be imposed, e.g., only intra-SMSA or intracounty moves will be considered as mobility. This arbitrariness is clearly no particular problem since the proportion of moves that would be classified differently by alternative areal frames is likely to be quite slight.

Definitions of Units

Another issue involves what should be the unit for which a move is to be recorded. The census has used individuals as units in its measures of both mobility and migration. In many ways, however, individuals are not the moving units since most individuals live in households that ordinarily move together. Of course, there are many one-person households and there are many moves which involve individuals splitting away from households. Nevertheless, the fact that many moves involve groups of individuals who move together also means that moves involve household decision making and are not simply the decision of any one individual within the household, as DaVanzo (1977) so correctly points out. Defining what is the moving unit is not a simple task[4] and any solution has implications both for the study of moving decisions and for the calculation of rates.

A rarely used unit of measurement that bears some consideration is what has been called "occupancy transfers," the sequences of occupants within particular dwelling units (Moore, 1978). The advantage of this approach is reputed to be that it focuses attention on the fact that residential mobility involves shifts of persons between dwelling units and that the characteristics of dwellings play a role in the shifts. Thus, the flow of persons and households can be viewed as transactions involving moves of particular classes of occupants among particular classes of occupancy units or dwellings. The "occupancy transfer" approach to mobility obviously requires longitudinal records kept by housing units, a circumstance that is rare, at least in the United States.

None of the researches reviewed has solved these measurement issues satisfactorily. Some have defined residential mobility over individuals, usually adults, attaching household characteristics to individual adults (e.g., marital status, employment statuses within the household, number of children, and such). This procedure may be suitable enough for studies which relate individual and household characteristics to residential mobility but falls short in possibly important respects in studies that are concerned with decision-making processes. These decisions may be made in significant proportions by negotiation and bargaining among several members within a household[5]

Time: Units and Perspectives

Another measurement issue concerns the time unit over which mobility is defined. Most of the studies of residential mobility are based on post hoc predictions, in which moves taking place over some prior period of time are related to the characteristics of movers at a later period of time or reconstructed characteristics of movers at a time prior to the move. The most notable exceptions are those studies that have used the Income Dynamics Study (Morgan, 1974, 1975), in which 5,000 families have been studied longitudinally since 1968 (see DaVanzo, 1977; Goodman, 1974; Duncan and Newman, 1975). Since the prevailing schemes accounting for mobility rely heavily on changes occurring in the situation of individuals, households, housing, or neighborhoods that occurred prior to moving, at best the studies have to rely heavily on the ability of households to reconstruct past states aided by interviewing.[6] The data collected by the census suffer from the same defects. Mobility and migration are measured by asking where individuals lived on a date a year (or five years) previous. Census tabulations present past period mobility by current occupation, location, marital status, and so on. Thus, some tabulations indicate that married persons are more likely to have moved in a previous period. But this finding may be seriously influenced by the fact that single persons who were married in the period, moved as a consequence, and hence are counted as married at the end of the period.

One of the unfortunate consequences of too heavy a reliance on retrospective accounts of mobility is a neglect of housing issues in residential mobility. The characteristics of the housing occupied by a household before it made its move into its present housing tends to be either not measured at all or measured very imperfectly.

Proceeding on the assumption that a move is preceded by an intention to move (and that a moving decision takes some time to implement), other studies have defined residential mobility as intentions to move, relating such intentions to current characteristics of the individuals or households involved (Duncan and Newman, 1975; Michelson, 1977). Although this approach gets rid of some of the defects of retrospective data, it does not do so entirely since an intention may be the function of events that have occurred in the past that are no longer reflected in the statuses of the present, e.g., the prior birth of a child currently two years old may have produced the sense of crowdedness that led to the intention to move. In addition, intentions may be defined over varying future periods, with longer periods being somewhat more problematic than shorter periods. Thus, Duncan and Newman (1975) find far fewer households implementing their intentions when defined over an indefinite future, as compared to *Why Families Move* which defined intentions over the next year. The paradox, of course, is that the shorter the period defined, the more accurately intentions presage actual subsequent moving, but the less interesting such predictions of moves will be.

Defining the Housing "Bundle"

Since the barebones definition of mobility offered above considers moving as involving shifts in residential addresses, an important conceptual and measurement issue arises over how should the residences involved be described. A residence implies a set of housing services—the housing "bundle," including the physical structure involved—its design, size, and such—the costs involved, the surrounding matrix of structures and their inhabitants, the locational characteristics of the dwelling, the symbolic meanings attached to the dwelling by inhabitants and significant others, and so on. The housing bundle description could be described in considerable detail in any or all of these respects and represent a data record of considerable length and complexity. For economists, housing costs may be particularly important, in which case the costs associated with occupying a dwelling may be considerably elaborated, a task that is especially formidable for owner-occupied units for which many costs are not clearly distinguishable, e.g., household labor used in maintenance. For geographers, the locational characteristics of dwellings may be very important in which case the aim is to distinguish the space-time relationships between a dwelling and common destinations for the household members. For those concerned with housing design and its impact, some mode of characterizing the space-configuration within a dwelling that is a complex of rooms of varying sizes with varying use definitions is most important, and so on.

Perhaps the most important aspect of housing in relationship to mobility is not so much a feature of the dwelling itself but of the tenure relationship between occupants and the dwelling. The mere fact of ownership, *ceteris paribus,* reduces the probability of moving to the extent that many researchers regard tenure as the most powerful predictor of mobility (e.g., Michelson, 1977). Of course, owning or renting is more than a simple dichotomy since there are degrees of owning (or amounts of equity) and in some localities forms of owning, e.g., sales contracts versus fee simple with mortgages, as well as differences in renting reflected in such arrangements as leases (if any), whether utilities are included in rental agreements, and so on. Indeed, these differences within tenure states have not been investigated to any great extent.

The influence of tenure on mobility poses a problem of some interest. From an economist's viewpoint, the main difference may lie in the costs of moving, including transaction costs conceived as being considerably greater for owners as compared to renters (Quigley and Weinberg, 1977). For the more sociologically oriented (e.g., Michelson, 1977), owning one's dwelling is an important housing goal in and of itself, one that is recognized by the surrounding society by according to home owners special privileges, e.g., easier credit, imputed stability in more than residential terms, and so on. I will return to these questions of interpretation in the next section.

Mobility researches have stopped far short (at least in their publications) of very complicated representations of the housing bundle. Housing design has been represented by number of rooms, structure type (detached, row house, high rise, and such). Perhaps the most interesting avenue taken is the attempt to arrive at a monetary value for housing physical features by regressing housing costs on dwelling characteristics in the construction of a "hedonic index" (Kain and Quigley, 1975). More recent research (Follain and Malpezzi, 1979) indicates that such indices are housing market specific with considerable inter-SMSA variation.

Housing costs have been defined more easily in the case of rented units. Costs for owner-occupied units have been estimated by summing interest payments, taxes, maintenance and utility costs, and estimating alternative returns on equity. Of course, the main obstacle to a precise estimate of housing costs for owner-occupied units is the difficulty of estimating the current value of such units, a step that is necessary to determine the amount of equity the owners hold in the dwelling.[7]

The locational characteristics of dwellings have been indexed by calculating distances from some central point (Duncan and Newman, 1975), a procedure that assumes that such distances are highly related to distances to the full set of destinations frequently visited by dwelling inhabitants. Other researchers have relied on respondent reports of distances (or time) to frequent destinations, e.g., work, nearest relatives, shopping, schools, and so on.

Neighborhood characteristics have been measured also in a variety of ways ranging from census tract summaries to respondent reports on neighborhood composition in housing or population terms.

Of the housing bundle characteristics that have been measured routinely, a persistently important factor has been dwelling unit size, especially when viewed in the light of household size.[8] In the Survey Research Center's Survey of Income Dynamics, a somewhat arbitrarily devised measure of household housing needs was devised by assuming that a household of any size needed at least two rooms, with additional needed rooms being determined by total household size conditioned by ages of household members (Duncan and Newman, 1975). The gap between this measure of needed housing size and actual housing size becomes an important predictor of mobility plans and subsequent moving. Other researchers (including *Why Families Move*) have found that a simpler index, persons per room, was also a powerful predictor of mobility.

Because of the important implications of the housing bundle characteristics for housing policy formation, it would seem that a logical direction for future research would be to develop better and more complex measures of these characteristics, a topic to which I shall return in the final section of this introduction.

Mobility Decision or Decisions?

In line with the conceptualization of other areas of consumer behavior, the decision to move is ordinarily broken into two parts, a decision to move from a dwelling and a decision to select an alternative dwelling. In the ideal typical case, a household becomes dissatisfied with its dwelling, decides to move, searches for a set of alternative dwellings that appear to be more satisfactory, and then decides among that set of alternatives. An alternative conceptualization (see DaVanzo, 1977) is to regard both the decision to move and decisions about the place to move to as occurring simultaneously or that knowledge about available and more desirable alternatives influences the decision to move.

That many households decide to move before having a housing alternative appears to be quite clear in researches that find many households with moving intentions but no chosen destination. But there are also many households that appear to move without having formed any moving intentions or without obvious dissatisfaction with their previous housing. In short, the ideal typical view of the process of moving requires modification in order to accommodate the fact that the process may be truncated by the omission of one or more stages or by telescoping states.

That the stages are often elided and frequently bypassed is shown dramatically in research from the Housing Allowance Demand Experiment (MacMillan, 1978). Renters in Phoenix and Pittsburgh often search for new housing without being particularly dissatisfied with their old housing and often moved without much searching behavior if good bargains happened to be brought to their attention. Even more important, for persons who were willing to move, the more dissatisfied they were with their old housing, the more likely they were to move. Thus it appears that the stages of mobility are not so much ordered steps but activities that can happen more or less simultaneously and most likely mutually influence each other.

In addition, some moves may be regarded as involuntary or derivative moves, brought about by being forced, for one or another reason, to leave a dwelling or moving because of another higher priority decision that implies moving. Dwelling units may be destroyed by fire or a natural disaster, or tenants evicted from a dwelling, or the state may take over a dwelling through the exercise of eminent domain. These and similar events can precipitate a move however highly satisfied a household may be. It should be noted that such events are by no means rare and are especially likely to happen to poor households.

Derivative moves may be defined as residential shifts that occur as a consequence of other decisions that, by definition, require moving. Such decisions include those that involve the formation or dissolution of households, i.e., marriage, divorce, or separation; accepting or seeking jobs in distant labor markets; entering institutionalized care; and events of that sort.

For some researchers, the death of one of the household heads also is regarded as an event that may likely precipitate a move, but I prefer to regard such an event as part of life cycle events to be dealt with separately below. Derivative moves are not as clearly precipitants of residential mobility as in the case of involuntary moves discussed above, in which the household has no choice but to move. For example, divorces and separation may mean that one of the partners must move, but the necessity of moving may be involved in the calculus regarding whether to divorce.[9] Similar considerations may be involved in decisions whether to take or seek jobs that might necessarily involve residential shifts.

The importance of such involuntary and derivative residential shifts is that the moves involved are generated independently of the residences involved. A certain amount of mobility (estimates are given in the next section) seems to be generated by vital processes and by markets other than the housing market, a fact which conditions severely the ability of housing policies to affect completely the amount of mobility in the society.

The Family Life Cycle

One of the major legacies of *Why Families Move* is the formulation that household housing needs are strongly conditioned by stages of family life cycles. The idea of family life cycle was, of course, hardly original (see Glick, 1947). It was used originally to reflect the fact that households change in a more or less regular way in response to vital processes—births, deaths, marriages, and divorces—and that the time-related character of such processes constantly shifts the size and age composition of members of the household. Accordingly, the housing needs of families at different points in the socio-economic life cycle will affect its need for housing and may be expressed in changes in housing demand.

Of course, the major difficulties with the concept of family life cycle, as Quigley and Weinberg (1977) point out, is that there is scarcely much agreement from researcher to researcher over the particular stages that are distinguished and that it is difficult to consider any operational translation of life cycle in any but nominal variable terms. Thus, some researchers distinguish households with any children under 18 as a child-rearing stage while others define that stage as households with children under 6. Whatever particular details are used to arrive at stages, all definitions stress heavily the presence or absence of children in a household and the ages of the primary couple (husband and wife). Indeed, when it came to using family life cycle to predict residential shifts, *Why Families Move* abandoned the life cycle stages formulation and simply characterized each household by the age of the head of the house and the number of members in the household, a cross-classification that seemingly captured enough of the explanatory power of the life cycle concept to be useful. MacMillan (1978) also found that approach useful in the analysis of mobility in the Housing Allowance Demand Experiment.

While cross-classification of age and family size places no restriction on the form of relationships between either variable involved and residential mobility, the use of age and family size in regression analysis usually involves assuming linear and additive effects. There is certainly a qualitative difference between 10-year intervals for, say, one-person households from age 17 to 27 and from 57 to 67, with the former being premarriage and the latter possibly representing either aging bachelordom or spinsterhood or widowhood. While it is possible that such qualitative differences may not be relevant to housing needs, it seems at least plausible that they are important. Certainly young unmarrieds and old widows or widowers do not seem to compete for the same sorts of housing.

The basic issue is what are the relevant aspects of households that more or less uniformly affect the housing needs of the individuals and/or families involved? It may well be that age and household size may capture much that is useful, with additional distinctions yielding only very small increments. It may also be the case that more complex characterizations of households may be of even greater utility. Clearly, this is another area where further research appears to be needed.

Area Mobility Rates

An alternate approach to the study of mobility that is particularly appropriate to investigating the particular interests of geographers in the spatial distribution aspects of mobility is through the study of area mobility rates. The proportions of persons five years old and over who were residents of the same house five years previous to a census year is available for census tracts and larger units, a prospect that must be tempting to many. Special data sets may also contain interchanges among small areas, the numbers of persons or household moving from one area to another for each area as an origin and as a destination (Moore, 1971; Brown and Longbrake, 1970; Moore, 1978). The stability percentage—persons who were residents of the same tract five years previous—is often used as a proxy for residential mobility, a tactic that is subject to some possible distortions. A stability percentage (or its complement) is affected by a number of processes in addition to a real turnover of population. Tracts experiencing a recent increase in its housing stock either through new construction or conversion to more extensive use of existing structures will have a mobility rate elevated by that fact alone (Moore, 1978). Tracts experiencing increases in vacancies will have upwardly biased stability rates. In short, stability or mobility rates based on proportions of persons resident in an area for a given period of time are affected by processes other than turnover which affect the growth or decline of the total population in that area over the period in question.

In addition, such mobility rates at best measure persons who have made at least one move in the period in question and also housing units that have experienced more than one change of tenants in that period will also be counted as having only one change. In short, multiple moves are under-counted and multiple turnover within a dwelling or tract will be under-counted.

A special caution must be sounded because the census typically tabulates mobility by individuals. Hence, large families weigh more heavily than small households in such rates to the extent that a tract which experiences a realtively large influx of such families will have its mobility rates inflated as a consequence.

Appropriate measures of mobility for small areas should take into account movements both into and out of areas, corrected for exits that are not residential shifts in the ordinary sense of the word, e.g., emigration, deaths, institutionalizations, dwelling unit destruction, and so on and for entrances that are not moves in the ordinary sense, e.g., the inhabiting of newly constructed units, household units that are formed within the period, births, and so on. Especially tricky is the problem of defining an appropriate unit, the most logical candidate being dwelling units, with rates being defined over changes in household units (or major parties thereto) over a period of time.[10] Approximations to these rates are currently available from the U.S. Bureau of the Census (1973-1976).

Of course the suggestions outlined above would be best fulfilled were there a continuous dwelling unit and associated population registers, measures that may be unacceptable on grounds involving threats to individual privacy, not to mention costs and record maintenance difficulties.[11]

At the present time, given the current statistics published routinely by the Bureau of the Census for small areas, it is possible to construct a stability rate which, when properly corrected for growth or decline of the housing stock of an area, measures the persistence over a period of time of the population in habiting an area at the beginning of that period. Properly employed, such measures may be used, for example, to ascertain the kinds of areas which have particular attraction to their inhabitants.

Some Summary Comments on Conceptual and Measurement Issues

The conceptual and measurement issues that were reviewed in this section loom larger to the residential mobility buff than to the reader who is primarily interested in what is known about residential shifting. The main thing to keep in mind is that some of the researchers distinguish clearly between long-distance and short-distance moves and some lump them together, a decision that does condition findings. In addition, some researches define moving units as individuals and other concentrate on households or intact families. Moving has been studied retrospectively and prospectively, over long and short periods of time. Finally, some of the studies have elaborated the characteristics of the housing occupied by movers and some have looked in fine detail at the characteristics of the households involved. While each of these technical decisions affects findings, there is still sufficient agreement among the outcomes of various researches to form a body of relatively firm knowledge about residential mobility, as the next section details.

CURRENT KNOWLEDGE ABOUT RESIDENTIAL MOBILITY

In this section, I review the substantive knowledge currently available on residential mobility in the United States. Some of the findings I will present are not current in the sense of being contemporaneous but are the best, existing estimates.[12]

Long-Term Trends in Mobility

Although relatively good time series exist since 1947, the evidence on mobility rates for earlier periods for the United States as a whole or for local jurisdictions is fragmentary and not very trustworthy. Albig (1933) found a steady decline in intraurban mobility rates using comparisons among city directories from more than 50% a year in 1903-1910 to about 20% in 1930-1932. Goldstein and Mayer (1963) found a similar decline for the same period but not as marked. Chudacoff (1972), in a study of residential persistence in Omaha, claims that mobility rates were lower in that city than for the United States as a whole in the 1940s. These studies rely primarily on comparisons year by year among city directories, documents that may suffer from severe underenumeration, particularly of the more mobile segments of the population, and from careless entries year to year. Hence it is difficult to know whether the evidence favors more the notion of a long-term decline or perhaps its opposite.

In 1948, the Bureau of the Census began publishing reports on annual residence change rates based upon questions asked in the April Current Population Survey, the results constituting an almost unbroken time series until very recently. Table I.1 presents the resulting data, consisting of the proportions of the total, noninstitutionalized population of the United States who resided at a different address one year prior to the survey date. For the entire period 1947 through 1971, the total persistence rate has shown a remarkable stability: At its height in the year 1950-1951, 20% of the population was found to have moved within the year to the address they were surveyed at in April 1951. At the lowest point in the series, 1970-1971, 18% had moved over that year. An additional low point is represented by

TABLE I.1. Proportions Moved 1947-1976 by Move
Type: (US Civilian, Non-Institutionalized Population
One Year Old or Over)

Period (April thru March)	Total Moved (%)	Inter-County (%)	Intra-County (%)
1947-48	20.0	6.4	13.6
1948-49	18.8	5.8	13.0
1949-50	18.7	5.6	13.1
1950-51	21.0	7.1	13.9
1951-52	19.8	6.6	13.2
1952-53	20.1	6.6	13.5
1953-54	18.6	6.4	12.2
1954-55	19.9	6.6	13.3
1955-56	20.5	6.8	13.7
1956-57	19.4	6.3	13.1
1957-58	19.8	6.7	13.1
1958-59	19.2	6.1	13.1
1959-60	19.4	6.5	12.9
1960-61	20.0	6.3	13.7
1961-62	19.1	6.1	13.0
1962-63	19.4	6.8	12.6
1963-64	19.6	6.6	13.0
1965-66	20.1	6.7	13.4
1966-67	19.3	6.6	12.7
1967-68	18.3	6.7	11.6
1968-69	18.8	7.0	11.8
1969-70	18.4	6.7	11.7
1970-71 [a]	18.0	6.5	11.4
1975-76	17.1	6.4	10.8

Source: US Bureau of the Census, Current Population Reports, Population Characteristics. Series P-20

[a] Data for April 1971 through April 1975 not available on annual basis. See Table 2.

1975-1976, a year in which the total moving rate dropped to close to 17%. Up to about 1965-1966, there appears to be no trend in the moving rate. After that point there appears to be a slow decline to the lower rates described above.

Similar trends appear in the components of the total moving rate shown in Table I1. The percentages that had moved between counties seems particularly stable, fluctuating between a range of 5.6 and 7.1. Intracounty moves, the larger of the two components and the closest proxy to the residential mobility, shows more apparent annual fluctuation, ranging from a high of 13.9% in 1950-1951 to a low of 10.8% in 1975-1976. Intracounty mobility

rates also show a trend, a more or less consistent small decline from
1965-1966 to 1975-1976.

Whether or not there actually is a decline in mobility rates since
1965-1966, as the data seem to suggest, the decline is not a very large one and
it is not particularly precipitous. Indeed, the most remarkable characteristic
of the entire series is the relative stability of the migration and mobility
statistics. For 30 years, the total annual moving rate has been about 20% and
the intracounty annual moving rate has been about 13%. This persistence in
magnitude is all the more remarkable when we take into account the fact that
the post-World War II period has been characterized by starting out with a
severe housing shortage, going through two small military engagements, two
relatively severe recessions, a large increase in the proportion of households
owing their homes, sharp changes in fertility, household formation and
dissolution rates, and at least two prosperity booms. Whatever it may be that
drives migration and mobility must be dominated by processes that are
relatively insensitive to such events in the economy, in vital processes, and in
the housing market. I will return to this seeming aggregate stability later on in
this section.

Computed over longer periods of time, the proportion who have ever
moved tends to increase, as Table I.2 indicates. Over a two-year period, the
proportion ever moved is 26.5%; over three years, 34.2%; and over five years,
41.3%. Cumulative proportions who have ever moved within counties range

Table I.2. Proportion Moved Over One Year, Two Year,
Three Year and Five Year Intervals: 1970-1978 US
Civilian Population, Non-Institutionalized of Appropriate
Ages[a]

Time Period	Dates	Total Moved	Inter-County	Intra-County
One Year	1975-1976	17.1%[b]	6.4%	10.8%
Two Years	1975-1977	26.5	10.4	16.1
Three Years	1975-1978	34.2	13.4	20.5
Five Years	1970-1975	41.3	17.1	24.2

Source: Current Population Reports: Population Characteristics: Series P-20

[a]Data consist of proportions of persons who lived in a different place as of survey data
at end of periods involved. Computed over persons one year or over, two years or over,
three years and over and five years and over, as appropriate in the period involved.

[b]Total proportions who did not move in the period listed cannot be computed as the
complement of the proportion moved since immigrants, persons returning from over-
seas, or deinstitutionalized persons are not counted as movers. In addition there is a
certain amount of missing data. All these non-move categories amounted to about 6%
of the population over a five year period. See Table 3.

from 10.8% for a one-year period to 24.2% for a five-year period. Clearly, some people move and stay for a while, while others may move several times within a given time period and are counted as moved only when the time period is short.

Still another way of looking at migration and mobility is shown in Table I.3, in which the origins and destinations of movers and migrants are taken into account. Table I.3 reports on origins and destinations of persons who have moved over a five-year period in terms of the rural or urban character-istics of the places involved. A bit more than half (52%) of the population reported in May 1975 that they had lived in their current residence five years or more. Among those who had moved from one civilian residence within the United States to another (42%),[13] a bit less than half had moved within a single urban place,[14] with the remainder making some kind of shift from between rural places or between a rural and an urban place.

The bottom panel of Table I.3 breaks down intraurban moves by origins and destinations within urban areas. Suburban areas and urban areas appear to have about as much residential mobility, according to these measures, with

Table I.3.   Moves by Origins and Destinations and by Race: 1970-1975 (Percent of Population 5 Years Old and Over as of April 1, 1975) Non-Institutionalized Civilian Population

	White	Non-Whites	Total
Non Movers	52%	48%	52%
Movers Total	42%	46%	42%
Inter-urban	7	4	6
Rural-urban	3	2	3
Urban-rural	4	2	4
Rural-rural	10	9	10
Intra-urban	18	29	19
Other and not reported[a]	6	6	6
Intra Urban Moves total	18	29	19
Within central cities	6	22	8
Within suburbs	8	4	8
Central city to suburbs	3	2	2
Suburb-Central city	1	1	1

Source: US Bureau of the Census, Current Population Reports. Population Characteris-tics, Series P-20, #285. October 1975. Data collected as of April 1, 1975 in Cur-rent Population Survey.

[a]Includes persons moving into the US from abroad or from non-civilian or institutional-ized addresses as well as cases with insufficient information given to allow characteriza-tion of origin and/or destination.

a preponderance of moves from central cities to suburbs as against moves from suburbs to central cities.

Table I.3 also shows the mobility differentials between whites and non-whites (predominantly black), indicating that the latter have considerably higher rates of residential mobility, 29% having made an intraurban move over the half decade in question, as compared with 18% of the whites. These gross mobility differentials between whites and non-whites, however, have to be considered against the considerable socioeconomic and housing tenure differences existing between the two groups, a theme to which I will return in a later section.

The distances involved in residential mobility shifts are not very great. Zimmer (1973), in a study of several metropolitan areas, estimates that the majority of moves are less than three miles, longer distances being involved in moves within suburban areas that have less dense settlement patterns and shorter moves within the more built up residential sections of central cities. Indeed, as Lansing and Mueller (1969) find, despite the number of moves a household may experience over its lifetime, most households are still living within the same metropolitan area in which they were formed and within 50 miles of such origins.

Whether the amount of mobility American households exhibited in the last 30 years is excessive is not an easy question to answer. According to some commentators, our mobility rates are as much as twice those experienced by Western European nations, but that difference may only mean that in Germany or Great Britain there is insufficient mobility. Indeed, the only way to make an attempt to answer this question is to come to some assessment of what is the optimum mobility rate, in some sense, for a political or other areal unit. Since there is little evidence that a large number of residential shifts has any negative (or positive) impact on a household or individual, there seems little reason to look to the individual or household level for clues for the answer. The main worry about residential mobility appears to stem from its impact on small areas. Highly mobile areas are areas that are susceptible to change and to which institutions that are sustained by change are attracted, and in which institutions that are sustained by stability do not flourish.[15] Instability, transiency, and the activities that are associated with these features are negatively viewed. It is not clear whether it is transiency and instability that is negatively evaluated or the activities (high crime rates, cheaper hotels, and so on) that are attracted to and flourish in such areas. Especially abhorred are areas that change from stability to transiency: The decline and fall of neighborhoods seems particularly deplorable. As Riis wrote about the Lower East Side around the turn of the century, "I want to arouse neighborhood interest and neighborhood pride to link the neighbor to one spot that will hold them long enough to take root and stop them from moving. Something of the sort must be done or we perish" (cited in Chudacoft, 1972). Riis's hysteria has persisted into the present: Area mobility rates can be perceived as excessive, and neighborhood stabilization is often the very elusive goal of community organizations and federal programs.

The Sources of Residential Mobility

This section takes up the main issue that was addressed in *Why Families Move*, namely, what are the sources of moving behavior for households? The literature reviewed on this topic typically sorts out the factors that leads a household to seek to move from those factors that influence its decision to locate in a particular destination. This distinction is clearly an analytical convenience, since in actual decisions made by households such a separation may not in fact exist.[16] Some of the literature (e.g., Speare et al., 1974) sees the first step toward residential shifts as a "decision to seek alternative housing." However, scarcely any of the literature distinguishes operationally (cf. MacMillan, 1978) between a decision to move and a decision to seek alternative housing, and in fact the operational definition always consists either of an intention to move or a move that has occurred.

Focusing upon the decision to move immediately brings to light the fact that for some households that decision is either forced upon them or is derivative (implied) by another decision made by the household or its members. Thus there are moves that are "induced" or precipitated by eviction; by dwelling unit destruction through fire, other hazards, or demolition; or by conversion to nonhousing uses. Some tens of thousands of dwelling units are removed from the housing market each year and additional thousands of households are evicted for one reason or another from their dwellings. Of course, some of these dwelling units are removed from the housing market because they are not occupied. Hence, the estimation of the number of induced moves in the United States or in any political subdivision is somewhat hazardous. In *Why Families Move,* I estimated the proportion of previous moves that were induced in this sense to be about 5%.

A much larger number of moves may be regarded as derivative in the sense that the move was implied by necessity in other actions taken by the household or its members. Typical derivative moves are generated by the formation and dissolution of households, through marriage, divorce, separations, deaths of marriage partners, imprisonment, induction into the armed forces, and other events that produce a radical shift in the composition of the adult components of a household. According to the 1975 Annual Housing Survey (U.S. Bureau of the Census, 1973–1976), about 26% of all moves made by families were made by households whose head of the household changed in the same year. Since this proportion includes migration moves as well as residential mobility, the proportion of residential moves that are associated with household formation, reformation, and dissolution is likely even higher.

The implications of this high level of derivative mobility are quite important. First of all, we begin to get some understanding of why annual rates of residential mobility are so stable. If a very large proportion of moves are dominated by vital processes that are not directly connected with housing market changes (at least within the range experienced in post-World War II housing market conditions), then a very large portion of residential mobility can only be affected by such glacial shifts that are typical of such vital processes. Indeed, the recent (since 1965) decline in residential mobility may reflect mainly those shifts in marriage patterns that have been noted by sociologists of the family. In particular, there has been a rise of several years in the average age at first marriage in the past decade, indicating that the rate of new household formation may be declining.[17]

A second important implication is that derivative residential mobility sets a rather hard limit on the amount of stability that can be found in any urban area. Without replacements, an urban area can be emptied of its inhabitants within a relatively short period of time through the operation of the normal processes of household formation and dissolution. Indeed, the difference between stable and mobile areas may be largely differences in composition, mobile areas being occupied by households especially susceptible to changes wrought by vital processes and stable areas being occupied by households with less susceptible characteristics.

Finally, the policy implications are also important. Recognizing the important role of derivative mobility is to recognize the limits of policy measures that might be taken to lessen residential mobility. For example, it focuses as much attention on replacement of households as it does upon stabilizing existing households.

If we add together the estimates of induced and derivative moves, it seems likely that perhaps as much as one in three residential (nonmigration) moves are "involuntary" in the senses used above.

There are other changes in household conditions which are similar to induced and derivative moves because they may force households to consider moving that would not have otherwise. In particular, drastic and abrupt losses of income or drastic increases in demands on income, as occurs in the case of catastrophic illness, may require a household to lower its consumption of housing and hence move. The impact of such events is buffered by savings and income transfer programs, at least temporarily, and hence may be translated into a move only after some delay.

For the two-thirds of the residential shifts that are not either induced or derivative, what can be said about the sources of these "voluntary" moves? First of all, these are the moves that we can envisage as possibly being dominated primarily by housing bundle considerations and hence they are of particular interest to the housing researcher. Second, these are moves of particular interest to policy concerns since their sources are likely points at which policy changes may make a difference (always assuming, of course, that policy may be sensibly directed toward the inducement of stability or mobility). Perhaps the most quoted sentence from *Why Families Move* is the following:

> The findings of this study indicate the major function of mobility to be the process by which families adjust their housing to the housing needs that are generated by the shifts in family composition that accompany life cycle changes [p. 61].

I think I had in mind primarily the "voluntary" shifts at the time I wrote it, but I am not quite sure. In any event, I would modify that general statement today along the following lines: Households tend toward equilibrium in their housing choices, an equilibrium which is represented by that choice in comparison to which an alternative choice would produce no additional benefits that exceed the costs of moving. This very general statement verges on the tautological, as Quigley and Weinberg (1977) put it, since another restatement of the sentence is that households move when it is clearly advantageous for them to do so, as they see it.

Incidentally, this statement also tends to explain why most households are satisfied with the housing they occupy at a particular point in time.[18] It also indicates why satisfaction with housing plays so important a role in studies of residential mobility, especially for the sociologists and the geographers. A direct indicator of whether a household or individual is close to its point of equilibrium is its expressed satisfaction with the housing it occupies. Those who stress, as did *Why Families Move,* that satisfaction with housing is an important determinant of moving are mainly restating the problem in social psychological terms. The central issue is what are the terms of the match between a household and its housing that lead to satisfaction (or equilibrium) and how are those terms changed over time.[19]

A useful theory of residential mobility is one that goes beyond the generality stated above to specify the terms of the equilibrium and the events, endogenous or exogenous, that move an individual or household away from its equilibrium position or which reduce the costs of moving or which change the nature of alternative locations vis-à-vis their current choice. I will attempt to set forth at least a beginning toward this goal in the remainder of this section on residential mobility sources.

The Mysteries of Housing Tenure

Nothing seems more firmly established as an empirical generalization in the residential mobility literature than the superior attractiveness to Americans of owning as opposed to renting their dwelling units. Not only do most prefer ownership tenure but owners are much less likely to move than renters. Both these apsects of home ownership hold up under a variety of controls, holding constant the confounding differences between households and individuals who typically own and rent their dwelling. Indeed, so strong is the inverse relationship between housing tenure and mobility that more than one researcher has asserted that tenure is the single most important predictor of mobility *ceteris paribus* (e.g., Speare et al., 1974; DaVanzo, 1978; Michelson, 1977; McCarthy, 1979).

The mystery alluded to in the title of this subsection is that we have only the softest data (if any) to provide clues as to why owning should be regarded as more preferable and more binding than renting. American norms concerning appropriate housing tenure apparently favor owning, but that only restates the mystery in an alternative form. There are many norms that die out or are flagrantly violated when they run contrary to personal or collective experience. Home owning is clearly more satisfying than renting, an experience that fortifies and reinforces the tenure norms.

It is clear that many of the major American institutions regard home ownership as a sign that marks an owning household as worthy of special merit and attention. Banks, policemen, retail store credit bureaus, and employers apparently regard home owners as more trustworthy and prestigious (in some sense) than renters. Of course, home ownership also means tangible assets that can be attached in case of default, a point that surely does not escape the credit-giving institutions. Still, home ownership does have some positive symbolic meaning, a proxy for good character and at least middle-class status (Warner et al., 1949; Hollingshead, 1949).

That home owners should be less likely to move than renters is somewhat understandable since the costs of moving are clearly higher for the former, involving the possibility of equity losses as well as the out-of-pocket costs of completing a sale transaction and the undoubtedly higher investment of time that would be involved in completing a sale. It seems doubtful, however, that the costs of moving are so much greater for home owners to account completely for their greater stability.[20] Clearly households that own their own home are more likely at any point in time to be closer to their equilibrium points. This suggests that owning one's own home enables one to adjust the housing involved to accommodate shifts in housing needs or housing aspirations. Home remodeling and modification in relatively radical ways are options that are open to owners (subject to building and zoning code regulations) and are only available within narrow limits ordinarily to renters.[21] Following this line of reasoning, owning provides the household with a more flexible housing bundle, at least as far as the housing unit itself is concerned. This freedom to modify, which also involves a freedom to use, may be the quality which is most important and which households may regard as an important positive attribute of homeownership.[22]

Quigley and Weinberg (1977) raise the fundamental question whether homeownership should not be considered an endogenous variable in relation to residential mobility. If households that desire to be stable express that desire through purchasing a home, then the greater stability of home owners borders on the tautological. It is difficult to evaluate this assessment, since it postulates some intrinsic desire for stability or mobility that is yet to be demonstrated.

Homeownership is, of course, more than the mere possession of a dwelling and a location. An owned home often represents the chief form of savings for a household, its net worth largely consisting of the equity invested in their home. To sell one's home therefore means to calculate in an uncertain market whether the sale will realize as much of the equity value as possible (or thought by the household to be fair in some sense). This uncertainty may also be a source of conservatism about moving, especially in times when housing prices tend to increase on the average. Indeed, for most households, investing in a home may be a more certain hedge against inflation than any other alternative open to a small investor and certainly better than savings accounts.

A second aspect of the mystery of home ownership is that its stabilizing effect, however strongly manifested in cross-sectional surveys, is not reflected in greater aggregate stability over time. In 1950, 55% of American dwelling units were owner occupied. By 1975, this proportion had grown to 65%. However, as we have seen from Table 11, residential mobility and general moving rates have remained remarkably stable over the same period of time. Perhaps renters have become more mobile over this period compensating for the larger proportion of households that have moved into the more stable home-owning category? Or, perhaps the other way round: Homeownership may not be as stable a state today compared with a generation ago? Whatever the ultimate explanation, it is clear that cross-sectional differences at a given point in time are not immutable.

Changes in Households: "Life Cycle" and Income

Households which remain intact necessarily change over time in size; socioeconomic level; and in the mix of ages, earning capacities, and accessibility requirements. Such changes are almost universally regarded as the more important sources of residential mobility operating by changing the housing expenditure capacities of the household and their housing requirements and aspirations. Indeed, *Why Families Move,* as indicated earlier, places life cycle changes at the top of the list of sources of residential moves. Such changes presumably shift households away from their housing equilibrium points.

Consensus over the importance of such household changes is not matched by complete agreement on the empirical evidence for that importance. In large part, the lack of agreement on details arises because the concept of life cycle changes does not lend itself easily to operational translation. Some researchers have distinguished stages (Lansing and Kish, 1957; Foote et al., 1960) consisting of combinations of presence or absence of children of various ages. *Why Families Move* used a combination of household size and the age of household head as an indirect measure of stages in household life cycle. Others have used the ages of major adults in the household (e.g., Speare et al., 1974; Fredland, 1974), household size or some measure of household composition (usually number of children within some age range), and marital status of individuals.

Perhaps the least ambiguous finding is that mobility decreases with age, with at least one research reporting (Fredland, 1974) that the relationship is best described as curvilinear. Less agreement is found concerning some of the other operational translations of life cycle, with some reporting that mobility increases with household size and others finding that rates peak for some household sizes in a way that precludes monotonic statements (e.g., Fredland, 1974). Similar ambiguities in findings exist for household composition.

Besides the problems presented by the definitional anarchy that exists, a more serious deficiency is that, typically, life cycle stages at a particular point in time are measured but *not changes* in life cycle. Thus, the size of a household is only a very indirect measure of whether a change has occurred in family size: Indeed, a small household size may indicate that the household has lost a member, or recently gained a member. The effects of household changes are typically not measured directly by observations over time but indirectly by measuring variables that could reflect the end results of changes, or, retrospectively as in *Why Families Move,* by reconstructing through interviews changes that precede moving.

It is also not clear what should be the time frame over which changes should be studied. The birth of a child, while immediately increasing household size, may not affect the household's housing equilibrium until the child is old enough to "need" its own bedroom. Similarly, the departure of a young adult to go to school or get married may not shift housing needs immediately but over some period of time. In short, while it is clear that households vary in their housing needs and aspirations in ways that are dependent on its rate of changes in size and composition, mobility researchers have not yet solved the problem of how to capture and measure these effects.

Even less well measured are the effects of income changes on residential mobility. There were some hints in *Why Families Move* that families that had experienced severe income stream changes downward were more likely to be precipitated into moving, but such changes also tend to be correlated with other changes in the household. Thus a separation, typically the cause of abrupt downward income shifts (Morgan, 1974, 1975), is also a change in household composition that is radical enough to be classified as one of the sources of involuntary moves, discussed earlier. The impact of unemployment[23] on households that remain intact would seem a priori to be important, but researchers have not paid much attention to such changes.

Upward shifts in income have also not been studied very well as far as residential mobility is concerned. Of course, there is a fairly strong correlation between household income and the amount and quality of housing consumed, but whether upward income shifts are translated quickly or slowly into increases in housing consumption appears not to be very well known.[24] It seems likely that one of the effects of such upward shifts would be to provide the resources for households to shift closer to their housing equilibrium points and hence to be translated eventually into a residential shift if that would be appropriate. In addition, it seems likely that upward income shifts may change housing aspirations.[25] Of course, at our present level of knowledge, the idea of housing aspirations, while intuitively attractive, is completely unstudied. In fact, we know very little about what people want in the way of housing, and we know only a little more about what actual choices they make in the way of housing. Indeed, it is not at all clear that it is possible to study housing aspirations except in the form of grossly measured preferences for one type of housing over another.

Perhaps the best information on the effects of income changes on the consumption of housing comes from analyses of the Housing Allowance Demand Experiment (MacMillan, 1978; Cronin, 1979; Weinberg et al., 1979). Random samples of renting households just above or below the poverty line were offered a variety of housing allowances, some tied to occupying housing of some minimum quality and other plans tied to paying more than a certain percentage of rent for "typical" housing in Phoenix and Pittsburgh. Some of the households were also offered plans which were not tied to either housing quality or amount of rent paid, but essentially amounted to income maintenance payments. Households offered constrained plans were induced to move slightly more than would be expected if the housing they occupied did not meet quality standards or if they were not paying the stipulated proportion of typical rents. Since payments on the average amounted to about a 20% increase in income, the monetary incentives were not trivial. Yet the response was to induce an increment of about .05 in the probability of moving over a two-year period. Households on the income maintenance plans (without housing quality or rent constraints) moved about a similar amount.[26] This increment in mobility was statistically significant in Phoenix but only borderline in Pittsburgh.

When mobility was not the only response possible to either income increments or the constraints imposed under some of the plans (e.g., repairs could have been made to the dwellings), the response was almost entirely limited *per force* to moving. Yet households were not stimulated to move by the prospects of additional income. Indeed, those most likely to move were those who were in those age and life cycle classes in which moving was very likely in any event.

Changes in the Housing Bundle

Housing has the distressing characteristic of being a very complex and diverse good. While not all possible dwelling units are found in our housing stock, the diversity is enough to be bewildering to the researcher who is attempting to measure its relevant characteristics in a parsimonious fashion. This is especially frustrating to the researcher on residential mobility since housing is what residential mobility is largely about. The concept of the housing bundle is one that reflects the frustration of the housing researcher by implying that housing is a complex of attributes that somehow are wrapped up together. It is useful to think of housing as composed of a number of identifiable attributes, as described next.

Housing as interior living space. In this connection we distinguish the amount of floor space that is usable as well as its particular configuration into rooms. In residential mobility research this aspect of housing is most frequently indexed as the number of rooms or as the number of bedrooms. Indeed, the closeness of a household to its housing equilibrium is often expressed as the number of persons per room.[27]

Housing as amenities. A housing unit also ordinarily provides shelter from the elements (heating in the winter and possibly cooling in hot weather) as well as facilities for cooking and eating meals, preserving food, washing, and facilities for all the other activities that go with housing. While some of these amenities are easily changed and modified at relatively low cost (e.g., a new refrigerator may quickly change the food preserving characteristics of a dwelling), others are more firmly embedded into the physical structure and require more in the way of modification and resources to change. The modifiability of a given dwelling is partly expressed by tenure, partially by its age and condition, and so on. The point is that a change in the amenities (e.g., the failure of a heating system) may shift a household toward or away from its housing equilibrium point.

Housing as location. Perhaps the most frequently studied aspect of the housing bundle is the position of the housing in space. On the grossest level, whether housing is located in the suburbs, in central cities, or in rural areas is a characteristic that is usually distinguished, and routinely so in the census tabulations. At finer levels of measurement, location has been measured in terms of distance from urban centers (e.g., Brown et al., 1970), in terms of time expended in journeys to work, and so on.

The problem with location as an attribute of housing is that the issue is location with respect to what? Places of employment, friends, relatives, shopping, elementary or high school, or to recreational facilities? And how should such distances be calibrated? In terms of straightline distances, the length of the shortest route, time expended in typical journeys, or in terms of the costs of travel? Furthermore, what is the impact of the telephone and television on the importance of location? If it is possible to be in contact by telephone, how important is it that one live near or far from relatives or friends? Since television brings entertainment quickly and cheaply into the home, what difference does one's location make with respect to a downtown entertainment district?

While 19th century city dwellers may have been dependent on locating near places of employment, late 20th century urbanites who have access to (so far) cheap and flexible personal automobile transportation are clearly less dependent on the locational aspects of their dwellings, at least as far as the journey to work is concerned. Indeed, in an analysis of moves in the San Francisco SMSA, Weinberg (1975) showed that employment mobility (changing place of employment) was as frequent a way employed to reduce the journey to work as changing residences.

The concept of place utility (Wolpert, 1965) as the "composite of utilities which are derived from the individual's integration at some position in space [location]" succinctly summarizes the concerns I have been expressing above. The problem is that it is difficult to give the concept operational forms and that it is also not at all clear from existing empirical studies whether place utility plays an important part in moving.[28] As the journey to work changes with job changes, as relatives and friends move about, as children change from one school level to another, as needs for medical care shift, so do the locational characteristics of a housing unit, along with the associated place utility. Existing evidence does not support the idea that such shifts in place utility play an important role in shifting households closer to or further away from their housing equilibrium points.

Housing and associated public services. An aspect of housing location is the public services that are provided by the political jurisdication in which the housing is located. Many public services are delivered on an areal basis—schools, police protection, certain types of publicly provided medical services, garbage collection, sewer systems, and so on. Perhaps the public service that has received the most attention as a determinant of residential mobility is the public school. The "white flight to the suburbs" is seen to some extent as a reaction to the racial integration of public schools within central cities (Coleman, et al., 1974). Whether the empirical findings, on balance, support the notion that at least some of the net central-city-to-suburb movement for whites is due to the desire to place children in all-white schools is certainly controversial (see Rist, 1976). Such considerations do not play a major role in the housing decisions as reported by movers, but this lack of salience to movers may not properly calibrate its importance at particular points in time.

It may also be the case that "place utility" considerations play a major role in residential location—where people move to when they decide to move.

Given the rather large amount of "unavoidable" mobility, it would take a rather short period of time to considerably reduce the household population of an area through outward movement. If replacements are not forthcoming because an area has lost relative attractiveness, it would be quite easy for an area to either become underpopulated or to start attracting a different population type than has left because of normal attrition. Thus it may not be white *flight* that has changed the racial composition of desegregated school districts but the dearth of white replacements for households that left the districts for unavoidable reasons.

Housing context externalities. Closely related to the locational aspects of a housing unit are the social and physical contexts in which the unit is placed, consisting of the mix of population types located nearby, the aesthetic appearance of neighborhoods, their social reputation in the eyes of significant others, the amount of noxious (or pleasant) stimuli emanating from the environment, and so on. Given the context of racism in our country, a great deal of attention has been given to the effects of racial compositions and shifts therein on residential mobility (Bradburn, et al., 1971). White residential areas that experienced an influx of blacks have largely turned into black majority areas, sometimes with surprising rapidity. The question which arises is mainly whether the change in neighborhood composition is accomplished mainly by an excessive loss of households that would not have otherwise moved or simply by the fact that new white households are not attracted to such neighborhoods.

Other changes in neighborhoods are not as dramatic or as rapid as changes in population composition. The aesthetic appearances of a neighborhood require some period of time to deteriorate as does the amount of air pollution. Indeed, the shifts that are important all seem to stem from population changes.

Changes in the Costs of Moving

Following the general statement of the mobility process presented earlier, another potential determinant of residential mobility is change in the cost of moving. Since none of the researches reviewed touch upon this topic, it may turn out to be either trivial in its impact or impossible to evaluate. It is mentioned here mainly in the service of completeness and consistency.

That the costs of moving (including transaction and search costs as well as the costs of moving goods and effects) can play an important role in residential mobility at least for relatively poor renting households is shown in analyses of the Experimental Allowance Demand Experiment (Cronin, 1979; Weinberg et al., 1979). Differences in moving costs between whites and blacks as well as between Pittsburgh and Phoenix helped to account for differences in moving rates stimulated by the housing allowances.

Changes in the Housing Market

Since a household's equilibrium is defined in part in terms of alternative housing and the latter's potential benefits, housing market conditions ought to play a role in residential mobility. This last sentence is put into a conditional form because, as we have seen from Table I.1, gross mobility rates appear to be less than responsive to the ups and downs of the national housing market in the post-World War II period. Nevertheless, since few households deal with the national housing market, or indeed for that matter with metropolitan housing markets, local conditions to which households might be responsive may be the housing market segments to which one should pay attention in the search for understanding the sources of residential mobility.

The Housing Allowance Demand and Supply Experiments provide an indepth analysis of the differences between four housing markets. In the Supply Experiment, Pittsburgh and Phoenix are compared. The much higher mobility rates in Phoenix are associated with a higher vacancy rate and with lower moving costs (Weinberg et al., 1979). The Supply Experiment permits a contrast between South Bend, Indiana, and Green Bay, Wisconsin, the latter being a declining area with a relatively high vacancy rate and relatively depressed rents and housing values (McCarthy, 1979). These differences, however, are not converted into striking differences in the mobility of the two populations, *ceteris paribus,* as in the case of the contrast between Phoenix and Pittsburgh. In short, the four cities present contrasts that are not consistent enough to provide reliable clues to the intermarket mobility differentials.

Alternative housing opportunities are most likely always within the awareness of households at all times. For example, most are likely to know something about market conditions through comparisons with the housing occupied by friends and relatives as well as the "For Sale" and "For Rent" signs seen in the course of everyday journeys to work, shopping, and other trips. While classified advertisements may not be routinely read by all readers, advertisements for new developments or for new apartment complexes are often in more prominent places in the newspaper. The point is that some assessment of the housing market and some knowledge of the market opportunities are probably always in the consciousness of adult household members. That such knowledge is partial and biased is also probably true in the sense that one knows best those opportunities that are available to households of one's kin and ken and along the more frequent pathways of travel.

Such passively obtained knowledge could conceivably change in response to changes in the relevant portion of the housing market. An increase in the vacancy rate within the passively known market might be reflected in friends' and neighbors' casual talk. Similarly, houses being offered for sale might also be brought to a household's attention. Hence, even without active information seeking it is possible that changes in the housing market as reflected in vacancies, properties offered for sale, and possibly even price changes would become known widely to households. Such knowledge, if perceived as showing a clear advantage in moving to one of the locations involved, might shift a household away from its equilibrium point and perhaps initiate entry into the market. Similarly, a sense of a tight market with very high prices conveyed in the same way to a household might shift a household closer to its equilibrium point.

The research literature does contain considerable information about where households are likely to move in terms of distances moved, types of housing moved to, given the household's characteristics (see, for example, the excellent review article by Simmons, 1968), and hence the end result of information seeking, passive and active, is known. But, how much market knowledge is present in households that are in a steady state is not very well known. Even the reputations of neighborhoods, an item which sometimes figures heavily in attempts to measure social status (Warner, 1949; Hollingshead, 1949; Coleman and Rainwater, 1978), are well known to city dwellers but not to researchers. Furthermore, how housing information is obtained when households actively enter the market has been studied only rather superficially.

Stochastic Modeling of Mobility

With the development of stochastic modeling in the 1960s, several attempts were made to see whether migration or mobility could be represented appropriately using one or another of a family of stochastic models. These attempts have not been very successful. It became clear very early that neither migration nor mobility could be described very well by the simpler models, as for example as a stationary Markov chain: The probability of moving is not identical even within particular population classes over successive time periods. In other words, mobility at one point in time is dependent partially on mobility in previous time periods and further varies systematically over different portions of the population, as preceding sections have indicated.

Considerable effort has gone into developing models that take these conditions into account. Several promising approaches have been attempted (Huff and Clark, 1978; Clark et al., 1979; Ginsburg, 1978). The virtues of these models are not immediately apparent. On the one hand, they attempt to provide terse descriptions of aggregate processes as derived from individual level data. In this sense, these models generate no new information. On the other hand, if appropriately descriptive, playing out the models over time enables one to make predictions about future states of the distribution of households, that may turn out to be useful.[29]

A Summary View of Sources of Residential Mobility

What seems to be best known from the literature are the stabilizing effects of home ownership, knowledge not without problems, and the unstabilizing effects of shifts in household composition and mix. The effects of locational characteristics of housing appear to be less well known and while there is much concern on how the changing social composition of neighborhoods affects households' propensities to move, firm evidence on the importance of this factor is not available.

RESIDENTIAL MOBILITY RESEARCH AND THEORY AND ITS RELEVANCE TO SOCIAL POLICY

The Housing and Home Finance Agency that provided the funds for the research reported in *Why Families Move* certainly did not do so out of the goodness of its heart, if any. And Merton, who wrote the research proposal, did not attempt to get the agency to start a basic research program with this effort. Rather, the main theme in the proposal was how important the understanding of the sources and consequences of residential mobility was to the policy needs of this agency.

I doubt whether anything reported in *Why Families Move* or in most of the subsequent studies of residential mobility contributed anything at all to the formation or the reformulation of housing policy in the United States. Indeed, since the agency stopped funding any social science research in the housing field shortly after 1949, perhaps the agency saw quickly enough how irrelevant in a direct way studies of this sort were to its policy needs. The best that can be said for the residential mobility research tradition is that it provides some sort of basic understanding of some of the major processes involved in housing market behavior that could serve as a sort of backdrop for policy deliberations.

If anything, the research on residential mobility relates a rather hopeless tale to the policy maker. Gross rates have been virtually constant for a long period of time and reveal only a slight hint that some glacial shifts downward may be in progress. The sources of residential mobility appear to be largely composed of processes that presently lie outside the control of social policy, especially by housing agencies, in the formation change and dissolution of households.

But, perhaps the problem is not stated properly? Is it the goal of housing policy to affect the rate of mobility or is it the goal of housing policy to provide decent housing in decent environments? If the latter, then residential mobility is only relevant to the extent to which it affects the ability of policy to attain such goals.

One of the major problems with the residential mobility literature is that we learn so little about how present or past housing policy impacts upon the phenomena. How were federal mortgage policies in the post-World War II period affecting households either as constraints or facilitations in the abilities of households of varying backgrounds and resources to reach their housing equilibria? Indeed, the connections between housing choice behavior, the institutional structures of mortgage banking, public housing programs, housing subsidies, real estate brokers, housing providers, developers, and the housing construction industry are not spelled out in the study of housing choice behavior. Even the housing market is only dimly revealed in the studies reviewed here,[30] reduced largely to household perceptual maps of housing opportunities.

Another major problem has been a lack of concern, especially in the social psychological study of housing choices, for the consequences of those choices within the institutional setting of our housing institutions. The residential mobility patterns in their relationship to housing equilibrium shifts can take a variety of forms that will produce equally equilibrating results. Here the point is not that housing policy should keep households away from their equilibrium points but that social policies ought to be concerned with "minding the store," i.e., attempting to see that social goals are fulfilled as well as individual goals. Hence, relevant research on residential mobility would be concerned with how changes in social policy might structure choices through a pattern of constraints and incentives both to satisfy household equilibrium needs and appropriate social goals. For example, a possible social goal of the future might be to reduce household energy consumption through less dispersed settlement patterns. Structuring housing choices so that more dense settlement patterns can satisfy households' housing needs would be the kind of research on mobility (or rather the equilibrating process that is responsive to changing household housing needs) that is needed.

Finally, it should be stressed that mobility per se is probably not the central issue of policy relevance. It is much more important that the relationships between mobility and the direct concerns of planners and policy makers be more clearly and pointedly articulated. In this context, the questions of who moves and why are less than illuminating. The critical questions center around the impact of specific programs and policies on the ability of population subgroups to maintain and/or improve their housing situations. For example, the present housing system may literally force persons to divorce their employment locations from their dwelling locations. An alternative housing policy might attempt to minimize travel time and/or costs in the interests of energy conservation and in the interests of sustaining the expansion of employment opportunities for women.

EPILOGUE

To write this introduction to the second edition of *Why Families Move* has been a sentimental journey for me. I hope that my indulgence in sentimentality has not obscured the cognitive content of this review of what has happened in research on residential mobility in the more than three decades that have passed since I collected the data that went into *Why Families Move*. Finally, I asknowledge the helpful comments of colleagues in an informal seminar on urban problems: Anne Shlay, Gary Hill, William Diggins, and Jerry Wilcox.

Peter H. Rossi
Amherst, Massachusetts

NOTES

1. Some earlier attempts to measure the amount of interaction within urban neighborhoods through per-capita rates of incoming telephone calls, trolley car trips, and other measures of communication are described in the annotated bibliography to the original edition of *Why Families Move*.

2. These themes are still alive and well and can be found in such popular social science fiction as Packard (1977).

3. None of the evidence for this statement appears in *Why Families Move*. About half of the questionnaires were taken up with items attempting to measure loneliness and alienation, none of which could be either explained or used to explain anything else. Chapters reporting these nonfindings were edited out of early drafts.

4. The problem lies in the fact that the moves of some individuals are not independent of others since individuals are not always independently moving units. Hence, a five-person household that moves together is counted five times in an individual-based measure while another unit with but two persons is counted only twice. In addition, both units involve two housing units and, hence, individual-based mobility rates are ambiguous surrogates of housing turnover.

5. Of course, this is a defect in *Why Families Move*. I did conduct a pretest in which both husbands and wives were interviewed, deciding on that basis that either husband or wife was a good reporter on the collectively agreed upon decision. Now that wives and husbands may be more frequently both participating in the labor market (as compared with 1950 patterns), the question of moving (or migrating) may be as much determined by wife's employment and earnings as by husband's (see DaVanzo, 1977, for evidence on this point with respect to migration).

6. This is the most serious deficiency in the analyses presented in Chapters 7 through 9 of *Why Families Move*. Information on changes that affected past moves of the households interviewed were obtained from questions asking why they moved, if they moved, and not from either measures obtained at the time changes occurred or which asked whether changes of the appropriate sort had occurred. Thus, estimates of the role played by household size shifts in precipitating moves are undoubtedly biased.

7. Some technical research has gone into the accuracy of owner-reported market values for housing, the outcomes of which have been widely cited as indicating that such reports are accurate "enough" for research purposes (Lansing and Kish, 1957).

8. I do not believe that *Why Families Move* contains an account of one of the major design deficiences of the study, fortunately, one that I was easily able to remedy. For some reason, the basic questionnaire did not call for any information on dwelling size. As I analyzed the data and came rapidly to an appreciation of space needs as a factor in impelling families to move, I undertook a postcard resurvey of the 924 families to ascertain this vital piece of information.

9. In societies with acute housing shortages, e.g., Yugoslavia, the availability of housing may condition marriage and divorce decisions.

10. Thus an outward mobility rate might be defined as the number of tenant households at T_0 who are no longer tenants at T_1 less deaths, institutionalization, and so on divided by the number of housing units available for occupancy and occupied over period T_0 to T_1. An inward mobility rate might also be defined in a similar fashion. (See Moore, 1978, for an accounting scheme that takes these considerations into account.)

11. Of course on a sample basis, such files are not difficult to maintain, although expensive, as the experience in the Rand Corporation's surveys of dwelling units and structures in the Supply Experiment that is part of the Experimental Housing Allowance Project shows (Rand Corporation, 1978).

12. Excellent literature reviews have been provided by Simmons (1968) and Quigley and Weinberg (1977).

13. Note that some persons did not report sufficient information to allow the Census Bureau to characterize either origin and/or destination or had moved from abroad or from a noncivilian residence (about 6%).

14. These figures are not quite comparable to those shown in Table I.2 since rural-to-rural residence shifts may be within the same county or involve crossing county borders. Hence, some of the rural-to-rural shifts are counted as intracounty moves in Table I.2.

15. Strangely enough, the one section of *Why Families Move* that is devoted to this issue is scarcely ever mentioned in subsequent literature. Chapter 4 is devoted largely to a qualitative analysis of interviews held with informants drawn from nieghborhood institutions–churches, retail stores, voluntary organizations, and the like–attempting to assess the effects of neighborhood stability or mobility (as the case may be) on the functioning of the organizations in question. Since I was unable to find very much beyond the very obvious (e.g., that voluntary organizations such as churches had difficulties in recruitment in mobile areas), perhaps the general mushiness of the results has led most readers to pass over this chapter.

16. Indeed, the fact that it makes sense to separate out the two decisions in post-World War II studies may only mean that in the housing market conditions prevailing over that period, some appropriate vacancy could be found for most every household. Hence, finding an alternative location was not problematic. One can imagine a housing market situation (or market segment) in which whether or not a household moved depended almost entirely on the existence of a vacancy. Such may be the circumstances faced by the very poor elderly or other population subgroups whose income is severely restricted or whose housing choices may be restricted by discrimination. With abundant vacancies of appropriate sorts, a household may decide to move confident that once that decision had been made an appropriate housing alternative could be found.

17. Of course, there are many compensating changes going on at the same time, including a sharp rise in the number of single-person households, a significant increase in the number of households formed by persons living together outside of formal marriage,

and a possible increase in the rate of divorce. In addition, the bulging cohort of post-World War II babies is currently entering upon the life cycle stage of household formation.

18. This also explains why quality-of-life studies (e.g., Campbell et al., 1976) which stress expressed satisfaction with domains of life are so sterile. Of course, most persons are satisfied at any one point in time since measurement intervenes at some point in an equilibrating process. Useful studies are those that attempt to specify the conditions under which feelings of satisfaction and dissatisfaction arise.

19. This statement makes equilibrium equivalent to satisfaction. Actually, we do not know whether this is the case. Nor do we know how stable are self reports of satisfaction. One can easily conceive of self reports of satisfaction with housing and neighborhood as being partially suffused with evaluations of other aspects of life (e.g., marriage, work, friendships, and so on) and partially dependent on transient fluctuations of mood. Clearly, a household that is out of equilibrium in an economic sense ought to be dissatisfied, but one can easily imagine circumstances under which that would not be the case (e.g., a family overconsuming housing, liking the housing even if they cannot afford it.) The appropriate translation of equilibrium into direct measurement requires the measurement of utilities, presumably related to satisfaction but not necessarily equivalent.

20. *Ceteris paribus* calculations that would sustain this statement are clearly difficult to make since housing units on the ownership and rental markets tend to differ considerably and the cost calculations involve making considerable inferences about the value of time spent on sales transactions and so on.

21. In this connection it is interesting to note that home-owning participants in the Supply Experiment in the Experimental Housing Allowance Project whose homes fell below quality standards were most likely to bring their housing into conformity by modifying their dwellings than by moving to another conforming unit.

22. Social psychological investigations of the meaning of homeownership have tended to come up with rather global positive attributes of home owning, e.g., owning is identified with the concept of "home" while renting is identified with the concept of "house," possibly indicating that households are not fully able to articulate in specific terms the specially attractive features of homeownership.

23. Part of the problem is that unemployment is not randomly distributed. Households subject to high risks of unemployment for their wage-earning members are also likely to have low levels of skills, low levels of earnings, when employed, and likely to occupy rented as opposed to owned units.

24. Interestingly enough, perhaps one of the strongest findings of the effects of negative income tax payments on poor and near-poor intact households in the New Jersey-Pennsylvania Income Maintenance Experiment (Rossi and Lyall, 1974) was an increase in home ownership as well as a general increase in housing expenditures. It should be kept in mind, however, that the rules of eligibility in this experiment favored relatively large families headed by males in low earning occupations, households which were very likely to be out of housing equilibrium but without the resources to move toward their equilibrium points.

25. One of the major reviews of *Why Families Move* characterized the volume as completely irrelevant since it was well known that residential mobility was almost completely an expression of social mobility with households changing their housing to be in line with their socioeconomic levels.

26. Similar results were obtained in an analysis of the housing effects of the Seattle and Denver Income Maintenance Experiments (Thomas, 1979).

27. Some researchers (e.g., Duncan and Newman, 1975) have weighted this index by the ages of the household members, reasoning that a married couple only need one

bedroom, while two children of the same sex under a certain age also need only one bedroom, while each unmarried adult person would need a bedroom apiece, and so on. Thus, quite sensibly, a household of a certain composition may be perfectly accommodated in a given dwelling unit while another of the same size but composed of different mixes of ages, sexes, and marital statuses might be considerably pinched for space in the same dwelling unit.

28. This is not to say that it does not play an important part in residential location, i.e., in the choice of a dwelling among a set of alternatives.

29. Frankly, I am not able to make very much out of this literature.

30. A major exception is the concern for the effects of housing allowance payments on residential mobility in the Supply Experiment of the Experimental Housing Allowance Project.

FOREWORD AND ACKNOWLEDGMENTS
TO THE FIRST EDITION

The study reported on in this volume was jointly sponsored by The Institute for Urban Land Use and Housing Studies and the Bureau of Applied Social Research, both of Columbia University. Senior staff members from both organizations served on an Administrative Committee which reviewed the work of the research staff.

The Administrative Committee was composed of Professor Ernest M. Fisher of the Institute, who served as Chairman, Professor Robert B. Mitchell, also of the Institute, and Professors Paul F. Lazarsfeld and Robert K. Merton of the Bureau. The research staff was headed by the author as Research Director.

The study was financed under a contract with the Housing and Home Finance Agency, the overall housing agency of the federal government. Dr. Ernest Jurkat, who was a member of the staff of the Division of Housing Research of that agency, was in close contact with the research staff of the project and at many points made valuable contributions to the project.

Mr. Norman Kaplan served as Research Associate and ably supervised the work of the interviewing staff in the field. He also contributed at many points to the analysis of the data, especially to the materials presented in Chapter 3.

Miss Mary Jean Huntington and Mrs. Joan Martinson May, both Research Assistants, also made important contributions to this study. Mrs. May conducted special interviews in Philadelphia and made the preliminary analysis of the effects of mobility on organizational life which is reported in Chapter 4. Miss Huntington did much of the preliminary analysis in Part III.

Mr. Joseph A. Rosenmiller conducted the check survey reported in Chapter 6 and made the preliminary analysis of the results reported there. Mr. Alvin D. Zallinger is the author of the annotated bibliography that appears in the appendix to this report [not reprinted in this edition].

From time to time, members of the staff of the Bureau of Applied Social Research made invaluable contributions to the conduct of this study. Mrs. Jeannette Green helped to organize the field work in Philadelphia. Miss

Babette Kass ably edited a preliminary report of the findings. Mr. Hanan Selvin constructed the sampling design and supervised its execution.

To the members of the Administrative Committee I am especially indebted for their guidance in the conduct of the study and their cogent help in writing this report. Whatever merit this study may have is primarily due to their help. Its faults arise from my inability to carry out their directives. Professor Paul F. Lazarsfeld took on the onerous task of supervising the revision of an earlier version of this report and I am extremely indebted for his guidance.

The members of the research staff through their excellent help and cooperation made possible the completion of this study within the short time span of 15 months. I am very conscious of the many contributions they have made to the design and analysis of the research.

I also wish to express my appreciation to Harvard University's Department of Social Relations and its Laboratory of Social Relations which, by easing my teaching and research assignments during my first year on their staff, facilitated the revision of the initial report.

My wife, Alice S. Rossi, took on the heavy task of reading the present manuscript, editing it, and at many points suggesting new modes of analysis and interpretation which have very materially improved this report. Her encouragement and expert advice have made substantial contributions to the present version of the report.

Publication of this research was made possible in part by a grant from the Eda K. Loeb Fund. Appreciation for such support is gratefully acknowledged.

The merits of this report arise primarily from the excellent help and guidance I have received from the research staff and the Administrative Committee. The report's defects are, however, entirely my own responsibility.

PHR
Cambridge, Mass.

PART I
INTRODUCTION

Chapter 1

OBJECTIVES AND OVERVIEW

RESIDENTIAL MOBILITY IN URBAN AMERICA

America's city dwellers are a mobile people. The decennial censuses provide documentation in their redundant accounts of rapid changes and growth in most of our great cities. But statistical evidence is hardly needed. The changes in our cities have occurred so rapidly that the perception of mobility is an integral part of every urban dweller's experience. Home towns are transformed in the intervals between visits. The neighborhoods of our childhood present alien appearances and the landmarks that anchored our memories have disappeared.

The city changes without cease. Homes give way to factories, stores, and highways. New neighborhoods arise out of farms and wasteland. Old residential districts change their character as their residents give way to different classes and cultures. Business districts slowly migrate uptown. Mansions of yesterday sport "rooms to let" signs today. Tenements once rented to immigrant European peasants, now house migrants from our own rural areas.

How do these dramatic changes in residential areas come about? In part, industry and commerce in their expansion encroach upon land used for residences. But, in larger part, the changes are mass movements of families— the end results of countless thousands of residence shifts made by urban Americans every year. Compounded in the mass, the residence shifts of urban households produce most of the change and flux of urban population structures.

How much mobility is there? About one person in every five shifts residences over a year's time. About three quarters of our urban citizens were living in 1950 in places in which they did not reside in 1940. America's city dwellers change their housing, it seems, almost as often as they change their cars.

Some of the mobility is an expression of the growth of our population. Every new family started ordinarily means another household formed. But the mobility that occurs is much greater than can be accounted for only by the addition of new households to our population.[1] The high level of mobility implies that established households are involved in a large-scale game of "musical chairs" in which housing is exchanged from time to time.

Residential shifts often accompany the dissolution of households, although not as consistently as in the case of the formations of new households. A divorce or separation forces at least one move, and often both husband and wife shift residences. Mortality sometimes precipitates a move on the part of the remaining members of the household. But, neither divorce nor mortality, when added to new household formation, can account for more than a very small part of the American mobility rate.

Another part of the high residential mobility rate might be traced to changes occurring in the labor force. American workers change jobs frequently and some of the residential mobility might be viewed as a consequence of job shifts. But most residential shifts do not involve long-distance movements. About three fourths of such shifts do not cross county boundaries and many of them take place within smaller areas. Neither can job shifts account for the overall picture of mobility, much of which is a kind of "milling about" within small areas of the city.

The larger part of residential mobility appears, therefore, to be above and beyond that called for by the growth of our population or the vagaries of the labor market. But the existence of a "mystery" does not, by itself, justify the expenditure of time and money on research. *Basic research into residential mobility is of importance because mobility is one of the most important forces underlying changes in urban areas.* Change in the urban residential neighborhood takes place through the ebb and flow of different populations. We need to know why residential shifts take place and how the characteristics of the neighborhood—its social composition, its location with regard to important urban activities, and its physical characteristics—tie into this phenomenon.

Besides this general concern with the dynamics of urban change, several other interests, some practical and some more general, are served by an inquiry into the nature of residential mobility. On the practical side, workers in the fields of public housing, real estate, and community organization have all expressed interest in ascertaining the motivational structure underlying mobility. Urban areas characterized by high mobility present severe problems to the community organizer. The builders of public or private housing, especially for the rental market, want to understand how they can build the kind of physical plant which will minimize tenant turnover and maximize tenant stability and satisfaction. By pointing out why families move, the practitioner may begin to see how his actions may be modified or changed to bring about the desired residential stability.

Research into residential mobility is of interest as well to the urban sociologist. Residential mobility has long occupied a central position among the concepts the sociologist has employed to explain the urban way of life. In part, the anonymity of urban life arises from the instability of many urban neighborhoods. To understand the social psychology of residential instability means to add to our knowledge of urban social structure.

What are the questions concerning mobility which we wish to raise in this research? Mobility can be studied on three different levels: We may raise questions concerning the mobility of urban areas, concerning the mobility of different types of families, or concerning the motivations underlying residential shifts.

On the area level, we wish to know what are the distinguishing features of mobile areas? Are they characterized by particular types of structures, or inhabited by particular types of residents? What effect does mobility have upon the residents or upon the social structure of the area?

On the household level, we wish to pinpoint the characteristics which distinguish mobile from stable households? How does mobility fit into the housing needs of a family? Do job shifts play an important role? Or, are household composition changes of greater importance?

Finally we wish to study individual residential moves. As families make decisions concerning whether to move or to remain, what are the things they take into account? What role does their dwelling play? What are the important dwelling features involved? What are the important changes which take place in the family which may make moving seem imperative to it? How do the perceived characteristics of the surrounding social environment fit into their decisions?

Objectives

It is far easier to write down a set of questions concerning residential mobility than to devise the instruments by which their answers can be provided. There is no dearth of studies of mobility, but most of them were conducted before the development of many of the modern social research methods. Hence a primary task of a program of research into this topic was to develop or adapt research instruments in an effort to provide answers to the questions raised previously.

Fortunately, it was not necessary to start from scratch in developing research techniques. A considerable and still growing body of social research methods was available for adaptation to this particular research problem. In order to explore fully the possibilities of social research methods, a main emphasis of this research became methodological. *A major purpose of the study design and of the analysis of the resulting data was to produce an example of how modern social research methods can be employed in the study of residential mobility.*

The aim of gathering additional empirical information about the nature of residential mobility has not been lost sight of, however, either in the study design or in the analysis of data. *We have been equally concerned with drawing generalizations concerning the social psychology of residential mobility.* Despite our interest in serving both methodological and substantive goals, it has not been possible to serve both aims with equal efficiency. The study design was constructed with primarily methodological aims in mind; hence, the generality of the empirical results may be strongly conditioned by the way in which the study design was laid out. *However, many of our empirical generalizations are so strongly supported in the data that they are almost certain to hold up in subsequent researches.*

The primary research technique employed in this study is the survey method. The basic instrument is the personal interview conducted by means of a structured questionnaire, with persons chosen according to sound sampling principles. The survey method is particularly well adapted to the study of large-scale social phenomena, and the use of this method seemed to have considerable promise if applied to residential mobility.

To indicate how the survey method has been applied to the study of residential mobility, and at the same time to give the reader an overall perspective on the findings, the remainder of this chapter will be devoted to a skeleton summary of the major methodological and substantive content of the report. The way in which this study was designed is described in Chapter 2.

An Overview

Three modes of analysis are presented in the body of this report, and each may be found in one of the major subdivisions of this report. In Part II, the focus of attention is on the characteristics of mobile and stable areas. Here the problem is: How can we study the features of urban areas which are associated with mobility? In Part III, the analysis considers the mobility of individual households. What are the characteristics which best distinguish households that are mobile from those which are stable? Finally, in Part IV, the topic under analysis changes to individual residence shifts, and the problem becomes the study of reasons given by households for making particular moves.

Area Mobility (Part II)

For an intensive study of the distinguishing features of mobile and stable areas, four samples of households were chosen: two samples were taken from two *stable* areas of Philadelphia, each of considerably different socio-economic status; and two samples were taken from two *mobile* areas, also of contrasting socio-economic status.[2] The major advantage of such a selection is that it allows an analysis of the effects of mobility for areas of roughly the same socio-economic status. This feature is of particular importance since, on the whole, mobile areas tend to be of considerably lower socio-economic status and many of the features deemed to be characteristic of mobile areas are really more properly attributed to their lower socio-economic status.

One of the illustrations of the use of the survey technique presented in Part II compares the way in which residents regard their areas with how these areas may be viewed by an objective observer. We find, for example, that areas which are objectively better located with regard to accessibility are regarded as very poor in that respect by their inhabitants. The subjective ratings of an area by its residents do not show very much correspondence to the way in which an objective observer might rank those areas.

One of the methodological innovations introduced in Part II is an attempt to measure the relative amounts of interpersonal integration in the four study areas. Integrated areas are ones in which there are many personal ties among residents. To measure the amount of such integration, the social relationships entered into by the households were studied. Addresses of best friends and closest relatives were obtained, as well as the number of families in the neighborhood with whom the households were friendly, and so on.

Upon analysis, it was found that mobility had little effect on the amount of social contacts entered into by a household. The number of friendships varied more with socio-economic status than with mobility and the residents of the two higher socio-economic status areas had on the whole more friends and did more visiting than the residents of the two lower status areas.

The effects of mobility were revealed, however, in the location of the household's significant personal ties. In the two stable areas, the residents' friends and relatives were found to be living close by; while in the two mobile areas, friends and kin tended to be dispersed more widely throughout the city.

Another methodological aspect of the study described in Part II is an attempt to gauge the effects of mobility upon the organizations and institutions found in mobile areas. A special canvass was made of ministers, businessmen, and other persons engaged in activities servicing one of the mobile study areas. It was found that the effects of mobility on the organizations in question ranged considerably. Some organizations, particularly those dependent on active participation on the part of residents, were particularly affected, while others had little or no concern with mobility. An evaluation was also made of such organizations as sources of information about mobility.

Some attention is also paid in Part II to the demographic compositions of the four study areas. Mobile areas were found to be occupied by large proportions of childless couples and single persons. The lower socio-economic status mobile area can be aptly described as the entry point of rural and small-town working class migrants to Philadelphia. The mobile higher socio-economic status area also served the same function for white collar and professional migrants to Philadelphia.

The demographic analysis also showed that the widely held opinion that single persons and childless couples are the most mobile elements in the populations of mobile areas is far from accurate for the areas studied. The most mobile elements in the two mobile areas studied were families with children.

Household Mobility (Part III)

In Part III, the focus of interest shifts from the area to the household. Here the central question is: What are the differences between mobile and stable households? Each household's mobility was defined as its desires and plans concerning moving in the future. The households in the sample differed considerably in this regard and the analysis of these differences turned out to be particularly fruitful.

It was found that the major social characteristics distinguishing mobile from stable households were variables closely related to the family life cycle. Large families were found to be more mobile than small families; young families, more mobile than older ones. Also of importance were the household's actual tenure and tenure preference. Renters were more mobile than owners, and renters who preferred to own were the most mobile of all.

Attitudinal differences were also found between mobile and stable households. Particularly important were complaints about dwelling units and neighborhoods. Indexes of complaints about six aspects of their dwellings and neighborhoods were constructed using advanced measurement techniques. It was found that complaints about the space within the dwelling, about the neighborhood, and about costs were particularly important in distinguishing between mobile and stable households. The more complaints registered by a household concerning these aspects, the more likely was the household to desire to move.

An equally important finding concerned the complaints which were not strongly related to mobility. Complaints about the journey to work, and about the distance from friends or relatives, for example, were found to be only slightly related to current mobility desires.

On the basis of these findings, two indexes were constructed: a *Mobility Potential Index* consisting of the background characteristics of households which predispose them to be mobile and a *Complaints Index* consisting of the number of complaints registered by the households concerning the important aspects of their homes and neighborhoods. Both indexes correlated very well with current mobility status, but not too well with each other. The combination of the two indexes showed a very high relationship to mobility status. *In other words, its position in the family life cycle and its attitudes toward its home and neighborhood are extremely good predictors of a household's current desires for moving.*

Another way of looking at these findings interprets the Mobility Potential Index as an indicator of a household's housing needs. At certain points in a family life cycle, the housing needs of the household are at their maximum. The Complaints Index may be looked upon as an expression of how the housing occupied meets these needs. The overall strong relationships between mobility desires and these two indexes can then be seen as a function of the housing needs of the family, as modified—either satisfied or frustrated—by the housing occupied by the family.

Of course, a family's current mobility, as we have conceived of it here, consists only of desires and plans about moving. Actual mobility behavior may or may not be closely related to attitudes toward moving. An attempt is made, therefore, to measure what the gap *actually* is between attitude and behavior in this area. Eight months after the initial interview with households, interviewers returned to the same dwelling units to ascertain whether or not the households had moved. In this way, it was possible to tell what the relationships were between attitudes toward moving and actual subsequent moving behavior.

It was found that of those households planning to stay where they were, 96% had done so. Of those who had planned to move, 80% had moved when the interviewers returned. The relationship between mobility plans and mobility behavior was very high. In order to gain some insight into the cases in which plans and behavior did not coincide, special interviews were conducted for these deviant cases.

Much of the data presented in Part III can be characterized as substantive findings concerning the determinants of mobility. Whether or not the strong relationships found here can be duplicated in the study of other samples of households is, of course, somewhat of an open question. As important as the substance of the findings are, the devices employed in the form of the analysis itself. The two indexes constructed are believed to be useful contributions. The finding that the relationship between attitude and behavior is so high in this area of behavior is confirmation of our faith in the relevance of survey methods.

The Decision to Move (Part IV)

Residential mobility, in the final analysis, is the compounded resultant of thousands of individual residence shifts. Each shift, looked at from the viewpoint of the household involved, can yield a valuable set of data concerning the social-psychological factors underlying residential mobility.

Residence shifts are the units of analysis of Part IV. Here we raise questions of the following order: Why did the households leave their former homes? How and why did they choose the dwellings they now occupy? Since the analysis undertaken to provide the answers to these questions is somewhat novel, detailed attention is given to a description of the method used. A scheme is presented for the analysis of moving decisions which may make a contribution to techniques for the study of residential mobility.

The "accounting scheme"—as the framework for analysis is called—presents a list of those data categories which are essential for an adequate understanding of why a household has moved. Reasons for moving are divided into those which pertain to the decision to move out of the former home—"pushes"—and those reasons pertaining to the choice among places to move to—"pulls." Within these basic categories of pushes and pulls, further distinctions are made concerning different stages in the decision process.

In addition, a technique is presented for assessing the relative importance of reasons. Rank orders of factors arranged according to their importance is residential shifts are devised. The assessment procedure employed is of general applicability to data collected by interview methods.

In brief outline, the major substantive findings of Part IV can be summarized as follows:

About one out of every four residential shifts must be classified as either involuntary or as the logical consequences of other decisions made by the household. Involuntary moves include evictions and destructions of dwellings. Moves which must be looked upon as forced by other decisions include moves made as a consequence of marriage, divorce, separation, job changes involving long-distance shifts, or severe losses in income.

Among voluntary moves—where the household had a clear choice between staying and moving—the most important factor impelling households to move was dissatisfaction with the amount of space in their old dwellings. Other factors, in order of their importance, were complaints about their former neighborhoods and about the costs of rent and maintenance in their old homes. No other category of complaints received any significant amount of mention as important factors in moving decisions.

The important things the respondents had in mind in choosing their present homes from all those available to them were, in rank order: space in the dwelling, particular dwelling design features, dwelling location, and, finally, cost. However, costs appeared as the major consideration in the actual choice, followed by space, location, and neighborhood in that order. Apparently, the most important attribute of a dwelling is its dimensions, but then if two or more dwellings of roughly equal size are considered, the cheaper one is finally chosen. Costs are the "clinching" factor in the choice point of housing selection.

An Interpretation

What is the meaning of residential mobility? Why do our urban areas experience so great a residential turnover? *The findings of this study indicate the major function of mobility to be the process by which families adjust their housing to the housing needs that are generated by the shifts in family composition that accompany life cycle changes.*

Mobility is greatest in the period when families are experiencing greatest growth. Most of the moves made by a family take place within a decade after its formation. Young families, especially those who have just added to their members, are those who are most likely to move. When such families find their housing inadequate to the demands generated by these shifts in composition, they are especially likely to move.

The housing aspects most sensitive to shifts in the family life cycle are those which tie in most closely to this life cycle interpretation. The space contained by a dwelling unit places a limitation on the ability of a household to make accommodations to life cycle changes. The social environment of the dwelling is also of importance. When space and social environment are found lacking, a family is especially likely to undertake a shift in residence.

Housing varies in the extent to which it is adjustable to such needs as are generated by life cycle changes. Large units are more flexible than small units. Because of the homeowner's control over his residence, owned homes can be modified to meet family changes—particularly those which impinge on the dwelling's interior characteristics. For these reasons, renters living in a small dwelling units are particularly inclined toward mobility.

Mobile areas derive their mobility primarily because of the housing they offer. The small dwelling units found there are particularly unsuited to the housing needs of expanding families. For such families, mobile areas can only serve as stations on the way to residential areas whose larger dwellings offer a more congenial housing.

The documentation for this interpretation can be found in the report which follows.

NOTES

1. In 1950 there were approximately one and a half million marriages involving, at the maximum, the moves of three million persons, and hence a mobility of about 2%.
2. Details of the area selection process are given in Chapter 2.

Chapter 2

THE STUDY DESIGN

A close analogy to a study design is the rough sketch made by an artist before he commits his vision to canvas. The broad outlines are drawn, the proper perspective achieved, and the total impact of the picture-to-be can be partially appreciated in advance. So it is with the design of research: It specifies in advance the kinds of statements that can be made on the basis of its findings and fixes the perspectives against which these findings are to be evaluated.

One major purpose of this study was to demonstrate whether or not the newer social research techniques could help in broadening and deepening knowledge concerning residential mobility. Construction of the design was guided by this goal of exploring new methods in the analysis of residential mobility. However, research techniques developed in one content area cannot be mechanically transferred to another. A new application often requires substantial changes and it is these innovative modifications which this study offers as its contribution.

Residential mobility has been the subject of many previous studies using a variety of research techniques. This study makes an additional contribution by using a design specifically planned to permit a comparison of several approaches.

The drawing up of the study design profited greatly from an extensive survey of previous researches on mobility, undertaken during the earliest stage of the project. It was found that most studies could be classified as belonging to one or more of three broadly conceived types: area studies, household studies, and motivational studies. Each study type had its characteristic design and mode of interpretation.

Area studies were the most frequently encountered type. Urban subareas, usually census tracts, were classified by their mobility rates and areas with high rates were compared with areas with low rates. A large number of generalizations concerning the close association between mobility rates and rates of divorce, delinquency, dependency, housing conditions, and so on emerged from these studies. Most of our knowledge concerning residential mobility derives from studies of this sort.

Household studies were much less frequently encountered in the published literature on mobility. The essential characteristic of this type was its focus on the individual household or, in some cases, individual persons. Mobile households or persons were compared with stable households or persons and significant differences were found with respect to relations with neighbors, the incidence of certain diseases, residence in certain kinds of housing, and such.

The third major study type—the motivational study—had a concern with the social psychological aspects of moving as its distinguishing characteristic. Such studies sought to answer the question: Why do people move? What reasons do people give for leaving one residence and taking on another? Attention usually was centered on housing conditions, neighborhood services, and such. Very few mobility studies were of this type.

Each of these three research designs has produced information of considerable importance. Yet no attempt was made in any of the studies to integrate one or more of these three design types. For example, there are no studies which integrate the social psychological aspects of moving with the general patterns of moving within urban centers. It became apparent that one of the major contributions a pilot study could make to both method and substantive findings would be to bring all three study types together in one design for the purpose of correlating their findings and evaluating their relative importance in producing data of use to the practitioner.

The study design finally adopted by the research team was to study the *moving decisions of different kinds of households* residing in *areas of contrasting stability and mobility*. Using such a design, *areas* of different mobility rates could be compared, *households* of different mobility could be contrasted, and the *social psychology of moving* could be analyzed all within the same study design, in such a fashion that the results of one approach could be compared with those obtained by another.

Although the advantages of this design were obvious, its disadvantages should not be underplayed. To study a representative set of urban subareas and at the same time a representative sample of households required heavier resources than this project could command. For this reason, the study abandoned representativeness in both respects and focused instead on *crucial types*. Rather than choose a large number of urban subareas, a small number of crucial types of subareas were chosen. Samples of households within these areas were taken without any attempt to insure that such samples would be representative of anything but the crucial type areas chosen. This expediency has meant that the substantive findings of this study have a somewhat more limited generality than its methodological findings.

Once the general outline of the design had been sketched, the next steps consisted of the selection of the crucial type areas and the specification of the kinds of data to be gathered from the households to be interviewed.

THE SELECTION OF PHILADELPHIA AND THE STUDY AREAS

Two major criteria were decided upon to guide the selection of a city. The city had to be somewhat "typical" of urban places in the United States with regard to both its housing types and its economic structure. Second, the city had to be fairly close at hand to New York, where the base office of the research organization was located. Within the geographic area circumscribed by this last criterion, Philadelphia seemed to be the most "typical" city. The proportion of owner-occupied dwellings and of multiple dwellings in Philadelphia is close to that of the national average for urban places. Philadelphia is also an economically diversified city, with no single dominating industry or commercial enterprise.

One further consideration also influenced the choice of Philadelphia. Close relations had been established by the Institute for Urban Land Use and Housing Studies with the Philadelphia City Planning Commission and several other local organizations interested in housing and planning problems. The help given by those organizations in the course of the field work justified our being influenced in this fashion.

The problem of how to select the crucial type areas within Philadelphia was a little more difficult. In the first place, it was necessary to choose some operational definition of "subarea." Census tracts, although arbitrary in their boundaries, were for our purposes the most convenient subdivision of the city.

Second, it was necessary to specify more clearly what was meant by "crucial types" of areas. Since one purpose of the study was to contrast mobile with stable areas, one element of being "crucial" was thereby specified. Another criterion was added as a result of the evaluation of previous studies. These researches showed that there was a strong inverse relationship between mobility rates and area indices of socioeconomic status. It was always difficult in such studies to disentangle what was related to mobility from what was more properly ascribed to socio-economic status. Hence, another criterion for selection of the subareas was socio-economic status.

Four areas—census tracts—were to be chosen, one of high mobility and high socio-economic status, one of high mobility and low socio-economic status, one of low mobility and high socio-economic status, and one of low mobility and low socio-economic status. By contrasting the first area with the second, and the third area with the fourth, the influence of mobility could be studied *independent* of socio-economic status. By contrasting the first and third areas and the second and fourth areas, conclusions could be drawn concerning the influence of socio-economic status *independent* of mobility.

Previous studies also showed that mobility rates were related to a large number of other area characteristics whose influence it would be necessary to remove if the effects of mobility itself were to be observed clearly. Areas with large proportions of foreign-born residents and with large proportions of Negroes were found to be among the most mobile. Hence, only census tracts with fewer than 20% Negroes and fewer than 15% foreign-born in 1940 were considered. There remained 213 residential census tracts from which the four crucial areas were to be chosen.

Each of these 213 tracts was classified according to whether it fell into the upper, middle, or lower third in a rank order according to median monthly rental (or estimated rent). The tract was simultaneously classified according to whether it fell into the upper, middle, or lower third in a rank order of the proportion of owner-occupied dwelling units. The 1940 Census was used as the source for the classification of areas. Median monthly rental was thus used as an index of the socio-economic status of the census tracts, and the proportion of owner-occupied dwelling units formed an index of mobility.

Tracts which were in the upper third in monthly rental and also in the upper third in home ownership qualified as the high socio-economic status, low mobility crucial type. Tracts in the lower third in monthly rental and the upper third in home ownership were candidates for the low socio-economic status, low mobility crucial type. The other two crucial types were defined in a similar fashion.

One hundred and one census tracts fitted into one or another of the four crucial types. The tracts which fitted the criteria for crucial type areas were not distributed at random throughout the city of Philadelphia. They tended rather to cluster into groups of contiguous tracts and only a few tracts were mavericks. About a dozen such groups of contiguous tracts were found and these groups, rather than the individual tracts of which they were formed, were the units which were considered in this final stage of the selection process.

At this point, when clustered tracts fitting the criteria were available for selection, the study enlisted the cooperation of persons professionally familiar with the city of Philadelphia. A conference was arranged with officials of the City Planning Commission, the Philadelphia Housing Association, and the Philadelphia Welfare Council in order to draw upon their intimate knowledge of the candidate areas and especially of the changes which might have taken place since the 1940 Census.

On the basis of this conference with the "experts," the choice was finally narrowed down to four clusters of tracts, one each of the four crucial area types. Four individual tracts[1] were finally selected, one from each of the four clusters. Wherever possible, these individual tracts were taken from the *centers* of the four clusters. From the point of view of the indexes of both mobility and economic status, and also in the opinion of the panel of experts, these four census tracts represented the four crucial types it was desired to obtain as closely as any empirical unit can approximate the ideal. More detailed descriptions of these areas and how they fulfilled the ideal patterns will be found in Chapter 3.

HOUSEHOLDS AS UNITS

The overall study design called for four samples of households, one from each of the four study areas. Each of the household units in the samples was to be interviewed with a schedule designed to ferret out the contrasting characteristics of mobile and stable households and also furnish reasons why households move.

Households rather than individual persons were chosen as the units to be studied since moving is ordinarily a group rather than an individual action. A household, for our purposes, was defined as a group of individuals, sharing the same dwelling unit, who ordinarily moved as a unit. This meant that households were operationally defined as nuclear families plus such other dependents who did not form another nuclear family.[2] Persons occupying a dwelling unit together but not forming a nuclear family were considered as forming one household only if related by blood ties.

Exploratory interviews indicated that it mattered little which adult individual in a household was interviewed. Data obtained from different persons within the same household varied from one to another within acceptable reliability limits. Accordingly, interviewers were instructed to obtain interviews with any adult member of a household with preference given to male adults when an alternative presented itself.

The final samples, therefore, consisted of adults selected from households found within probability samples of dwelling units taken within each of the four crucial type areas.[3]

HOUSEHOLD MOBILITY DEFINED

Since mobile and stable households were to be contrasted and their differences studied, it was necessary to be clear about the operational meaning of household mobility. Two ways of defining the term could be employed. A household's mobility could be viewed as its past mobility behavior—essentially the number and character of moves made in the past—or it could be viewed as its present mobility behavior—essentially the household's present desires and plans concerning moving in the future.

In principle, both definitions could be employed in the same study. But in actual operation, an emphasis on one exludes extensive consideration of the other. To study *past* mobility, it is necessary to know a great deal about the past behavior of the household in other respects—for example, occupational career, shifts in family composition, and so on. To study *present* mobility behavior, data on present occupation, present attitudes toward the dwelling unit occupied are more relevant. Since interviews are limited in length, it was necessary to choose one over the other definition.

The choice of present over past mobility was determined by the relative ease with which the validity of present mobility measures could be ascertained and by its greater utility to the practitioner. The validity of past mobility measures depends ultimately on how accurately persons can recall past mobility behavior. It is hard to design a measure of the accuracy of recall over the long periods of time represented by the average lifetimes of urban households. The validity of measures of present mobility can be ascertained by observing, over a period of time, whether or not households *acted* upon their reported desires and plans.

How to measure and study present mobility seemed to be of some utility to the practitioner, for his interests frequently focus on the question of what, at a given time, affects the future mobility or stability of a given population.

Past mobility was not entirely neglected, however, in designing the questionnaire. A full mobility history was obtained from each household. These data have been used as corroboratory tests of certain interpretations arising from other parts of the analysis. They are referred to at several points in the analysis of present mobility.

MOBILITY DYNAMICS

Another important goal of the study design was to devise methods of studying moving decisions. Was it possible to discern some of the reasons why a household left one dwelling unit and took up its abode in another? What were their dissatisfactions with the old and the anticipated benefits of the new?

Similar problems had been encountered in the study of other kinds of behavior—why people purchase certain items, why individuals shift their allegiances from one candidate to another in elections, and so on. Although the methodological problems had not been entirely solved, a body of previous experience was available for guidance and help.[4]

An ideal study design for the study of the social psychology of moving would involve following a group of households through the various stages of moving, from the initial beginnings of desires to the actual move itself. A panel of households observed repeatedly over a span of some years would fit the needs of such an ideal design. Given the time limitations of the present study, however, it was necessary to rely upon recall to reconstruct the histories of moves. Since we know that memories become less and less reliable the further in the past they refer to, the decision was made to study the last moves made by the households only if they took place within the previous five years.

THE EFFECTS OF MOBILITY

The effects of mobility upon the organizations which serve an area have received attention in many previous studies. But empirical evidence on these effects has been either entirely lacking or of a very impressionistic character. In addition, little attention has been paid to a specification of the ways in which mobility affects such organizations and whether organizations differ in the magnitude and quality of the effects felt. This pilot study makes a contribution to our knowledge of the effects of mobility upon organizations. Qualitative interviews were conducted in one of the mobile areas with leaders of many organizations, such as local clubs, churches, schools, and businesses. The analysis of these interviews attempts to point out what kinds of organizations are strongly affected by mobility and through what mechanisms mobility accomplishes these effects.

* * * *

The major outlines of the study design have now been laid out. Its rationale, limitations, and strong points should be borne in mind by the reader as he evaluates the sections of the report which follow.

NOTES

1. The tract numbers are as follows: 15A, known throughout this report as Central City, 25B, called Kensington, 46A, called West Philadelphia, and 42F, known as Oak Lane.

2. Thus a dwelling unit occupied by a man, his wife, and unmarried children would be counted as containing but one household. A dwelling unit containing a man, his wife, and his married daughter with her husband would be counted as containing two households.

3. The dwelling units were sampled from enumerations of all the dwelling units within each tract. Sanborn maps were used to enumerate single dwelling unit structures

and canvassers were employed to enumerate the dwelling units within multiple dwelling unit structures. Each sample was constructed by taking every n^{th} dwelling unit on the enumeration lists—the n varying with the size of the list so as to insure samples of approximately equal size in each of the areas. Dwelling units containing more than one household were treated as a separate universe and so sampled that no bias toward the underrepresentation of such households arose. Mr. Hanan Selvin, a staff member of the Bureau of Applied Social Research, constructed and supervised the design of the sample.

4. Professor Paul F. Lazarsfeld, a member of this study's Administrative Committee, has been particularly concerned with the general problem of the analysis of reasons. The analysis of this material in this study owes whatever worth it has to his advice and guidance.

PART II
AREA MOBILITY

Chapter 3

AREA COMPARISONS

INTRODUCTION

One of the major purposes of this study was to show how the interview method could throw light on the different natures of mobile and stable urban areas. To accomplish this purpose, four small areas, each comprising one of Philadelphia's census tracts, were selected to represent four *crucial types* of areas.[1] *Oak Lane*[2] was chosen to represent an area of low mobility and high socio-economic status. *West Philadelphia* serves as a representative of high status and high mobility areas. *Kensington* and *Central City* are both areas of low status but of low and high mobility, respectively (see Note 2).

It is essential to the validity of the findings to be presented in this chapter that each area adequately fulfills its representative role. One major purpose of this chapter is to give the reader an opportunity to judge for himself how closely each area resembles the ideal type it was chosen to represent. Obviously ideal types are never completely found in reality; there are only varying degrees of approximation to be found in the empirical world. Beyond the important question of how adequate the process was by which those four areas were selected, there are several other purposes to be served in this chapter.

Most of the knowledge available concerning residential mobility comes from ecological analyses. Such ecological studies have built up a considerable body of empirical knowledge through the study of the characteristics which distinguish mobile from stable areas. Is anything gained above and beyond this knowledge by the use of survey methods in the study of residential mobility? Are there types of data which result from interviews which add to or refine knowledge concerning mobility? Are there ways in which these two methods yield quite different results and how can these differences be resolved?

The interview method, as we shall see in this chapter, can obtain data which goes considerably beyond what is ordinarily available from ecological analysis. In the first place, ecological studies are generally restricted to census data plus a few other items which are collected and tabulated on an area basis. Such data can only inferentially throw light on the social pyschological aspects of urban areas. For example, areas can be ranked and ordered according to their dilapidation and inferences made about the desirability of such areas to their residents, but it is only through interviewing the residents that we may obtain direct evidence on their views concerning the area's desirability.

Two important social psychological aspects of the four study areas will be considered in this chapter. First, how do the attitudes of each area's residents toward the area compare with how an observer would rank the areas in more "objective" terms? Second, how do these areas compare according to the strength and frequency of personal ties among their residents? The answers to these questions will illustrate how the addition of social psychological dimensions enriches knowledge concerning residential mobility.

A last topic illustrates certain dangers inherent in ecological analyses. All too often researches have come forth with statements that generalize from the characteristics of mobile and stable areas to the characteristics of mobile and stable families or individuals. Some studies, for example, indicate that because small families and single persons are found in heavier proportions in mobile areas, then these household types are the most mobile types in urban areas. The difficulties which make such generalizations methodologically unsound are illustrated with data on the household compositions of the four study areas.

THE STUDY AREAS

Anyone acquainted with the variety of neighborhoods to be found in a large American city will find each of the four study areas somewhat familiar. Their locations within the city, their population compositions, and their physical appearances will undoubtedly recall some memory of a counterpart area in the city of his acquaintance. The familiar ring to the description of each area is no chance event. In the process of selecting the four study areas, an attempt was made to remove from consideration any area which had idiosyncratic features. The only pecularities which the study areas have were imposed by the criteria of selection: They tend to be on the upper and lower ends of both the ranges of mobility and socio-economic status.

Oak Lane, of high socio-economic status and low mobility, is located on the city's northern border, almost directly north of the central business district. It is a 15-minute bus ride beyond the last stop of Philadelphia's main north-south subway line. Oak Lane is almost exclusively residential, with no industrial establishments and with just a few retail establishments serving primarily the area itself. The predominant structure in Oak Lane is the small, brick (six- or seven-room) row house. In front of each house there is a short expanse of grass, and in warm weather the back yards present a familiar picture of grass and lawn furniture.

Oak Lane has experienced three waves of growth—in the housing booms of the twenties, the late thirties, and after World War II. Consequently, the area has a newness of appearance reflecting these relatively recent constructions. Its streets are spacious and lined with trees. The general impression is of neat, middle-class living.

The basic street design in Oak Lane is a grid system upon which several diagonal avenues have been imposed. One small portion, built in the earliest wave of growth, in the 1920s, has streets conforming to the curves of the land's contours.

Family living is the predominant pattern in Oak Lane. Few single persons occupy separate dwellings in the area. Most of the dwellings are occupied by married couples with young children. Home ownership is a predominant pattern.

Few of the householders work in factories or do routine clerical work. Rather, it is middle-class occupations which predominate: managers, officials, proprietors, and professional people, earning well above the average income.

West Philadelphia is an area of high socio-economic status and high mobility. It is located due west across the Schuylkill River from Philadelphia's central business district and can be reached from that point by trolley, bus, and elevated railway in 15 minutes.

West Philadelphia was once one of the city's most fashionable residential areas and a reminder of this past is found in the number of large old-fashioned, three- and four-story "town houses," which are now subdivided and converted into small "utility" apartments. During the twenties, several of Philadelphia's largest apartment developments were built in this area. The mixture of fairly modern high-rise apartments and old-fashioned town houses presents a very jagged sky line.

The basic street pattern is a grid system with narrow streets running north and south and wider streets running east and west. Most of the latter streets are main transportation routes and traffic along them is heavy. The Market Street elevated line runs along the northern border of the area. A sprinkling of commercial establishments can be found in the perpetual shadow of this elevated line, but most of the land is devoted to residential structures.

Unlike Oak Lane, few persons own their own homes or apartments in West Philadelphia. Family living is not the major pattern: Many single persons and couples with no children occupy the small apartments in the large developments or in the subdivided mansions.

Occupationally, West Philadelphia is as middle class as Oak Lane. Two out of three breadwinners earn their living at the more responsible white collar occupations—proprietors, managers, professionals.

Mobility is high in West Philadelphia: 3 out of 10 of its households moved into the area during a two-year period.

In sharp contrast to West Philadelphia is the low status-high stability area, Kensington. This district is located about two miles northeast of the central business district. It is a residential peninsula surrounded on the north, south, and east by large industrial establishments. On the east, a freight rail line runs its heavy cars on tracks in the middle of a wide avenue. On the west, another freight line runs in a cut. Marked off in this fashion, Kensington is a residential enclave which cannot escape continual awareness of its noisy, smoky, industrial borders.

The predominant housing pattern in Kensington is the familiar Phila-delphia two-story, five-room, brick row house, built close to the street with little free space to the front or the rear. These residential structures were built during the latter part of the 19th century as low-rent housing for working-class occupancy. They are not "hand-me-downs" from older middle-class occupancy.

Most of Kensington's residents own their homes. The houses are neat in appearance, newly painted, and in good repair. In the summer, colorful awnings protect the windows from the sun's glare. But the grid-pattern streets are so narrow two automobiles can barely pass each other. The general appearance is of land crowding, with few open spaces.

Kensington makes its living from industrial occupations. Three out of four breadwinners work in blue collar jobs. The average annual family income of $3,197 reflects this occupational pattern.

Few of Kensington's residents are newcomers to the area. Only 14% of the households have moved into their dwellings in a two-year period.

The fourth study area, Central City, contrasts sharply with the other three. Its mobility is extremely high: 41% of its households have lived there two years or less. Its shabby appearance, the "Furnished Rooms" signs in ground floor windows, the institutions that cater to a transient population, all testify to Central City's low status and high mobility.

Central City is located immediately to the northwest of the central business district. Several trolley lines run north and south through its streets, providing excellent transportation to the heart of the city. A short 15-minute walk connects its outer fringe with the very center of the city itself.

Residential structures in Central City were once the finest in the city. The old three- and four-story mansions have long passed their pinnacle of fashion. The spacious interiors have been altered through conversion to furnished rooms and small apartments. Their general appearance is of shabby exteriors and crowded, poorly maintained interiors.

Family living is not the pattern of life in Central City. There are few households with young children and many are composed of single adults. Home ownership is slight and restricted primarily to the owners of rooming houses who live on their premises.

Occupationally, Central City is blue collar. Two out of three of its workers make their living at low-status factory jobs or in the poorer white collar occupations. The average annual household income is $3,149.

The most striking characteristic of Central City is its shabbiness. The streets are dirty, the interiors of the houses are grimy and poorly lighted. Institutions which serve transiency are firmly entrenched in the area: missions, cheap restaurants, the "bachelor's shirt laundry," and the all-night delicatessen.

The reader probably knows areas in other cities comparable to the four described above. Oak Lane is a typical, middle-class, semisuburb. West Philadelphia is a middle-class apartment house district. Kensington is a typical blue collar residential area. Central City resembles every city's rooming house and furnished apartment district.

The criteria of selection dictated that Central City and Kensington resemble each other in socio-economic status, and similarly, that Oak Lane and West Philadelphia be matched in this respect. Furthermore, Oak Lane and Kensington were to resemble each other in mobility, and West Philadelphia and Central City were to form another matching pair in this regard. The success of this selection procedure can be evaluated by the data presented in Table 3.1.

With regard to socio-economic status, Oak Lane and West Philadelphia resemble each other more than each resembles either Kensington or Central City. In the same way, the mobility levels of West Philadelphia and Central City are closer to each other than to either of the other two areas. While the pairs of areas which were chosen to match each other do not do so precisely, their similarities override the degree of difference.

Closely related to the mobility level and socio-economic status of the four areas are many other distinguishing characteristics, some of which have been touched upon in the brief descriptions given earlier. To sharpen and summarize the comparisons among the study areas, Table 3.2 presents some of these salient differences.

The two stable areas, Oak Lane and Kensington, contain large proportions of households in the child-rearing stage, composed of parents and their unmarried children. The two mobile areas contain few such households, and, correspondingly, larger proportions of both single-person households and families without children (presumably either before or after the child-rearing state) are found in West Philadelphia and Central City. Mobile areas are childless areas, containing high proportions of persons living outside families.

TABLE 3.1   Socio-Economic Status and Mobility in the
Study Areas

	Oak Lane HL*	West Phila. HH*	Kensington LL*	Central City LH*
I. SOCIO-ECONOMIC STATUS:				
Proportion with high status occupations**	61%	53%	12%	20%
Average annual household income	$4,902	$4,103	$3,197	$3,149
Proportion attended college	39%	34%	3%	11%
II. RESIDENTIAL MOBILITY				
Proportion of households living in area less than 23 months	16%	30%	14%	41%
Number of households interviewed in each area	(215)	(286)	(214)	(209)

*The code letters under each area's name designate the crucial type it represents: Thus Oak Lane, the *high* status *low* mobility area is given the code "HL", and Central City, *low* status and *high* mobility area is given the code "LH". The codes will be used on all tables in this report which are concerned with area comparisons.
**"High status occupations" comprise proprietors, managers, professionals and semi-professional workers, and "responsible white collar" occupations (white collar jobs of a non-supervisory character but requiring considerable initiative and responsibility).

Both stable areas are characterized by high proportions of home owner-ship. Nine out of 10 of Oak Lane's residents and three out of four Kensing-tonians own their own homes. Only 3 out of 20 in the two mobile areas are homeowners. Many of these latter are rooming-house landlords living on the premises.

The origins of the residents of the four areas suggest that the two mobile areas serve as ports of entry, as it were, for migrants from smaller towns and rural areas. A little less than half of the residents of the two mobile areas were born in Philadelphia and about the same number spent their childhoods in small cities or rural places. In contrast, two out of three of the residents of Oak Lane and Kensington were born in Philadelphia, and only one in four spent their childhoods outside of a large city. Migrants to the city, lacking in first-hand knowledge of the city's neighborhoods and perhaps just entering the labor market, may find the small apartments and the accessibility of Central City and West Philadelphia congenial to their immediate housing needs.

This interpretation receives confirmation when we consider what the households' plans were when they first moved into each area. About half of

TABLE 3.2   Statistical Profiles of the Study Areas

		Oak Lane HL	West Phila. HH	Kensington LL	Central City LH
I.	HOUSEHOLD COMPOSITION				
	Households containing parents and their unmarried children	71%	24%	67%	36%
	Single person households	1%	22%	4%	21%
	Households containing married couples with no children	20%	36%	16%	25%
II.	DWELLING UNIT DIFFERENCES				
	Home ownership	91%	16%	76%	17%
	Average number of rooms	6.04	3.71	5.68	3.52
III.	ORIGINS OF RESPONDENTS				
	Born in Philadelphia	62%	48%	67%	40%
	Childhood spend in small city or rural areas	25%	40%	24%	53%
IV.	MOBILITY				
	Original intentions were to stay permenently	56%	27%	48%	18%
	Desiring to move	36%	51%	43%	62%
	Expect to move within year	3%	10%	3%	16%
	Number Interviewed	(215)	(286)	(214)	(209)

the households in the two stable areas intended to settle permanently, whereas less than one in four in the two mobile areas had such plans in mind. To the bulk of their residents, the mobile areas are seen as expedient residential way-stations.

The mobility of each area apparently will remain at very much the same level in the future. More than half of the households in Central City and West Philadelphia desired to move. In contrast, only one in three in Oak Lane and two in five in Kensington had such desires. But even more striking differences between the mobile and stable areas are found when expectations about moving in the very near future are considered. Three percent of the residents of Oak Lane and Kensington expect to move within a year; 1 out of 10 of West Philadelphia's and 3 out of 20 of Central City's households expect to move out within the year following their interviews.

HOW THE HOUSEHOLDS REGARD THEIR
HOUSING AND NEIGHBORHOODS

A set of neighborhoods may be easily compared and ranked according to the degree to which they fulfill certain criteria of adequacy. Some neighborhoods, as either census data or inspection of maps will tell us, are more accessible than others or contain a more adequate ratio of open space to occupied land, or are located closer to objectionable land use such as factories or heavy transportation. The information is readily available and most observers will agree that the ranking coincides more or less with the desirability of residence in the areas.

Such rankings, however, may or may not coincide with how the residents of such neighborhoods regard the matter. For one thing, residence is to a large degree a self-selective phenomenon: households which desire a particular neighborhood characteristic tend to locate themselves in areas where this aspect is maximized. For some households, accessibility to main lines of transportation is extremely important; for others this may be a relatively minor concern.

To illustrate this generalization, the material presented in this section will compare how an objective observer may rank the four study areas with the way in which the residents of these areas view the matter. The subjective data are indexes of satisfaction with certain aspects of each of the four areas: the physical design of the area, its location in the city, and the space available in its dwelling units.

Each of the indexes was constructed from a battery of questions asking respondents to indicate whether they were satisfied or dissatisfied with specific aspects of their dwellings or neighborhoods.[3]

We will begin by considering the relationship between the objective observer's appraisal of the location of each area and subjective satisfaction of the residents with its location. The location of each area will be considered with reference to the network of fixed transportation routes in Philadelphia. The measure for comparison is distance from the central business district. The business district is the most frequent of all destinations in a large city and is the point of convergence of the major fixed transportation routes.

The location of the four study areas is perhaps best judged from the following descriptions:

Oak Lane is about four miles to the north of Philadelphia's central business district and can be best reached from the latter by a combination of subway and bus, requiring a trip of about an hour. Oak Lane is the least favored of the four areas in accessibility to both central business district and the other areas of the city.

Kensington is somewhat more favored. This area lies about two miles to the northeast of the central business district and is served by an elevated line and several trolley and bus lines. Although it is closer than Oak Lane to the central business district, it is relatively inaccessible to other parts of Philadelphia.

Central City is located directly northwest of Philadelphia's central business district. Although it is closest to the city's main business center, it does not enjoy the use of any major transportation facility. Several trolley lines connect the area to other lines leading to the center of town. Trips to the other sections of the city are perhaps best accomplished by going to the central business district for connections with the subway and other transportation lines.

West Philadelphia has the best location of the four areas. An elevated line runs along its northern border and brings West Philadelphians to the heart of the city in a few minutes. Fast trolley lines run along several of its east-west streets and lead directly into the central business district.

According to the descriptions shown above, the rank order of "goodness" of location, starting with the best location, is: West Philadelphia, Central City, Kensington, and Oak Lane. However, when the views of the residents in each area are considered, quite a different ranking occurs, as we may note in Table 3.3.

In fact, there seems to be little relationship between the two rank orders. Central City, which we have objectively placed as second best, is the area about whose location the residents are least satisfied.

An index registering satisfaction with certain physical aspects of each area affords another opportunity to contrast objective and subjective rankings. This index is composed of complaints about such matters as street noises, amount of air and sunlight, and amount of open spaces in the neighborhood, matters which are easily noted by an objective observer. The following thumbnail descriptions will allow the reader to rank each of the areas in this respect.

TABLE 3.3   Subjective and Objective Views of Area Location

	Oak Lane HL	West Phila. HH	Kensington LL	Central City LH
Proportion of households with no location complaints	69%	78%	81%	58%
Subjective rank order	III	II	I	IV
Objective rank order	IV	I	III	II

Oak Lane easily ranks first with regard to its physical structure. Many of the houses are detached, although most are attached row houses. Its streets are wide and lined with trees. The monotonous gridiron street pattern has been broken by several diagonal avenues, and in the eastern portion of this tract the streets follow the contours of the land. Street noises, particularly those which arise from through-traffic, are relatively few. Oak Lane is rather pleasant looking, almost suburban in many respects.

Kensington ranks far below Oak Lane in this respect. Its structures crowd the narrow streets and are built side by side in the monotonous row pattern. There are few open spaces in the area and, although traffic is not very heavy, the narrow streets restrict escape from the street noises which do occur. The freight trains rumbling by on southern and eastern borders contribute to the noise as do the factories in the area itself and on its other borders. Smoke from nearby heavy industries leaves a gritty film on the visitor's car and, when the wind is favorable, factory odors pollute the air.

West Philadelphia, with its tall apartment buildings built around open courts and its rows of converted town houses interrupted by open spaces, is not too badly off with regard to air and sunlight. Its east and west streets are main thoroughfares; an elevated rumbles along its northern borders and trolleys and buses grind through most of its other east-west streets.

Central City, with its three- and four-story structures crowded together on narrow streets, is probably worse off than all the other areas with regard to air and sunlight. Little through-traffic passes along its streets, however, so that traffic noises are not great. No open spaces appear between the structures, giving the impression of considerable land-crowding.

The resultant ranking of the four areas, from "good" to "bad" is then as follows: Oak Lane, West Philadelphia, Kensington, and Central City. The residents' own views on the physical aspects of the areas they inhabit are given in Table 3.4. Again there appears to be little relationship between the observer's ranking and that derived from the residents' attitudes toward their neighborhood. Particularly striking is the discrepancy between Kensingtonians' views about their area and that derived from an observer's appraisal. The objectionable features of landcrowding, heavy industrial noise, and air pollution count little to the inhabitants of this area.

Last to be considered is an index measuring the degree of satisfaction with the amount of space in the dwelling units of each area. As shown in Table 3.5, homes in Oak Lane are most commodious, followed in order by Kensington, West Philadelphia, and Central City. The levels of satisfaction defining

TABLE 3.4   Subjective and Objective Views of Physical
Aspects of the Study Areas

	Oak Lane HL	West Phila. HH	Kensington LL	Central City LH
Proportions of households with no complaints about physical aspects	61%	53%	62%	45%
Subjective Rank Order	II	III	I	IV
Objective Rank Order	I	II	III	IV

the subjective rank order, also shown in Table 3.5, almost coincides with the objective rank order, the exception being that Oak Lane follows very closely behind Kensington with regard to space satisfaction.

What conclusions can be drawn from the way in which the objective and subjective measures of the four study areas vary? We have seen that in two out of three comparisons which were made, the correspondence was very slight. In only one comparison was the correspondence fairly close. Residents' views of their areas seem to be a composite effect of the objective standing of the area and their general feelings about the area as a place in which to live. Kensingtonians seem to regard their area highly without regard to how poorly placed it is in comparison with other areas. In the same way, the residents of Central City regard their neighborhood poorly even if, objectively, it is relatively well off in some one respect. Ratings in specific respects, therefore, seem to be generated more by the overall views of the areas than by an objective appraisal of the area's standing in some one aspect. This can be seen by that fact that the subjective rank orders vary but slightly in the three tables presented in this section while the objective orders vary considerably.

It is significant, however, that the subjective-objective correspondence is greatest with regard to the matter of dwelling unit space. We will see later on

TABLE 3.5   Subjective and Objective Views of Dwelling
Unit Space in the Study Areas

	Oak Lane HL	West Phila. HH	Kensington LL	Central City LH
Proportion of households with no complaints about space	63%	52%	64%	40%
Average dwelling size	6.04 rooms	3.71 rooms	5.68 rooms	3.52 rooms
Subjective Rank Order	II	III	I	IV
Objective Rank Order	I	III	II	IV

that dissatisfaction in this respect is one of the strongest motives impelling households to move.

AREA INTEGRATION

One of the main reasons why students of urban life have paid so much attention to residential mobility stems from the notion that high mobility substantially molds the character of the social organization of an area. A neighborhood whose residents are stable is likely to be characterized by the growth of close interpersonal relations within this area. Organizations—clubs, churches, civic associations—flourish. Residents take pride in living there and derive satisfaction from close association with others like themselves. In contrast, mobile neighborhoods, with their continuous turnover of residents, are characterized by anonymity, dearth of organizational life, and little community pride. These factors affect the area by providing a setting for the flourishing of deviant behavior, crime, delinquency, and so on. The effects upon the individual resident is to loosen his bonds to the larger society itself and to deprive him of the satisfactions inherent in close association with his fellow men.[4]

Although this thesis has occupied a central position in discussions of residential mobility, little research has been done directly on the problem. Correlations have been found between mobility rates and rates of delinquency, divorce, suicide, and insanity, and these relationships have been interpreted in terms of the lack of integration within mobile areas, but few researches have directly attempted to measure whether mobile areas are, in fact, characterized by this lack of integration.

There have been several difficulties in the way of such research. First of all, integration as a concept has been variously defined to cover a wide variety of phenomena, ranging from the amount and quality of personal ties among individuals to the "degree of moral consensus." Second, whatever definition is employed, the translation of the definition into research requires the use of some sort of interview methodology, collecting data which goes beyond what is ordinarily available in printed sources.

In this section, we will attempt to show how survey methods may be employed to do research into this important problem. We will also present some empirical findings which raise some important questions concerning the interpretation of mobility and its effects on interpersonal integration.

As a first step, it is important to delineate the aspects of integration which will be studied here. An area may be considered integrated if the division of labor among its inhabitants is such that all the major needs can be filled within its borders. Certainly few urban subareas are integrated in this sense. Or, any area may be considered integrated if there is a high degree of moral consensus among its inhabitants—agreement concerning standards of behavior, life goals, and so on.[5]

Or, an integrated area might be viewed as one in which its inhabitants perceive each other as substantially alike in important status dimensions. Or, finally, an integrated area might be considered as one in which there is a substantially large number of personal ties among its residents. Additional definitions can also be constructed.[6] The lack of a unique definition points to the complexity of the concept of integration.

For illustrative purposes, only two kinds of integration will be considered: the extent to which residents of the four areas perceive themselves to be like or different from their neighbors and the extent to which there are close personal ties among them. The data will show how these two different kinds of integration are related in contrasting fashions to area mobility.

PERCEIVED LIKENESS OR DIFFERENCE

There are many ways in which the respondents could perceive themselves to be like or different from their neighbors. One of the more important ways in our complex socity is social class, and the data to be considered concern what the respondents see as their own and as their neighbors' social class.[7]

By considering both their self evaluations and their evaluations of their neighbors (as in Table 3.6), it will be possible to judge the extent to which the residents of each of the four areas perceive themselves to be like or unlike their neighbors.

The two upper economic status areas show a decided preference for middle-class affiliation, with 83% and 76% choosing "middle class" as their

TABLE 3.6 Comparison Between Personal Class
Affiliation* and Class Affiliation Ascribed to Neighbors

Class	Oak Lane HL		West Phila. HH		Kensington LL		Central City LH	
	Self	Neighbors	Self	Neighbors	Self	Neighbors	Self	Neighbors
"Labor"	12%	8%	11%	8%	51%	56%	37%	64%
"Middle Class"	83	88	76	81	45	40	51	27
"Upper Class"	2	1	8	5	2	1	2	—
Don't Know	3	3	5	6	2	3	10	9
100% Equals	(215)		(286)		(214)		(204)	

*Based on responses to the following question:
"To which of these groups do you feel closest? Labor, middle class, or upper class?"
"How about most of the people who live around here? Where do they belong? Labor, middle class, or upper class?"

own position. In contrast, Kensingtonians show a strong preference for "labor" as the group to which they feel closest. Residents of Central City, although of roughly the same economic status as Kensingtonians, show a dominant preference for "middle class." Very few respondents in any area elected "upper class." West Philadelphia, with 8% of its respondents affiliating themselves with "upper class," is the only area with any significant number of persons electing that class.

It is important to note the difference between Kensington and Central City. The slight differences which exist in the objective economic level favor Kensington, whose breadwinners tend to be of slightly higher occupational level than those of Central City. Yet, the difference in subjective class affiliation is quite striking. Kensingtonians elect "labor"; Central City residents are "middle class."

The differing portions of "don't knows" in each of the four areas is also a significant piece of information. The highest "don't know" percentages are in Central City and West Philadelphia—the two mobile areas. If a "don't know" response to this question is looked upon as indicating a lack of self identification, it may be seen that larger proportions of persons who feel they have no particular place in the class system are in the two mobile areas. It should be noted that this proportion is particularly large (10%) in Central City.

Somewhat different distributions are found when the placement of neighbors is considered.[8] Respondents in Oak Lane and West Philadelphia tend to ascribe to their neighbors higher class positions than their own. In Kensington and Central City, on the other hand, respondents tend to ascribe a lower class position to their neighbors. The tendency to ascribe neighbors to a lower position than oneself is especially marked in Central City; only 37% of the respondents claimed that they were "closest to" labor as compared with 64% who stated that their neighbors belonged to that group.

The degree to which respondents in each of the areas consider themselves and their neighbors to have the same class status is perhaps best expressed by presenting correlation coefficients (as in Table 3.7) between self affiliation

TABLE 3.7 Correlation
Between Self Affiliation
and Ascribed Affiliation
of Neighbors[*]

Oak Lane (HL)	.68
West Philadelphia (HH)	.50
Kensington (LL)	.85
Central City (LH)	.33

*The coefficients in this table are product moment correlation coefficients computed from fourfold tables (omitting the response categories "upper class" and "don't know").

and ascribed neighbors' affiliation. The larger the coefficient, the greater the agreement between self affiliation and ascribed affiliation. Reasoning one step further, the higher the coefficient, the greater the degree of integration of an area.

The rank order of these correlations coincides with the rank order of the stability of the areas. Kensington, the most stable of the four areas, has the highest correlation coefficient, and Central City, with the lowest stability, has the lowest correlation.

Apparently an area's integration in this sense is dependent on its mobility. The more mobile the area, the less integrated it appears to be.[9] Socio-economic status has apparently no effect on this type of integration.

The way in which respondents perceived their neighborhoods to be friendly or unfriendly affords further evidence for this thesis. The more mobile the neighborhood, the less friendly it appears to its residents (Table 3.8).

INTERPERSONAL TIES

The strength of interpersonal ties will be considered next as a measure of the integration of the four study areas. The greater the number of interpersonal ties in a neighborhood, the more highly integrated that area will be considered to be.

To judge the extent of such ties in each of the four areas would seem at first glance to be a rather simple matter. All that seems necessary is to count the number of persons in each area who have some sort of personal relationship with other persons in the same area. Those areas with large proportions of persons with many intraarea personal ties could then be judged as having achieved a greater integration. But the problem of interpretation is not that

TABLE 3.8   Perceived Neighborhood Friendliness*

Friendliness Rating	Oak Lane HL	West Phila. HH	Kensington LL	Central City LH
"Extremely friendly"	33%	31%	59%	25%
"Just somewhat friendly"	58	54	37	43
"Indifferent" or "Unfriendly"	9	15	4	32
100% equals	(208)	(248)	(211)	(164)
Don't know and NA	(7)	(38)	(3)	(45)

*Based on answers to the question: "How would you say the people around here acted toward each other? Extremely friendly, just somewhat friendly, or indifferent and unfriendly?"

easily solved. Individuals differ in their "sociability" and an area may appear to be more integrated than another area because its residents have many more personal ties in general and hence more ties within the area. Proportionate to their total number of ties, they may have no more intraarea ties than the other area.

This point of interpretation is particularly important since many studies have shown that a person's "sociability" is closely related to his economic status.[10] Hence we can expect that the lower socio-economic areas will evidence less integration than the higher socio-economic status areas, because lower class people have fewer personal contacts than higher socio-economic status people.

This problem of interpretation is illustrated dramatically by the data on visiting relationships within the four study areas (Table 3.9).

Respondents in the two higher socio-economic status areas have, on the average, more ties with their neighbors than respondents in either of the two lower status areas. Differences between areas of different mobility levels are overshadowed by differences between areas of unlike socio-economic status. Apparently, upper status persons have more contacts with their neighbors than lower status persons regardless of the mobility of the neighborhood in which they live.

However, if we compare areas of similar socio-economic status, as, for example, Kensington with Central City and Oak Lane with West Philadelphia, some evidence on the effect of mobility on visiting relationships can be found. Fewer West Philadelphians than Oak Lane residents have large numbers of visiting relationships. Similarly, Central City's residents have fewer than Kensingtonians. Mobility does affect the appearance of visiting relationships, but its effect is somewhat overshadowed by the effect of socio-economic status.

The threads of interpretation will become clearer if further data from our study are considered. Table 3.10 presents measures of the different levels of "sociability" of the residents in the four areas. By "sociability" we mean simply the number of interpersonal contacts entered into by respondents regardless of the location of the partners in these relationships.

TABLE 3.9   Visiting Relationships in the Study Areas

Number of Visiting Relationships	Oak Lane HL	West Phila. HH	Kensington LL	Central City LH
None	14%	26%	31%	44%
One to three	27	33	36	33
Four or more	59	41	33	23
100% equals	(213)	(282)	(211)	(202)

These data were obtained by asking each respondent to designate where his three "best friends" lived, where the three relatives he "liked most" lived, and the formal organizations of which he was a member.

Many respondents were unable to name three best friends or most-liked relatives, indicating they had fewer than three. Likewise, fewer than half claimed membership in some sort of formal organization. The data in Table 3.10 presents the proportions of residents within each of the four study areas who fell short of naming a full quota of friends or relatives, or who were not members of organizations.

The striking findings on each of these indicators is that persons residing in the two lower socio-economic areas have a considerably more restricted sociability than the persons residing in the two higher socio-economic areas.[11] Economic status counts for considerably more than mobility, at least in this respect. Within the same socio-economic level, living in a higher mobility area makes for slightly less sociability, but these differences are small and not consistently in the same direction for each of the indexes.

The level of sociability shown by respondents within the area is not quite the same as the extent of interpersonal contacts within an area. To judge interpersonal integration, it is necessary to know where the "best friends," "most liked relatives," and organizations are located. These data are presented in Table 3.11.

The data indicate that interpersonal integration is greater in the two stable areas, Oak Lane and Kensington. In Oak Lane and Kensington, greater proportions of the respondents have their best friends and relatives residing predominantly in the near vicinity. The corresponding proportions for West Philadelphia and Central City are consistently smaller.

The mobility of an area is more clearly related to the location of relatives than to the location of friends. Differences between mobile and stable areas

TABLE 3.10 Levels of Sociability in Study Areas

Sociability	Oak Lane HL	West Phila. HH	Kensington LL	Central City LH
Proportion designating less than three friends	17%	23%	41%	42%
100% equals	(211)	(275)	(213)	(206)
Proportion designating less than three relatives	18%	24%	32%	41%
100% equals	(212)	(275)	(213)	(204)
Proportion belonging to no organizations	45%	54%	72%	66%
100% equals	(214)	(284)	(213)	(207)

TABLE 3.11   Intra-Area Sociability

	Oak Lane HL	West Phila. HH	Kensington LL	Central City LH
Proportion of households whose friends reside locally*	71%	62%	71%	58%
100% equals	(206)	(259)	(187)	(177)
Proportion whose relatives reside locally*	49%	27%	65%	19%
100% equals	(208)	(271)	(202)	(186)
Proportion members of local organizations*	40%**	24%**	22%**	17%**
100% equals	(118)	(132)	(60)	(71)

*A household was categorized as having its friends or relatives residing locally if a majority of the persons designated resided either in the area itself or within the larger ward of which the area was a part.
A local organization is defined as one which the respondent said was composed primarily of people in the neighborhood.

**Proportion shown of persons who are members of organizations.

within each socio-economic level in this respect are considerably larger than the corresponding differences for friends. Since a person's relatives are a relatively static set of social relationships, with enlargement or contraction beyond the control of the individual, it is especially significant that the residents of the two stable areas should have so large a proportion of their most-liked relatives in the vicinity. This finding suggests that the relationship between the residential location of relatives and the residential mobility of households be thoroughly investigated in future studies.

The pattern of differences among the study areas with regard to memberships in local organizations is not very clear-cut. Only in Oak Lane, the high status stable area, is there a high proportion of local memberships among residents who are joiners. Residents of the other areas show about half as many members of local organizations. Although differences among the four areas are small (with the exception of the one noted above), there is a definite tendency for the two lower status areas to have fewer residents involved in local organizations. Status apparently plays a stronger role than mobility in setting the character of organizational membership in an area.

The evidence presented here concerning the amount of interpersonal ties among residents in areas of differing status and mobility points to the generalization that higher status areas are more integrated *regardless of their mobility levels,* primarily because upper status persons enter into more personal relationships than lower status persons do. Residence in areas of different stability does have an effect, however, on the kinds of relationships entered into by residents. In stable areas, more of the personal ties are made with persons within the immediate vicinity. Persons residing in mobile areas tend to have their personal ties less often with their neighbors.

Taking into account the findings concerning the perceived similarity of neighbors and the perceived friendliness of a neighborhood, the effects of mobility upon the integration of an area may be summarized as follows:

(1) The more mobile the area, the greater the difference perceived by its residents between themselves and their neighbors.
(2) The more mobile the area, the more unfriendly the neighborhood is perceived to be.
(3) The more mobile the neighborhood, the less likely are its residents to form personal ties with their neighbors.
(4) The higher the status of a person, the more likely he is to enter into personal ties with others, either through membership in organizations, by maintaining close ties with relatives, or by cultivating friendships.

This analysis was undertaken primarily because mobility has been assumed by many writers to play an important role for the informal mechanisms of social control within neighborhoods. Where mobility is high, public opinion cannot act as a restraint on the appearance of deviant behavior. Where families do not know their neighbors and do not care how their neighbors act, or care what their neighbors think of them, public opinion cannot operate as a means of social control.

What implications do our findings have for this view of the role of mobility? It has been shown that the number of personal ties is more a function of the socio-economic status of a neighborhood than its mobility. The two low socio-economic status areas evidence fewer visiting relationships among their residents than do the two high status areas. Hence, mobility alone cannot account for the anonymity of mobile neighborhoods. Low social status areas, *in general,* are areas of anonymity.

Yet, mobility does have an effect which is consistent with the notion that it lessens the impact of informal social controls. Residents in the two mobile areas think less highly of their neighbors: They view their fellow residents as lacking in friendliness and think of them as having lower status than themselves. If their opinions of their neighbors are so low, the neighborhood's opinion climate presumably will have little effect on their behavior.

In other words, mobility may undermine informal controls not so much by reducing the personal ties among residents as by producing a lack of concern for what public opinion climate may exist.

AREA MOBILITY AND HOUSEHOLD MOBILITY

Much useful knowledge has been contributed by the application of the ecological approach to the study of residential mobility. Many empirical generalizations concerning the character of mobile areas are founded on data from studies which correlated rates of mobility with rates of delinquency, divorce, insanity, and so on. Indeed, it has been primarily the findings of such studies which have focused the attention of students of urbanism on the importance of this phenomenon.

However valuable such studies have been, they have not been useful in the study of the mobility of households. Although area studies have been used as the basis for generalizing about the mobility of families, such generalizations do not follow from their results. For example, many ecological studies report that in mobile areas one may find greater-than-ordinary proportions of familyless households and childless couples. Some writers have concluded from these findings that single persons and childless couples therefore move around more than other segments of the urban populations. But, it may very well be the case that such households are in fact very stable and that it is families with children who contribute most of the mobility in mobile areas.

The importance of emphasizing the restrictions on the interpretation of ecological studies becomes obvious when other findings from such studies are considered. One study indicates that the divorce rates of mobile areas are much higher than in stable areas. This cannot be generalized to the statement that divorced persons are more mobile. All the findings indicate is that, proportionately speaking, more divorced persons can be found within mobile than within stable neighborhoods.

The danger of generalizing from area correlations to individual behavior can be illustrated with data from the present study. In many ecological studies, mobility rates have been found to be positively correlated with the proportions of single-person and childless households. Mobile areas have more than their share of such family types. The findings of the present study also bear out this generalization (see Table 3.12). West Philadelphia and Central City both have much larger proportions of "incomplete families" (childless couples) and single-person households. These two household types together account for more than half of the households in the two mobile areas as compared with about one household in five in the two stable areas.

Despite their preponderance in the mobile areas, it cannot be said that single persons and childless couples are more mobile household types. It may equally be the case that the high mobility of these two areas is completely accounted for by the fact that families with children find such areas so uncongenial that they move out as soon as they arrive. Or, it may be the case that *all* household types are more mobile in the mobile areas.

TABLE 3.12   Household Compositions in Study Areas

	Oak Lane HL	West Phila. HH	Kensington LL	Central City LH
Full Family*	71%	24%	67%	36%
Incomplete Family*	20	36	16	25
Single Persons*	1	22	4	21
Miscellaneous*	8	18	13	18
100% equals	(215)	(286)	(214)	(209)

*The definitions of the terms employed are as follows:

> *Full Family* consists of husband and wife plus children and perhaps blood relatives of either spouse.
> *Incomplete Family* consists of just husband and wife with no children and/or dependent blood relatives.
> *Single Persons* consists of persons living alone.
> *Miscellaneous Families* consists of household groups containing broken families (either spouse missing), persons unrelated by blood or marriage (e.g. two friends sharing an apartment), or persons of fairly distant blood relationships (second degree or more removed as e.g., cousins, nephew and uncle, etc.)

Table 3.13 measures the mobility desires of the different household types within each area. In the mobile areas, every type is more mobile than the corresponding type in the two stable areas.

Similar findings can be presented from this study concerning a number of other differences between the stable and the mobile study areas.[12] Generalizations concerning individual behavior cannot be made from such findings on the characteristics of areas.

What interpretation can be given to area correlations?[13] Do data of this sort yield any information of value? A rate computed for an area should be

TABLE 3.13   Mobility Desires of Household Types
Within Study Areas

Household Type	Oak Lane HL	West Phila. HH	Kensington LL	Central City LH
Full Families	38%	60%	46%	82%
100% equals	(154)	(70)	(143)	(75)
Incomplete Families	37%	53%	33%	58%
100% equals	(43)	(103)	(34)	(52)
Single Persons	*	29%	*	30%
100% equals	(3)	(62)	(9)	(44)
Miscellaneous	20%	51%	41%	66%
100% equals	(15)	(49)	(27)	(38)

considered an indicator of the kind of environment in which are found the families and individuals residing there. Thus a mobility rate indicates the amount of turnover which the area's residents experience in the environment about them. The fact that more divorced persons, or more insane persons, are found in mobile areas indicates only that divorced or insane persons are found more often in environments of this sort.[14] Whether or not divorced or insane persons are themselves more mobile than other population elements can only be determined by relating the characteristics of individuals to their particular mobility experience.

SUMMARY AND CONCLUSIONS

One of the major advantages of the employment of the survey method in the study of residential mobility is its ability to collect data on some of the social psychological aspects of mobile and stable areas. The primary purpose of this chapter was to illustrate how the addition of social psychological depth in analyzing the differences among the four study areas would lead to different formulations of the characteristics of mobile areas.

The first illustration presented concerned how much difference there was between "objective" rankings of the four study areas and the attitudes toward those areas expressed by residents. It was found that little relationship existed: the objective "goodness" of an area in three respects—location, physical structure, and space adequacy of housing—differed radically from the way in which residents viewed their neighborhoods. The residents' ranking seemed more a function of their overall estimation of their neighborhood than a function of an appraisal of the particular quality in question. Thus, the residents of a neighborhood more advantageously placed (in terms of transportation to the city center) viewed their area as poorly located, and vice versa.

What implications have these findings? They indicate that the views of an area held by its residents may vary widely from that arrived at by the appraisal of an expert. An action program designed to remedy defects as revealed to the "expert" may find considerable popular resistance. The possibility that such resistance might be found among families living in what seems "obvious" substandard condition should be taken into account when action is contemplated directed toward such areas.[15]

The usefulness of survey methods was also illustrated by an attempt to measure the extent to which the four study areas were integrated. Two types of integration were considered: how the residents of a neighborhood regarded each other and the frequency of personal ties among them. The analysis attempted to show whether mobility had any effect on integration as defined in these two ways.

Mobility was shown to play a very important role in determining how an area's residents regarded each other. In the two mobile areas, neighbors tended to see each other as unfriendly and to relegate their neighbors to a lower social status than themselves.

The pattern of interpersonal contacts was more complicated because socio-economic status played so strong a role in this area. Both high status areas showed more interpersonal interaction than the lower status areas, and in this sense were better integrated. Higher status individuals have more contacts in general and hence more contacts with their neighbors. But, once the level of interaction was held constant, it was found that the residents of stable areas had a stronger tendency to have friends and relatives within the local area. Mobility's effects were shown in the geographical range of one's close contacts.

The implications of these findings with respect to integration are of some importance. Many students of urbanism deplore the anonymity of urban life and ascribe much of this to mobility. The findings here indicate that socio-economic status plays a very important role in restricting the amount of interaction in which a household may engage. Research into the way in which status leads to interaction restriction is obviously indicated. An understanding of this connection may give clues to how anonymity may be reduced.

An illustration of some of the pitfalls in the interpretation of ecological correlations was given. Many area studies have incorrectly generalized their findings to the level of individual behavior. It was shown here that the fact that mobile areas contained more of their share of single-person households and childless families did not mean that such persons were among the more mobile segments of our society. Rather, it was shown that all household types within mobile areas had higher mobility than their counterparts in more stable environments. The mobility rates of each of the four areas seemed to be a characteristic of the area itself rather than a function of the household types which are to be found there.

NOTES

1. The rationale behind the construction of these types and how the tracts were selected are described in Chapter 2.

2. It was symptomatic of the differences between mobile and stable areas that popularly given names were available for the two stable areas but not for the two mobile areas. The name *West Philadelphia*, which we have given to Tract 46A, is given in popular usage to a much larger section covering this tract and some dozen or more others. *Central City*, the name given to the mobile low economic class tract, 15A, is popularly given to Philadelphia's central business district upon which this tract borders. In contrast, the two stable tracts had names which corresponded roughly in popular usage

to the tracts and but one or two other tracts. In addition, the place names employed for the two stable tracts were very much a part of popular usage in designating those areas.

3. The construction of these indexes and the specific questions of which they are composed are discussed in detail in Chapter 5.

4. The argument presented here is a composite paraphrasing of a dozen or more discussions of the effects of mobility.

5. See Robert C. Angell, "The Moral Integration of American Cities" *American Journal of Sociology*, LVII, 1, July 1951.

6. See Werner S. Landecker, "Types of Integration and their Measurement," *American Journal of Sociology*, LVI, 4, January 1951.

7. Our main concern here, it should be noted, is not with the class position of the households—as perhaps determined by their occupation, income, or prestige—but with their own image of their class position. A full picture of the stratification of the four areas would require a consideration of many characteristics beside social class identification.

8. Parenthetically, it should be noted that there is more agreement among respondents concerning where their neighbors belong than about where they themselves belong.

9. This should not be interpreted to mean that those respondents who saw themselves and their neighbors as alike in class affiliation were more stable. No relationship was found between household mobility and perception of difference or likeness in class affiliation.

10. See Knupfer, Genevieve "The Portrait of the Underdog." *Public Opinion Quarterly*, Vol. II (1947) for an excellent summary of studies of participation and economic status.

11. The four areas differ in other respects as well as economic status and the reader may well question whether the variations shown above are due possibly to these other differences. One important factor in this regard is educational level. Interviews with respondents of lower educational attainment generally show greater constriction in responding to questions on almost any topic. It might be expected, therefore, that the differences shown in Table 3.10 might be a function of the differences in educational attainment among the populations of the four areas. Inspection of the relationship between education and sociability in each of the four areas showed that the differences between the areas hold for respondents of every educational level. Variations shown in Table 3.10 therefore cannot be ascribed to differences in educational attainment. Length of residence, another factor of presumed importance in determining whether a family would have few or many ties within an area, also turned out to be of no importance. (Another recent study of mobility has also shown the same lack of relationship between length of residence and personal ties: Theodore Caplow and Robert Forman "neighborhood Interaction in a Homogeneous Community," *American Sociological Review*, 15, 3, June 1950.)

12. For example, households with close friends or relatives in their immediate neighborhood are no more likely than other households to desire to remain in the area, although stable areas show a higher proportion, holding economic status constant, of close ties among their residents.

13. For a more detailed discussion of the problems of interpretation of ecological analyses, see William S. Robinson "Ecological Correlations and Behavior of Individuals," *American Sociological Review*, 15, 1, June 1950; Patricia L. Kendall and Paul F. Lazarsfeld "Problems of Survey Analysis" in Robert K. Merton and Paul F. Lazarsfeld (eds.) *Studies in the Scope and Method of The American Soldier*, Macmillan, New York, 1950.

14. Environment can also be interpreted in several ways. For example divorced persons may be found more frequently in mobile areas because, once divorced, they find

the mobile areas to have the kind of housing they need—small units, suitable for single person households—or that persons living in such areas, free from the informal social controls flourishing in more stable areas, find divorce an easier course to accept than persons in more stable areas. In other words, an area as environment may operate through some selective attraction or through more direct impact on its residents.

15. Note that it is *not* suggested here that action programs should be guided by popular opinion, but rather that action programs should take popular opinion into account as one of the relevant factors aiding or hindering, as the case may be, the carrying out of such programs. The function of the professional expert is to set up standards, and this function should not be left to a public opinion poll. Popular opinion on a matter is a social "fact," as much a part of the data on a planning problem as the contours of an area's land surface, and, as such, needs to be treated in the same way, as a datum to be taken into account in drawing up projected plans.

Chapter 4

THE IMMEDIATE IMPACT OF AREA MOBILITY ON HOUSEHOLDS AND ORGANIZATIONS

INTRODUCTION

The effects of any complex social phenomenon can be felt at many different points in a social system. Residential mobility is, of course, no exception in this regard, and the investigation of its effects can proceed along what may be considered quite different lines. In the immediately preceding chapter, one line of investigation has already been considered. Mobile and stable areas were contrasted with regard to certain strategic variables and it is reasonable to assume that at least some of the differences found are causally related to mobility. In this chapter, two additional lines of investigation into the effects of mobility will be considered.

In order to interrelate the various lines of investigation, it is necessary to consider some of the ways in which mobility might affect a household and modify its behavior. To begin with, the *number of moves* made by a household may affect it in some way. Another way in which mobility might work to produce modifications in a household's behavior is by creating a particular type of environment, either limiting or enlarging, as the case may be, the set of opportunities confronting a household for the fulfillment of its needs. For example, in an area with a large transient population, a household may be deprived of opportunities for the kinds of satisfying personal friendships it may consider important. This kind of effect operates through the modification of the household's surrounding social environment. Parenthetically, it may be noted that it is not necessary that a household be aware of the effects of its own mobility on its life or on its social environment. In the previous chapter we have found some evidence that the mobility or stability of an area does affect the ability of a household to establish contacts with other persons in their area and to participate in organizational life. Later on this chapter will consider certain further evidence on this score concerning the effects of mobility on organizational life.

But there is still a third important way in which mobility may operate to affect households.[1] Mobility is a fairly visible social phenomenon and the direct perception of mobility as a neighborhood quality may change the attitudes and behavior of members of families in that area. The mobility of an area may be seen by its residents as *the* characteristic which makes that area so undesirable. Moving may beget moving, as it were, by altering the way in which residents regard their neighborhood. Or, the perception of mobility may have an effect on families through the kinds of families which are seen to be entering and leaving the neighborhood. It is with effects of these kinds that the first sections of this chapter will be concerned. In this connection, two general questions will be raised: *First, is the mobility or stability of an area perceived at all by its residents? Second, are they affected in any way by the mobility which they perceive?* Do they feel that mobility detracts from the area's reputation? Are they sorry to see families leave?

In addition, we will also consider in this chapter some of the effects of mobility upon the organizations found within an area. This is a line of investigation which is somewhat removed from the direct impact of mobility on area residents but it is of some importance since organizations form a significant part of the social structure of an area. Organizations, whether retail businesses or informal social clubs, are directly dependent on the maintenance of contacts with the population they serve. Mobility affects their operations in a very direct fashion and as a consequence modifies and molds the surrounding social environment of an areas's residents. In this connection we will raise questions of the following sorts: *How are organizations affected by mobility? Are there significant differences among organizations in their sensitivity and reactions to mobility? What are the explanations for such differences as we may find?*

In summary, the focus of this chapter is on the direct and immediate effects of area mobility on households and on organizations. It should be very clearly understood that whether or not these effects are considerable or insignificant has little or no bearing on whether mobility has or has not important kinds of other effects on either households or organizations, effects which may operate below the level of direct perception which is considered here.

HOUSEHOLDS–PERCEPTION OF MOBILITY

A neighborhood's mobility may affect its residents through their awareness of the turnover taking place and of the kinds of families entering or leaving. Awareness of mobility may change a family's evaluation of its environment and ultimately determine its attachment to the neighborhood. However, awareness cannot be taken for granted. Studies of social factors in perception have all pointed to the way in which human beings are selectively aware of their environment, their attention being strongly directed by their needs, fears, and hopes. Before the effects of mobility can be weighed, it is necessary to study how much awareness of turnover can be found.

Residential mobility entails a certain amount of physical activity and it might be expected that its "visibility" is fairly high. The presence of moving vans, the loss of friends and acquaintances, and the appearance of new faces might conceivably lead to a considerable awareness of the mobility within a person's neighborhood. Yet, in response to a question asking respondents to estimate how much moving took place in their neighborhood over the previous year, a fairly large proportion were unable or unwilling to make such estimates.

The level of awareness of mobility varied from area to area. In Oak Lane, 85% of the respondents were aware of mobility in the sense that they felt able to estimate how many families moved out in 1950 (see Table 4.1). Next in awareness were the residents of Kensington (67% making estimates). In West Philadelphia and Central City, where the mobility was actually much higher, only about half of the respondents were able to give estimates. In short, *those areas in which the amount of mobility is small, have the greatest awareness of mobility.*

TABLE 4.1   Households: Perception of Mobility*

	Oak Lane HL**	West Phila. HH**	Kensington LL**	Central City LH**
Don't know how many families moved in 1950	15%	52%	33%	48%
Know how many moved	85	48	67	52
Including:				
No families moved	9%	2%	24%	3%
Just a few moved	57	47	44	25
One in 10 moved	17	16	9	9
Two in 10 moved	9	13	10	13
Three or more moved	8	22	13	50
100% equals	(213)	(279)	(205)	(208)
No information	(2)	(5)	(9)	(2)

*The wording of the question used to elicit the data in this table is as follows: "Thinking back over the last year or so, how many families that lived in this neighborhood in 1949 would you say have moved out to some other place?"

**Following the practice established in the previous chapter, the symbols under area names refer to the socio-economic status and mobility, respectively, of the area. Thus "HH" indicates the high status, high mobility area.

When given, estimates varied considerably. In areas where mobility was objectively low, many respondents overestimated the amount of mobility. In areas of high mobility, underestimation was fairly frequent. Yet it cannot be said that the estimates were random in character. The estimates tended to cluster about the actual, objectively measured, mobility rate in each area.[2]

The proportions of respondents in each area who perceived the level of mobility in their areas more or less correctly are presented in Table 4.2. Note that there are three sets of figures in this table: The first line (from Table 4.1) contains the proportion of respondents who made estimates; the second line, the proportion of respondents making correct estimates; and the third line, the proportion of respondents making correct estimates based on the total number of respondents making estimates. Oak Lane's households were by far the most accurate in their perception of mobility. A majority of the households in the area estimated mobility correctly. Next in accuracy were the residents of Kensington, but their showing is somewhat marred by their poor level of awareness. Least accurate were the West Philadelphians with only 17% of the respondents making correct estimates.

Occupying a position close to West Philadelphia and behind Kensington is Central City. The residents of this highly mobile area did not fare too badly in their accuracy of perception: 26% of the respondents made correct estimates and when we consider the accuracy of estimation only among those who made estimates, we see that half of the estimates given were correct.

TABLE 4.2   Households: Accuracy of Perception of Mobility

	Oak Lane HL	West Phila. HH	Kensington LL	Central City LH
Proportion making mobility estimates	85%	48%	67%	52%
Proportion making "correct" estimates**	63%	17%	35%	26%
Proportion making "correct" estimates** (of those making estimates)	74%	35%	68%	50%

**The proportion of households in each area correctly perceiving mobility was computed by considering the following responses as "correct" perception:

   Oak Lane: "Few" and "one family in ten"
   West Phila: "Two in ten" and "three in ten"
   Kensington: "None" and "few"
   Central City: "Three in ten"

Note that the accuracy of perception in each area does not materially change if different definitions are employed of what is the "correct" perception for that area. The reader is directed to table 4.1 where it can be seen that incorporating any of the adjacent response categories into the "correct" category would not alter the considerable differences between the mobile and the stable areas.

Awareness of moving does not seem to be related to the amount of moving. *Paradoxically, it appears that the residents of mobile areas are least aware of the mobility which their neighborhoods are experiencing. Furthermore, the accuracy of awareness shows the same pattern: Residents of stable areas tend to be more accurate in their estimations of the amount of turnover taking place in their neighborhoods.* The direct impact of mobility through the awareness of families can therefore only affect portions of the populations. These portions are smallest in areas where mobility is greatest and largest where mobility is least.

What kinds of families are those who are potentially open to the effects of mobility which may work through conscious awareness? Can the differences between mobile and stable areas be accounted for by the fact that there are more families of this kind in stable areas?

Perhaps awareness of mobility depends primarily on how closely each of the areas is integrated by the existence of personal ties among its residents. In Chapter 3 it was shown that residents of stable areas tend to have more of their friendships and relatives located nearby. Because of these close local ties, families living in stable areas may have more opportunities to notice mobility and, perhaps more important, more motivation to do so. This line of explanation appears to be at least part of the answer: In each area, the more local ties a family has, the more likely it is to be aware of residential mobility.

Another measure of opportunities for the observation of mobility is length of residence in the area. The longer a person lives in an area, the more likely he may be to know—at least in the sense of recognizing faces—other persons who live in his neighborhood and hence be more aware of turnover. Such appears to be the case.

In Table 4.3 families in each of the four study areas have been classified according to whether they have few or many local ties and also according to whether they are recent arrivals or "old timers." Recent arrivals with few local ties are least aware of the mobility about them, and "old timers" with many local ties are most aware. Length of residence gives a family a greater opportunity for perception of mobility, but both characteristics together discriminate very strongly between families of greater and lesser mobility awareness.

It should be noted that within each of the subgroups distinguished in Table 4.3, the greater awareness of Oak Lane residents is still maintained although the differences among the other areas are somewhat minimized. Apparently there is some quality of Oak Lane as a neighborhood which makes its mobility considerably more visible than that of the other areas studied.

The degree of awareness of mobility can also be shown to vary with most[3] indexes of interaction within the study areas. It was found, for example, that households with children were more likely to be aware of mobility than

TABLE 4.3   Length of Residence, Local Ties and
Awareness of Mobility

	Oak Lane HL	West Phila. HH	Kensington LL	Central City LH
Proportion who know about mobility:				
RECENT ARRIVALS*				
Few local ties**	64%	27%	45%	34%
100% equals	(14)	(45)	(20)	(62)
Many local ties**	73%	35%	58%	57%
100% equals	(40)	(55)	(19)	(47)
OLD TIMERS*				
Few local ties**	79%	47%	68%	53%
100% equals	(29)	(64)	(75)	(45)
Many local ties**	93%	64%	73%	71%
100% equals	(128)	(111)	(89)	(48)

** "Few local ties" are households with none or just one visiting relationship with neighbors. "Many local ties" are households with at least two visiting relationships.

* "Recent arrivals" are defined as households who have been living in their present dwelling units since December 1947. "Old timers" are defined as households living in their
present dwelling units since before December 1947.

households without young children. Another factor of importance is the
location of the respondents' best friends. None of these indexes, however,
showed as strong a relationship to mobility awareness as the two factors
considered in the previous three tables.

*Awareness of mobility is greatest among those whose ties to their neigh-
borhoods are greatest. Paradoxically, mobility awareness has its largest potential impact upon those whose rootedness in the neighborhood appears
strongest.*[4]

Up to this point we have discussed primarily the factors associated with
awareness of mobility regardless of the accuracy of the perception. Are there
any factors which determine whether a respondent will correctly estimate the
amount of mobility in his neighborhood? In this connection it is necessary to
report a negative finding. None of the variables reported on above or any
others which seemed relevant had any significant relationship to the accuracy
of perception. Old timers, for example, were just as likely as recent arrivals to
estimate their area's mobility correctly. The accuracy of perception is then
apparently related to other factors as yet unknown.[5]

HOUSEHOLDS–IMPACT OF MOBILITY

While awareness of mobility is a precondition for the effects of mobility to be directly felt by the households, perception per se is neutral in character. The question might now be raised whether the households have any positive or negative reaction to the mobility which they perceive? Are they concerned about the movement of households in and out of their neighborhoods or are they, by and large, indifferent to the matter?

Considering first the respondents' reactions to the families which were moving out of the area, Table 4.4 indicates that few respondents saw any differences between the out-going families and those that remained in the area. Central City residents were the most likely to see differences (36%), but in all areas a clear majority of respondents saw no differences between the out-going families and the others in their neighborhoods.

Not only are differences not perceived but, by and large, this movement of families does not seem to affect respondents. When asked "What do you feel about the families moving out?," less than a third of the respondents reacted in any fashion that could be classified as positive or negative in affective content (see Table 4.5). In practically every area more than half of the respondents replied to this question that they were unaffected by the movement. The direct reported effects of mobility upon the inhabitants of our study areas are apparently very slight.[6]

Turning now to reactions to incoming mobility, very much the same sort of analysis can be presented. Few of the families saw the incoming families as any different from the other families in their neighborhoods.

When differences were perceived, however, they were considered to be somewhat more unfavorable than in the case of outgoing families (see Table 4.6). Four out of five West Philadelphians who saw the incoming families as different claimed that they were "worse." Two out of three Central City families said the same about the new families in that area. In the two stable

TABLE 4.4   Perceived Difference of Outward Moving Families*

	Oak Lane HL	West Phila. HH	Kensington LL	Central City LH
Families moving out are different	25%	15%	17%	36%
100% equals	(154)	(116)	(96)	(96)

*The wording of the question used was: "Are the families moving out any different from most of the other families?

TABLE 4.5   Reactions to Outgoing Families*

	Oak Lane HL	West Phila. HH	Kensington LL	Central City LH
Sorry to see them go	24%	26%	22%	8%
Glad to see them go and envy them	7%	4%	5%	8%
TOTAL AFFECTIVE RESPONSES	31%	30%	27%	16%
Doesn't affect me	60%	48%	54%	57%
Impersonal responses	14%	26%	25%	32%
TOTAL NEUTRAL OR UNCONCERNED	74%	74%	79%	89%
100% equals	(151)	(128)	(102)	(99)

*Note that the percentages add up to more than 100 percent. Some respondents' answers could be classified in several ways, as for example "I'm sorry to see some of them go, but most of them have to leave to get more room for their growing families." An impersonal response was one which merely described what kinds of people were moving or where they were moving to without giving any indication of what the respondent's reactions to such moving was.

areas, Kensington and Oak Lane, very few respondents had any such strong positive or negative reactions to the incoming families.

In other words, the negative impact of mobility upon the residents of mobile areas comes through the perception of *new* residents as undesirable neighbors. Change is regarded as bringing about a deterioration of the population composition of the area. It should be noted, however, as one may gauge from the fact that only one out of every three households perceive the incoming residents as different from present residents, that this unfavorable impact of mobility affects only a small number of the inhabitants of the two mobile areas.

Summarizing our findings, it is apparent that whatever other effects mobility has upon households, its direct impact upon them is very slight. There was greatest awareness of mobility in the two areas where mobility was least, but even in these areas there was a substantial proportion who felt they knew so little about local mobility that they could not estimate the proportion of movers in their areas.

Even more significant than awareness of mobility was the lack of personal concern with mobility. Most respondents saw no difference between the mobile portions of the populations of their area and the stable portions. Very few respondents had any unfavorable reactions to mobility. Residents

TABLE 4.6   Perceived Differences of Incoming Families*

	Oak Lane HL	West Phila. HH	Kensington LL	Central City LH
Families moving in are				
different	25%	32%	17%	36%
100% equals	(154)	(116)	(96)	(96)
In what way are they different?				
Better	8	3	--	9
Worse	18	79	19	63
Total affective responses	26%	82%	19%	72%
Different ethnic group	45	3	31	23
Younger families	37	21	37	9
Older families	5	10	--	--
Other	--	7	31	20
Total mentioned	87%	41%	99%	52%
100% equals	(38)	(29)	(16)	(35)

*The actual question asked of respondents was as follows: "How about the families that are moving in — are they different from most of the other families around here?"

of the two mobile areas were most likely to react unfavorably to the changes in the population composition brought about by the influx of undesirable population types.

These findings, then, are essentially negative with regard to the direct impact of mobility upon households. They indicate that the search for the major effects of mobility must proceed along other lines of investigation, and we will turn now to an account of a preliminary effort to gauge the effects on organizational life.

THE SURVEY OF ORGANIZATIONAL PERSONNEL

On an *a priori* basis it can be anticipated that the organizations[7] to be found in an area would be more sensitive to residential mobility than households. The typical household's existence is not threatened by changes in the population resident in its neighborhood. The important social relationships entered into by a household may not involve any other person in its neighborhood, and all households physically would survive rapid turnover of the neighborhood's population. In contrast, at least some local organizations are directly dependent on the maintenance of specific kinds of relationships to their locality's population. Business organizations must maintain a minimum number of clients; clubs, associations, and churches need members, and so on. The turnover of population can directly affect the very existence of an organization by disrupting its necessary social relationships.

While these considerations may seem fairly cogent to the reader and have enjoyed widespread endorsement in the literature on residential mobility, there has been relatively little empirical evidence gathered in a systematic fashion concerning the effects of mobility on organizations. In an attempt to fill the need for a firmer empirical base for our knowledge in this regard, a special survey of organizational leaders and key personnel was conducted in one[8] of the study areas, West Philadelphia, supplemented by a few interviews in Kensington.

The necessity for this special survey was indicated by the obvious deficiencies of a household survey in obtaining information of the sort desired. Only persons strategically placed within organizations had the information necessary to answer the question of how mobility affected the organization, and the chances of picking up a significant number of such persons in a household survey are very slim indeed.

Several Philadelphia-wide organizations furnished our interviewer[9] with introductions to leaders in the two areas studied. Further contacts developed from the respondents themselves who were asked to suggest other persons who might serve as informants. In the final analysis some 60 interviews were used, about two-thirds obtained from persons in West Philadelphia, covering a wide variety of organizational personnel: ministers, club leaders, businessmen, real estate brokers, and local political party workers.[10]

The interviews were quite informal and followed no set routine of definitely structured questions. Rather, the respondent was encouraged to talk about the problems of his organization with the main task of the interviewer being to see that three main topics were adequately covered: How does the organization learn about mobility? How important is a stable population base to the functioning of the organization? What are the adjustments which the organization has had to make to mobility's effects? In addition, information about the organization's structure and activities was obtained to help in the later interpretation of the elements related to sensitivity to mobility.

The analysis of these interviews affords some insight into the ways in which mobility affects the organizations which serve a mobile area. It should be stressed, however, that the effects studied are only those of which the personnel of these organizations are aware. There are undoubtedly others which are somewhat indirectly connected with mobility but nevertheless stem from it. It may be the case, for example, that it is easier for an organization to accomplish its ends in a social environment where there is a great deal of interpersonal contact among residents. The small-store owner may best be able to compete with the large chain when his customers find shopping in his store a significant daily social event where friends meet to talk and gossip. Where few personal contacts develop among neighbors, as in highly mobile areas, the small-store owner may be at a definite disadvantage, yet not be aware that his disadvantage is at least in part due to the mobility of his clientele.

Another type of effect which may be missed stems from the obvious limitation that we could only interview organizations that had survived high mobility. Organizations which ceased to exist under its impact or organizations which may have considered West Philadelphia as an area for operations but rejected it because of high mobility could not, of course, be studied. However, some of the organizations studied upon which the impact of mobility was particularly strong will probably go out of existence, and it is reasonable to assume that they are in many respects like those organizations which have died in the past.

On the whole, the organizational personnel interviewed were quite sensitive to the existence of mobility or stability in the areas studied. Their degrees of awareness and concern must be rated much higher, on the average, than those of the households in the same areas. Virtually every person interviewed knew that his area was either mobile or stable, as the case may be, and many could pinpoint quite accurately the amount of mobility not only during the present but also going back several decades. Yet there were striking differences among organizations and there were quite a few persons interviewed whose perception of mobility was distorted or who evidenced a considerable lack of concern with the problem. These differences, as we shall see later, are closely related to differences in the activities and structures of the organizations involved.

The range of differences which appeared among the organizations with regard to the perception of mobility was considerable, even though, on the average, awareness and accuracy were keener than in the case of households. Some of the organizational personnel were only aware of mobility in the highly mobile West Philadelphia area because they were residents of the area and not because their organization had experienced mobility directly. Other persons, for example, the local political party workers, could give very precise accounts of the mobility within the sections they worked. The content of the perception of mobility also varied. Some persons saw the mobility taking place in West Philadelphia as merely the replacement of out-going households by equivalent (as far as they were concerned) families. To these persons, mobility was not as serious a matter as to those who saw West Philadelphia's families as changing radically by the "invasion" of different social types.

Variations were also observed in the way in which mobility affected organizational life. Some types of organizations are apparently exempt from its effects; others were so seriously affected by mobility as to have their existence threatened. Some were affected only when certain types of residents moved; others were sensitive to any amount of mobility among any groups. One completely unanticipated finding in this regard was that some organizations considered mobility an asset rather than a liability, and several businesses in Kensington complained that they were suffering because of its stability.

Upon examining the interviews, it was found that there were two characteristics of organizations which by and large determined what the perception of and the reaction to mobility would be: *its degree of specialization in particular kinds of populations and the character of the relationship between the organization and the population it served.*

Each organization ordinarily orients itself primarily to special portions of the population of an area and rarely to the population as a whole. For our present purposes, there are two important kinds of specification: geographic and segmental. Organizations restrict themselves to the populations of particular areas and also to particular segments of the population within a subarea. Some of the organizations were either oriented entirely to a different area than the one in which we were interested or were concerned with an area of which our own was but a part. Such *metropolitan-oriented organizations,* as we called them, were by and large exempt from the impact of mobility because their population base was not experiencing turnover to the extent involved in our study area. The Philadelphia Electric Company officials in West Philadelphia, although very much aware of the mobility taking place in the area, were not particularly concerned[11] because their district included a considerably larger area than the census tract we were studying. *Locally oriented organizations,* concerned with the population inhabiting the entire census tract or some subportion of it, were much more sensitive to mobility. In fact, the smaller the area involved, the more the organization appears to be vulnerable. The West Philadelphia Y.M.C.A.—aware of the area's mobility and suffering somewhat from its effects—is a good example of a locally oriented organization.

Our findings with respect to geographic specialization are fairly obvious and could have been anticipated. Yet what makes this distinction of particular importance was the somewhat unanticipated finding that a typical successful adjustment to the impact of mobility is to shift from a local to a metropolitan orientation. Some of the smaller stores—a German-style bakery, for example—have survived the loss of the populations they once served by developing clienteles which are metropolitan in character. Interestingly enough, this is also a typical survival mechanism for organizations which suffer from the stability of an area. A real estate broker and a moving company located in Kensington have survived stability by enlarging the base of their operations to include other neighborhoods.

Organizations specialize in particular population types as well as in particular areas, and when an organization is oriented to a type which is stable, the impact of mobility is, of course, not felt. In such cases, the mobility of the remainder of the population sometimes goes unnoticed. The local West Philadelphia branch of the Philadelphia Department of Public Assistance experiences little mobility in the area because the elderly persons who are its clients are among the most stable of the population types in the area. At the other extreme, organizations specializing in the mobile population segments are generally the most hard hit. A good example of the latter organization type is the local Y.M.C.A., whose members are among the most mobile of the population types in the area.

Another important structural feature of organizations is the character of the relationships between the organization and the population it serves. The most important distinction here is between client-oriented and member-oriented organizations. A *client-oriented organization* is one in which the major amount of interaction, within the organizational context, is between the individuals served and the organizational personnel, with relatively little interaction between the clients. The best example of a client organization is the retail business where the store's personnel and the clients interact as clerks and customers but with no necessary social relationship existing among customers. The chief concern of client-oriented organizations is with the maintenance of these relationships.

In contrast, *member-oriented organizations* constitute social groups with the populations they serve. Members have particular social relationships with each other as well as with the organizational leaders or other key personnel. The functioning of member-oriented organizations depends not only on the maintenance of organization-member relationships but also on the maintenance of member-member relationships as well. Parenthetically, it may be noted that there are many more relationships which must be maintained by member-oriented organizations than by client-oriented organizations. The best examples of member-oriented organizations are social clubs, church groups, fraternal groups, schools, and so on.

There are, of course, some organizations which are in some respects both client- and member-oriented. Political parties, when observed as local political clubs, are member-oriented; but when we consider the relationship between the party and the rank-and-file voter, a political party must be considered a client-oriented organization.

Client-oriented organizations are generally not so strongly affected by mobility as member-oriented organizations. Mobility among clients generally means that the organization has to find replacements for the old clients who have left. The relationship between the organization and the client is quite specific and the problem of replacement consists of establishing new relationships between the organization and other individuals. The loss of members in a member-oriented organization is a much more serious matter.[12] Not only is the specific relationship to the organizational personnel disrupted but in addition all the relationships which the lost member had to other members have been broken. The recruitment of newcomers means the induction of new members into a large number of relationships and hence usually is a more difficult task. The effect of mobility on member-oriented organizations is particularly strong when the lost member was a particularly active one with many relationships with other members.

Following out this line of reasoning, it is easy to see why it is that the local schools, churches, and social clubs are the organizations which have been hardest hit by mobility and which are most concerned with the problem. The local grammar school in West Philadelphia experiences approximately 30% annual turnover in its student body. The school's office staff is under pressure as a result of the paper work involved in the January and September transfers. The teaching staff has found it necessary to institute special programs for initiation of incoming students.

West Philadelphia's Protestant churches have also been hard hit not only by the problem of membership turnover but also because the proportion of Protestants in the area has seen a considerable decline in the past 30 years. Those churches which have best survived the effects of mobility are those which have made special attempts to recruit and *integrate* newcomers into church life.

Thus at one extreme we see that awareness of[13] and concern with mobility are at a minimum with client-oriented organizations which serve a large geographic area and are at a maximum for local member-oriented organizations. The activities and structure of the former are least affected while the latter's are often considerably modified.

When mobility has an impact, modes of adjustment have to be worked out if the organization is to survive intact. The modes of adjustment which were encountered in this study covered a wide variety: modification of structure, changes in location and geographic orientation, shifts in population base, and the initiation of special activities designed to meet the problems of dealing with a mobile population. Some adjustments, of course, do not succeed and there is evidence in our interviews with old residents of West Philadelphia that the organizational life of that area was once considerably richer both in quantity and quality. According to the local West Philadelphia retail trade association, there has been a 75% turnover in retail business ownership over the past few years, at least part of which was attributable to problems occasioned by high residential mobility. The Philadelphia Boy Scout Council has not been successful either in establishing a troop in the West Philadelphia area.

One of the more successful adjustments to mobility has been geographic expansion. The local Jewish woman's organization, Hadassah, has adapted itself to the mobility of the West Philadelphia area by drawing its members from the larger section of which the study area is but a part. The local American Legion Post in the same area has also adapted in this fashion and now claims that its resultant metropolitan orientation is a definite asset since "the boys like to get away from neighborhood gossip and away from the little woman!" As we pointed out previously, geographic expansion may also be used as a defense against stability by those organizations which consider mobility an asset, particularly real estate brokers and moving companies.

Some organizations hard hit by the mobility of the populations they once served have modified their structure, an adjustment sometimes involving radical changes in function. A local fish-store owner in West Philadelphia, finding his old clients gone and the new residents won over to the chain stores, changed his store into a restaurant and caters primarily to clerks who run the local chain stores. The local movie house in the same area, once a first-run show and before that a vaudeville theater, is now a third-run cinema.

Still another mode of adjustment involves the establishment of special procedures designed to meet the specific impacts of mobility. The West Philadelphia grammar school, referred to previously, has instituted several new procedures for the induction of new students into the student body, some of which have been so successful as to invite imitation from other schools in the Philadelphia system. The program centers about a system of making old pupils responsible for the initiation of the new. Each teacher appoints "Big Brothers" and "Big Sisters" who are put "in charge" of new children to help them get around and to influence their acceptance by the others.

The minister of a Presbyterian church in West Philadelphia has adjusted to mobility by intensifying his efforts to make personal contacts with the young transient Presbyterians and to bring them into his church by providing social and religious activities which he considered more congenial to such an age group. That his efforts have been very successful can be seen when his growing congregation is compared with the declining congregations of the other two Protestant churches in the area.

Unfortunately, the small scale of the survey reported here does not afford more detailed treatment of how more than a small handful of organizations adjusted to mobility's impact. The study of the structural innovations made by such organizations in an effort to cushion their organizations against mobility's effects is of prime importance. American urban areas probably will be experiencing high mobility for some time to come. The maintenance of strong local organizational life under conditions of high mobility requires further and more systematic study of what sorts of modifications can be introduced into organizations so that operation under such conditions becomes possible.

For membership organizations, there are two primary problems: How can such organizations constantly attract to their folds sufficient new members to maintain organizational strength? Second, how can new members be rapidly inducted into the social group without continual disruption of the structure of the organization itself? Some of the devices employed by membership organizations in West Philadelphia can be seen to have general applicability. But there are undoubtedly other organizations in other areas and in other cities who have faced the same problems and solved them in a more or less satisfactory way. The further study of these successful adjustments may prove of immense value to those who wish to decrease the anonymity of metropolitan living.

SUMMARY AND CONCLUSIONS

In this chapter two of the ways in which mobility may affect the social life of an area were assessed. First, those effects which stem from the residents' awareness of area turnover were discussed. The main questions raised in this connection were: How aware are the families in each study area of their neighborhood's mobility? Are there family types which are especially sensitive to turnover? How is this turnover regarded? With approval, disapproval, or without concern?

Second, the impact of mobility upon an area's organizational life was assessed. What kinds of organizations are particularly sensitive to mobility? What are the adjustments in activity made by organizations to minimize the impact of turnover upon them?

Concerning the direct effect of mobility upon families, it was found that fairly large proportions in each area were unaware of the mobility taking place about them. When mobility was perceived, the accuracy of perception was fairly small. In other words, for many families, the turnover of residents in their neighborhoods was a social phenomenon below the threshold of attention.

Awareness of mobility was sharpest in the two stable study areas. Where mobility was greatest, its attention value was least. One of the reasons behind this finding is that a family's awareness of mobility depends on the strength and duration of its ties to its neighborhood. Families with many local ties who had been long residents of an area were the most aware of mobility. More such families can be found in stable areas than in mobile areas.

Most families regarded the mobility they perceived with neutrality. Mobility was largely seen as *not* altering the essential elements of a neighborhood's social composition. Approval or disapproval of residential turnover was confined to a small minority of the households in each area.

The impact of mobility through the direct awareness of families was found to be slight. Whether a neighborhood is mobile or stable does not seem to be a salient characteristic to its residents. Furthermore, turnover is viewed, by and large, with equanimity. A family's regard for its neighborhood stems from other characteristics, and whatever effects mobility may have on a family's attitudes come not through direct perception but through other means.

In contrast, considerable awareness of mobility and sensitivity to its impact were found among the key personnel of various organizations serving two of the study areas. Most organizational leaders were aware of their area's turnover and many were concerned about the effects they could discern on their organization's viability.

Sensitivity to mobility, however, varied according to two main organizational characteristics: the kind of population it served and the type of relationship the organization had to its population. Organizations which specialized in serving the population of a very small area or which specialized in a particularly mobile segment of that population were most aware of mobility and most strongly affected by it. In addition, membership organizations which sought to weld their members into a social group were more affected by mobility than those who regarded families as clients rather than members.

Highly specialized membership organizations were the types of organizations most severely threatened by an area's turnover. Unspecialized client-oriented organizations were least affected.

The adjustments made by organizations to the impact of mobility varied considerably. Some organizations altered their sensitivity to residential turnover by changing the kind of population they served. For example, local organizations often became oriented to the population of larger sections of the city, or to the metropolis as a whole. Some organizations intensified their efforts to maintain their clients or members and developed devices for the attraction of new clients or members. Some membership organizations instituted novel procedures for rapidly inducting new recruits.

The analysis of mobility's impact on organizational life uncovered one of the most serious sources of concern over this phenomenon. Organizations which try to weld the residents of a neighborhood into social groups find that mobility makes their work difficult. Particularly important, however, is the finding that there are institutional devices which, while costly in time and energy, can cushion mobility's impact. Since mobility is probably a permanent characteristic of urban life in America, it is especially important that these devices be studied in a more detailed and systematic way so that the benefits of a strong organizational life can be experienced by the residents of mobile areas.

NOTES

1. This short discussion should not be taken as a complete inventory of the possible ways in which households may be affected by mobility. There are undoubtedly other mechanisms which are at work and all we intend here is to point up those which have received more prominent treatment in this report. For example, considerable attention has been given in previous literature on the effects of mobility on the informal means of social control. Mobility, some writers have maintained (see especially Park, Robert R., *The City,* University of Chicago Press, 1925), breaks down the informal mechanisms by which social order is maintained. In mobile areas the individual is free to act as he wishes without the restraining influence of gossip and public opinion. Hence mobile areas are also those where vice and crime flourish. Still another important way in which the effects of mobility may be felt by a household is by modifying the attitudes of a household's friends and relatives to the area in which the household lives. Mobile neighborhoods may be looked upon as somewhat disrespectable places to live in by a household's significant friends and relatives and affect the household's behavior and attitude in this fashion.

2. Since the spatial frame of reference employed by the respondents in giving estimates may have been considerably smaller than the total study areas, each area was broken up into smaller sections approximately four blocks in area. The mobility rates for these smaller areas were computed and compared with the mobility estimates given by respondents within these smaller sections. The accuracy of estimation was slightly higher for each of the subsections of an area as compared with the total area. The mobility of these smaller areas varied somewhat from that of the total area. At least some of the inaccuracy of perception recorded in Table 4.1 and Table 4.2 is due to the employment of smaller reference frames by respondents in answering those questions.

3. There was one index of opportunities for interpersonal contacts which did not discriminate between levels of awareness. It was thought that female respondents, the greater part of whose lives are spent within the neighborhood, would be more likely to be aware of mobility than male respondents. However, a breakdown of respondents by sex failed to produce any significant difference in degree of awareness of mobility.

4. There is some equivocal evidence that awareness per se does affect a household's attachment to its neighborhood. Larger proportions of households wanting to move can be found among those who are aware of mobility than among those who are unaware. The percentages desiring to move among those who are aware and those families who are unaware of mobility are presented below:

	Oak Lane HL	West Phila. HH	Kensington LL	Central City LH
Aware of mobility	37%	54%	43%	72%
100% equals	(182)	(134)	(122)	(157)
Unaware of mobility	26%	47%	41%	52%
100% equals	(31)	(144)	(83)	(83)

In every study area, households aware of mobility are much more likely to move than those who are not. Especially large differences percentage-wise are found in the two mobile areas. But it is not clear whether the desire to move leads to greater awareness of mobility or whether awareness of mobility leads to greater moving desire. Some evidence for the first interpretation is found in the fact that those who see higher amounts of mobility in their areas are not more likely to want to move than those who see smaller amounts.

5. All the factors which we have used as indexes of opportunities for perception— location of friends, number of visiting relationships, presence of children in the household, and so on—were not at all related to accuracy of perception. Other factors such as education, occupation, income, and so on also turned out to be irrelevant to accuracy of perception.

6. The direct effects of mobility are somewhat higher for those respondents who perceive differences between the outward-moving families and the stable families in an area. If a respondent sees the mobile families as different, he is more likely to have an affective reaction to their leaving.

7. The term *organization* is used in this chapter to cover all formally organized social systems other than families or households. Included under this term are businesses, clubs, churches, schools, governmental and private social welfare agencies, and political parties.

8. Since the special surveys took much longer than had been anticipated and turned out to be relatively expensive operations, the original intention of covering all four study areas had to be abandoned.

9. The interviews with special persons and a preliminary analysis of the data were undertaken by Mrs. Joan Martinson May. The Philadelphia Housing Association was particularly helpful in furnishing introductions to local leaders.

10. The local party workers were interviewed in detail about the amount of turnover within each of the blocks included in their jurisdiction. The blocks were then ranked according to the turnover as rated by the political workers and also as determined from our household survey. The correlation between the two rank orders was approximately .8, indicating that for rough estimates of relative mobility, local party workers—at least in Philadelphia—are fairly accurate sources of information. It should be added that where the household survey and the party workers were in poor agreement, it turned out that the blocks in question were of mixed character, e.g., one side of the street highly mobile and the other fairly stable and so on.

11. Of course, both out-going families and incoming families use electricity, and mobility hardly affects the *amount* of electricity used. It does, however, create certain "bookkeeping" problems for the electric company, since meters have to be turned off and on, billings changed, and so on.

12. Client-oriented organizations are most vulnerable when they are in a situation competing with other organizations. In this regard, the small storekeeper is particularly vulnerable. One of the small storekeeper's defenses against the competition of chain stores is the development of personal relationships with his clients. In an atmosphere of mobility, personal relationships have little opportunity to develop and the small grocer becomes what one such interviewee termed "a rainy day grocer."

13. Some metropolitan- and client-oriented organizations are quite aware of mobility because in their operations a mechanism exists for the automatic recording of mobility. The local branches of the telephone company and electric company are both quite aware of the mobility in West Philadelphia because each residential shift entails some record handling.

PART III
HOUSEHOLD MOBILITY

Chapter 5

THE DETERMINANTS OF MOBILITY INCLINATIONS

INTRODUCTION

Few studies of residential mobility have used individual households as the units to be analyzed. Perhaps the major reasons why this approach has been neglected are connected with the availability of extensive Census data on the mobility of urban subareas and the relative newness and expense of survey techniques. Area studies could be undertaken without resort to much beyond the data already published in Census volumes; households studies required funds and personnel ordinarily out of the reach of social scientists in the 1920s and 1930s when most of the mobility research was undertaken.

Households will be the units of analysis in this and the next chapter of this report. Our personal interviews obtained each household's views concerning its future mobility. The data consists of two basic types of information: the household's *inclinations toward moving or staying on and its expectations concerning mobility* in the near future. Eight months later, interviewers returned to each dwelling unit and ascertained whether or not the same household remained in it. *Actual mobility behavior,* thus measured, serves as a check on the validity of the reported desires and expectations of the households studied.

Two major questions will be raised concerning this material: *What are the major differences between households inclining toward mobility and those inclining towards stability? Further, how close is the relationship between these reported inclinations and expectations and the actual mobility behavior which ensued?*

The analysis is designed to show how predictive schemes can be built from interview materials and how these predictive schemes can be validated against actual behavior. At the same time, our empirical results can cast considerable light on the dynamics of residential mobility.

In this section, the households are treated without regard to the areas from which they were chosen, the separate samples from each area being combined

117

in one overall sample. The question may be raised as to whether it is "legitimate" to make such a combined sample from four such disparate areas? The answer to this question depends, in part, on what kinds of statements the analysis is made to yield and, in part, on whether or not the empirical findings fall into certain patterns. Considering the first point, combining households from all four areas does not necessarily increase the representativeness of the combination of the four samples. The *specific* results therefore cannot be generalized to the whole of Philadelphia or to the whole of urbanized areas in the United States. The combined sample, because of the nature of the component subsamples, is heavily weighted toward the extremes of the distributions of mobility and socio-economic status. Therefore, the relationships to be found are probably higher than would be found in a more representative sample. *But it is hardly likely that the direction of the relationships found and the relative weights of the factors evaluated would be very different in a more representative sample.* In other words, when the statement is made that the relationship between family size and mobility is such that X% of the small families and X% + Y% of the large families are likely to move, the chances are that the values X and Y would be different in a more representative sample, but Y would hardly be negative.

Considering the second point, there is a danger that the correlations shown are spurious in the sense that they merely restate the differences between the four areas in another form. Thus, large households may be found to be more mobile than small households because the large households are all found in the mobile areas and small households are all found in the stable areas and within each area large households are no more mobile than small households. All the relationships described in this section were checked to see whether they held within the areas as well as for the combined sample. Relationships which did not meet this criterion were discarded. Thus the reader can rest assured that the correlations shown are *not* merely restatements of the differences between the four areas.

MOBILITY INCLINATIONS DEFINED

The mobility of the future has its beginnings in forces at work in the present. At any given time, a survey of households will find some that are at the point of moving, others feeling vaguely that they would like to do so, and still others can be found who are firmly wedded to their present residences. Inclinations toward mobility will be found to vary along a continuum.

What distinguishes a household strongly desiring to move from one whose desires are to remain? In this chapter we will attempt to answer this question by considering two types of factors: characteristics of the structure of the household itself and its attitudes toward the dwelling unit and neighborhood.

in which it lives. A household's structure defines what we have called its *Mobility Potential*. The household's attitudes toward its home and environment will be studied by cataloging its *Complaints*. We will see that a combination of these two types of factors goes a long way toward distinguishing between households inclining toward mobility from those desiring to remain.

To measure each household's predisposition toward moving from or remaining in its present dwelling unit, a single, straightforward question was found sufficient. The questions employed was, "If there were no housing shorgage,[1] would you like to stay on here or would you like to move from this place?" This was followed by a question designed to measure the intensity of the attitude displayed, "Are you very anxious to stay here (move out) or doesn't it matter too much to you?" Based upon the answers given to these questions, each household was classified as falling into one or another of the four categories shown in Table 5.1. Note the fairly even distribution of households among these four, graded steps of inclination toward mobility.

The remainder of this chapter is devoted to ferreting out the main differences between households wanting to stay and those wanting to move. Obviously, desire and actual behavior are not identical. The next chapter explores what their relationship is. The reader may take it for granted at this point that the relationship is strong enough to permit the statement that whatever is related to mobility inclinations is also related to mobility behavior.

If both behavior and desires are available in this study, why is so much time spent on desires? Might it not be more fruitful to go directly to the study of mobility behavior? There are several good reasons for studying mobility desires as intensively as has been done in this chapter.

First of all, if we look at moving as a process, desires and behavior become stages in a connected sequence. If we want to understand how behavior comes about, we need to know what has given rise to the motivation behind the behavior.

TABLE 5.1 Mobility Inclinations

Anxious to stay	36%	
Stay, but not anxious	16	
Total desiring to Stay		52%
Move, but not anxious	23	
Anxious to move	25	
Total Desiring to Move		48
100% equals	(924)	

Second, this study ran but for a short period. Eight months elapsed between our initial interviews with families and the subsequent measurement of their mobility behavior. Few persons (13%) were found to have moved in that period. Yet the motivational "reservoir" of which this moving was expressive consisted of the 48% of the households desiring to move. From this "reservoir" would have come a much larger number of movers—if we had had the time to make a longer observation period. Those desiring to move, as will be shown in the next chapter, are close to the actual movers in many important respects. What is gained by studying households with inclinations toward mobility can be generalized to the universe of movers.

Finally, by studying both behavior and motivation, it is possible to learn about the conditions under which motivation is crystallized into behavior. Some of the most valuable findings of this study concerns the conditions under which such moving desires are precipitated into action.

TENURE AND TENURE PREFERENCE—ATTRIBUTE AND ATTITUDE

Without exception, previous residential mobility studies have shown that renters are considerably more mobile than owners. So firmly established was this relationship that tenure was used as a major criterion in the selection of the study areas, and the findings of the previous section indicates the reliability of this criterion.

Tenure status is an attribute of the household which is ascertainable, both in principle and in practice, without resort to personal interviews. The relationship between tenure and mobility potential, as we can see in Table 5.2 is very high. Few owners are mobile and few renters are stable.

TABLE 5.2   Tenure Status and Mobility Inclinations

	Tenure Status			
Mobility Inclinations	Renters		Owners	
Anxious to stay	24%		52%	
Stay, but not anxious	15		15	
Total Wanting to Stay		39%		67%
Move, but not anxious	25		20	
Anxious to move	36		13	
Total Wanting to Move		61		33
100% equals	(477)		(429)	

The well-established character of this relationship, and hence its appearance of obviousness, tends to deter one from considering it in further detail. Tenure status is a complex variable. In part, renting or owning has an attitudinal aspect, expressing how a household regards its housing in terms of rejection or acceptance of the high valuation placed on home ownership in our country. In part, tenure status indicates something about the dwelling unit itself, for rental units in a large urban center have different characteristics than owner-occupied units. Furthermore, regardless of attitude or dwelling unit characteristics, tenure status denotes a kind of commitment to a dwelling unit. For one thing, a renter's financial tie to his dwelling unit ceases when he moves. An owner has a financial commitment which persists whether or not he actually occupies the dwelling. In this sense, renters are freer to move than owners.

The importance of considering the specific meanings of tenure status, as far as mobility is concerned, is dramatically illustrated when instead of considering tenure as a gross variable it is broken up into its components. As we mentioned previously, part of the difference between owners and renters reflects a difference in value orientation, adherence or nonadherence to the value of home ownership. If the household's attitudes toward home ownership are considered, it becomes obvious that the greater mobility inclinations of renters can be partially accounted for by the fact that many renters want to change their tenure to accord with this cultural emphasis. If renters are classified into those who prefer to rent and those who prefer to own, as in Table 5.3, it is clear that the most mobile group is composed of renters who desire to own their homes.

TABLE 5.3   Preference for Renting or Owning and
Desire to Move

	Renters who prefer to rent	Renters who prefer to own	Owners*
Anxious to stay	36%	15%	52%
Stay but not anxious	21	11	15
Total desiring to stay	57%	26%	67%
Move but not anxious	22	27	20
Anxious to move	21	47	13
Total desiring to move	43	74	33
100% equals	(206)	(271)	(429)

*Only nine cases were found of owners who desired to rent.

Renters who prefer to own are considerably more mobile than renters preferring to rent, 47% as compared with 21% being anxious to move. Note that the distribution among the four levels of mobility for renters preferring to rent is almost the mirror image of the same distribution for owners. Renters who prefer to own are just about as anxious to move as owners are anxious to stay (47% and 52%, respectively).

This analysis is presented to illustrate a general point. The addition of a social psychological variable can help specify in greater detail the relationship between a so-called objective characteristic and an item of behavior. Although tenure status and mobility inclinations were highly related, when attitudes toward renting and owning are introduced we account for much of the higher mobility inclinations displayed by the renters.

Although a great deal of the variation in mobility desires has been "explained" by the two variables brought to play so far, there are still many households whose inclinations seem to call for additional explanations. For example, there are owners who nevertheless desire to move, renters preferring to own who are not mobile, and renters preferring to rent who still want to move. To account for more of the households' mobility, we will have to consider additional items of information.

HOUSEHOLD STRUCTURE AND MOBILITY

The structure of a household, its age and composition, affects its mobility inclinations. In an earlier chapter (3), it was found that in all areas full families were the most potentially mobile of all household types. Table 5.4 recapitulates these data separately for owners and renters.

TABLE 5.4   The Mobility Inclinations of Different
Household Types

	Proportion Wanting to Move			
Household Type	Renters (100% equals)		Owners (100% equals)	
Full families (both parents and unmarried children present)	81%	(165)	34%	(274)
Incomplete families (childless couples)	57%	(144)	33%	(82)
Broken families (one spouse absent)	76%	(24)	*	(4)
Single persons	32%	(93)	15%	(20)
Miscellaneous	53%	(47)	26%	(50)

*Too few cases to present percentages.

The major differences in mobility are still accounted for by tenure status but there are significant differences among household types. Full families have the highest mobility inclinations and single-person households, the least.

Perhaps if household types are considered in other terms, clearer relationships will emerge. One of the differences among household types, as they have been defined here, is that of age. Households where husband, wife, and their children are all present are likely to be households where the parents are between the ages of 25 and 50. In part, the distinction among types is one of sheer numbers of people. In fact, if these two household structural characteristics are taken together, they go a long way toward explaining the differences between mobile and stable households.

Three important generalizations can be seen in the interrelationships between age, household size, and mobility:

(1) The younger the head of a household, the higher its inclination toward mobility.
(2) The larger the household, the higher its mobility.
(3) Age and size are independently related to mobility, although age is somewhat more strongly related than household size.

The evidence for these generalizations is presented in Table 5.5.

TABLE 5.5   Household Size, Age, and Mobility Inclinations

I. Renters — Proportion Wanting to Move

	Number of Persons in Household			
Age of Head of House	1	2	3	4 and 5
Under 35	67%	65%	83%	95%
100% equals	(12)	(55)	(30)	(34)
35–49	36%	53%	76%	81%
100% equals	(28)	(64)	(34)	(42)
50 and over	22%	56%	72%	69%
100% equals	(59)	(78)	(18)	(19)

II. Owners — Proportion Wanting to Move

	Number of Persons in Household		
Age of Head of House	1 and 2	3	4 and 5
Under 35	54%	48%	56%
100% equals	(13)	(21)	(36)
35–49	48%	33%	34%
100% equals	(27)	(51)	(77)
50 and over	20%	40%	22%
100% equals	(124)	(40)	(41)

Why do age and household size affect mobility so strongly? A good part of the answer is that both of these variables are indicators of family life cycle stages. The family life cycle, in turn, is a strong determinant of the housing needs of a household.

If we look on residential mobility as a process in which the housing requirements of a household are gradually brought into congruence with its needs, then a main determinant of mobility should be those factors which change or modify the housing requirements of the household.

The housing needs of a *young* household are most likely to be "out of balance," as it were, with its actual housing. This is the period in a family's life cycle where the greatest amount of change in household size and composition takes place. It is also the period in which the household, because of the financial demands made upon it by these rapid changes in size and composition, is least likely to be able to bring housing into line with its needs. Older households, on the other hand, particularly those headed by persons beyond middle age, are most likely households whose requirements have been contracting either through the death of household members or through the loss, through marriage, of children.

This interpretation is consistent with the findings of Table 5.5. The younger the family and the larger its size, the more inclined it is toward moving. Note that these differences, percentage-wise, are greatest in the top half of this table, where the data are presented separately for renters. The renters' desires for moving are expecially sensitive to these two household characteristics. The proportions desiring to move tend to increase across the rows (reading from left to right) and up each of the columns.

The bottom half of Table 5.5 shows the same relationships for families owning their homes. The relationships here are not as high although there is a general tendency for the proportions wanting to move to increase with the greater youthfulness of the households. Owning families are less sensitive to the housing demands created by age and size. There are two plausible reasons for this lack of sensitivity. First, owner-occupied dwelling units tend to be larger in size than renter-occupied units (the modal sizes of owned and rented units in this study being six and three rooms, respectively). Owned homes can therefore sustain a greater expansion in family size before space pressure is felt. Thus, family size, as can be seen in Table 5.5, has little effect on the mobility inclinations of owning families. Rented units are sold by the number of rooms, as it were, and cannot be changed by their tenants, while an owner may change the space within a structure by alterations and additions to it.

The question may be raised whether it is not the peculiarities of the household sample which produce the strong relationships between age and mobility potential. Certainly, the four areas from which our households were selected cannot be presented as a representative sample of urban areas.

A check can be made on this interpretation by inspecting the past mobility records of these households. This examination of past mobility[3] agrees with the results we have obtained about the present. Table 5.6 shows that households which are 10 or more years old have completed an average of 3.16 moves during their lifetimes. During the first decade of their existence, we can see that, on the average, they have completed 2.80 moves. In other words, most of the moves undertaken by a household throughout its entire existence take place in the first decade of its existence. The first decade is precisely the period when there is the greatest expansion in household size and inferentially the period in which housing is most likely out of line with the shifting housing needs.

THE INDEX OF MOBILITY POTENTIAL

There is an important common quality to the household characteristics which have thus far been found to have strong relationships to mobility inclinations. The tenure preference expressed by the family, the age of the head of the house, and the number of persons in the family are all qualities of a household which are *independent* of the dwelling in which a family may find itself. These attributes define what might be called the family's intrinsic *mobility potential*. A family whose characteristics dispose it toward wanting to move can be considered a household with a *high* mobility potential.

TABLE 5.6 Number of Addresses Occupied by Households

Number of Addresses	During Entire Existence of Household	During First Decade
One	12%	9%
Two	31	44
Three	24	23
Four	14	13
Five	9	7
Six and over	10	4
100% equals	(915)	(632)
No information	(9)	(41)
Not in existence one decade		(251)
AVERAGE NUMBER OF ADDRESSES	3.16	2.80

Correspondingly, households whose characteristics predispose them to stability can be considered families of *low* potential.

Combining these three family attributes into an index,[4] we can express each family's mobility potential as a score, a convenient way of expressing the degree to which a household's characteristics predisposes it toward mobility. The efficiency of such an index in predicting whether a household wants to move is presented in Table 5.7.[5] The higher the score, the greater the mobility potential.

The relationship between Mobility Potential and wanting to move is fairly strong. Among households with zero scores, only 17% want to move; among families with the highest score, 87% want to move. The proportions with inclinations toward mobility tend to increase as the Mobility Potential Scores increase. Note, however, that the proportions wanting to move do not increase in a regular fashion. The greatest differences occur between families scoring zero and those scoring one; and between families scoring one, two, or three, and those scoring four or five.[6]

Knowing a household's Mobility Potential Score, particularly when the scores are either very low or very high, allows a fairly close prediction of whether the household is going to want to move or want to stay. Why does this index afford so good a prediction? The answer to this question lies in the nature of the characteristics which are the components of the index.

More than anything else, the index measures the stage in the family life cycle in which a household may be found. High scores are made by families

TABLE 5.7   Mobility Potential Index and Mobility Inclinations

	Mobility Potential Scores*					
	0	1	2	3	4	5
Proportion wanting to move	17%	45%	42%	49%	75%	87%
100% equals	(177)	(139)	(190)	(196)	(141)	(55)

*The Mobility Potential Score was computed using the following weights:

Age	Household Size		Preference (Renters Only)
Under 35 = 2	One person	= 0	Renting = 0
35–49 = 1	Two persons	= 1	Owning = 1
50 and over= 0	Three persons or more	= 2	

A household's score was obtained by summing the various weights obtained by the household on each of the factors: for example, renting household, desiring to own (weight = 1), whose head of the house was between 35 and 49 (weight = 1), and whose household size was two (weight = 1) received a Mobility Potential Score of 3.

which are young and large and who prefer owning to renting. These are most likely to be households caught at that stage in their life careers when their housing needs and actual housing are most out of joint. Furthermore, these are the households whose needs are hardest to satisfy. Their large size means, on the average, a lower per-capita income and at the same time a higher demand for dwelling space. They need large units at a reasonable cost, a combination difficult to find even in the most favorable of housing markets.

Despite the Mobility Potential Index's high relationship to mobility inclinations, the correlation is by no means perfect. There are many families with large scores who nevertheless want to remain in their dwellings. There are many with small scores who want to move. There is apparently more to the desire to move than can be explained by considering just the age, size, and tenure preference of each family. After all, each household can be found within a particular dwelling unit, and these units may or may not satisfy the particular level of housing demand which is seemingly determined by the Mobility Potential Scores.

To learn more about mobility inclinations, we must also consider the family's attitudes toward their dwelling units and neighborhoods, to which task we turn in the next section.

FAMILY SIZE AND DWELLING SPACE

The Index of Mobility Potential measures characteristics of families which are independent of the housing it occupies. It is a measure of a family's housing needs in so far as these needs are determined by the characteristics which compose the index. Needs, however, can either be met or remain unsatisfied by the housing which the family occupies. To fully explain residential mobility, it is necessary to add to the dimension of "objective" needs the social psychological dimension of how families regard the way in which their dwellings satisfy these needs. To illustrate how objective characteristics and subjectively defined needs interact to produce inclinations toward mobility, we will consider in this section the relationship between family size, dwelling unit size, and how families regard their housing as meeting their space needs.

Household size, as a variable, can have many meanings for residential mobility. In part, household size indicates different family compositions. Most obviously, a single-person household is quite different from all other household sizes because the single person is living outside of a family. Two-person households are most likely childless couples, and the difference in size between large and small households is probably almost entirely accounted for by the presence of children.[7]

Household size may exert its influence on inclinations toward mobility by producing more or less crowded conditions within the home. The more persons in the household, the greater the demand for housing space and the harder it may be for the household to command the space needed to satisfy these demands. This is the sheer quantitative aspect of household size.

To test this interpretation, we can see whether the mobility inclinations of households of the same size vary with the size of the dwelling units they occupy. Table 5.8 presents a set of such comparisons. There we find that there is a tendency for small households in large dwelling units to have stronger inclinations toward mobility than small households living in smaller units.

Correspondingly, large households in small dwelling units have stronger mobility inclinations than families of comparable size in larger dwellings. However, this tendency is not as marked as the tendency for all large households, regardless of the size of the residence, to have greater desires for mobility.

Perhaps it is not so much the objectively available amount of space which produces the desire to move, but the subjective evaluation of that space as fulfilling or not fulfilling household requirements. In Table 5.9 renters and owners are divided into households of different sizes. Households in which

TABLE 5.8   Household Size, Dwelling Unit Size, and
Mobility Inclinations

| | Household Size (Renters Only)* | | | | |
| | One Person | | Two Persons | | |
	1 – 2½ Rooms	3 or more Rooms	1 – 2½ Rooms	3 – 3½ Rooms	4 or more Rooms
Proportion wanting to move	28%	33%	52%	66%	56%
100% equals	(65)	(24)	(59)	(64)	(57)

| | Three Persons | | | Four or More Persons | |
	1 – 2½ Rooms	3 – 4 Rooms	5 or more Rooms	1 – 4 Rooms	5 or more Rooms
Proportion wanting to move	80%	75%	72%	83%	81%
100% equals	(10)	(36)	(22)	(34)	(42)

*This table refers only to renters since sufficient cases of owned dwelling units of varying sizes were unavailable.

there are complaints about the amount of space in the dwelling unit are compared with households in which there are no complaints.

In the first two columns at the left, the mobility inclinations of the renters are shown. If the figures in the two columns are compared row by row, it can be seen that households dissatisfied with their space are much more likely to want to move than households which are satisfied with space within the dwelling unit. For one-person households the contrast is especially striking. Among satisfied one-person households, only 19% want to move, as compared with 57% of the dissatisfied one-person households. Similar, although not quite as large, differences appear between satisfied and dissatisfied households of other sizes. Note, however, that regardless of satisfaction, an increase in family size leads to a higher level of mobility desires.[8] This can be seen from the fact that the percentages increase down each column with increasing household size.

In the second pair of columns to the right, the same information is displayed for owners. Here again we note that dissatisfaction with space makes for higher mobility desires. However, family size, holding space dissatisfaction constant, does not make for higher levels of mobility inclinations among owners (as it does among renters). The percentages do not tend to increase down the two right-hand columns of this table. In other words, if an owning household is satisfied with the space in the dwelling unit, inclination toward mobility does not increase with the number of persons in the family.

A general point can be drawn from the findings of this section. Objectively defined needs allow a fairly good prediction of behavior, but when such needs

TABLE 5.9 Complaints About Dwelling Unit Space*
and Mobility Inclinations

	Renters wanting to move		Owners wanting to move	
Household Size	No Complaints	One or More Complaints	No Complaints	One or More Complaints
1 Person	19%	57%		
100% equals	(70)	(33)	19%	50%
2 Persons	45%	71%	(125)	(44)
100% equals	(103)	(99)		
3 Persons	67%	86%	21%	63%
100% equals	(40)	(43)	(67)	(46)
4 Persons			21%	54%
100% equals	66%	93%	(66)	(46)
5 Persons or More	(35)	(72)	24%	50%
100% equals			(21)	(22)

*The index of space complaints consists of the respondents reporting satisfaction or dissatisfaction with privacy, number of rooms, and closet space. The construction of the index is explained more fully in the Appendix.

are also felt as pressing, prediction of behavior is considerably increased. There is even some evidence in these data that felt needs afford better predictive ability. Thus, we found that the objectively measured space within a dwelling unit is not as good a predictor of whether a household wants to move as the family's estimation of that space as appropriate or not to its needs. The objective situation per se tends to be correlated with attitudes; but attitude, at least in this case, is more important for the understanding of the family's mobility inclinations.

The findings of this section point to the direction in which the analysis should go in order to add more to an understanding of residential mobility. We need to add to the data considered so far an attitudinal dimension which will measure the way in which each family sees its dwelling as fulfilling its needs.

HOUSING AND NEIGHBORHOOD COMPLAINTS

Each household faces a particular kind of housing situation. Dwelling units vary in their size, their design, the utilities, conveniences furnished, their ecological setting, and so on. Households can therefore be expected to vary in the extent to which they see their present dwelling unit as fulfilling or not fulfilling their housing requirements and needs as they view them. This section investigates the ways in which complaints about dwelling units and neighborhoods affect mobility desires.

Obviously, a dwelling unit is a complex of many elements, all of which may be relevant to the household's perceived housing needs. What are the relevant kinds of satisfactions or complaints toward which we should direct our attention? Out of all the various possibilities, this study has focused on six aspects, the selection being guided in part by the current interests in the field of housing and in part by preliminary work done in connection with this particular project.

Complaints were solicited from the respondents by asking the following question about 14 aspects of housing commonly thought to be sources of dissatisfaction, "Now, about this place, would you say you were satisfied, dissatisfied, or doesn't it matter to you about. . . ." The proportions claiming dissatisfaction or indifference are shown in Table 5.10.[9]

The complaints given in Table 5.10 are in the order of their frequency. Thus the most frequent complaint was given concerning the amount of closet space, and the least frequent complaint concerned shopping facilities. In the column to the extreme right are listed the proportions of respondents who claimed that particular housing aspects "didn't matter" to them, a measure of indifference to the aspect in question.

TABLE 5.10 Complaints About and Indifference to
Selected Aspects of Housing

Housing Characteristics (Arranged in rank order of complaints)	Proportion Complaining*	Proportion Indifferent*
"Amount of closet space"	33%	0%
"Open space about the house"	28%	6%
"Street noises"	23%	16%
"Amount of room"	22%	2%
"Heating equipment"	16%	0%
"Rent (or maintenance)"	15%	1%
"Nearness to friends and relatives"	15%	15%
"Amount of air or sunlight"	14%	2%
"Kind of people around here"	13%	9%
"Amount of privacy"	12%	1%
"Nearness to church"	9%	8%
"Travel to work"	8%	10%
"Kind of schools around here"	6%	41%
"Shopping facilities"	6%	1%

*"Complaints" and "dissatisfactions" are identical in the sense used here. "Indifference" is the respondent's report that a particular housing aspect "didn't matter too much" to him.

By and large, the households are fairly satisfied with each particular aspect. Only with amount of closet space do as many as one-third of the households register a complaint. Three dwelling unit characteristics—open space about the house, street noises, and amount of room—receive complaints from about one-fourth of the respondents. Next in importance are heating equipment, rent (or maintenance costs for home owners), nearness to friends and relatives, air and sunlight, "kind of people" in neighborhood, and privacy. Lowest in the proportion of complaining households are nearness to church and travel to work, schools, and shopping.

Few of the possible dissatisfaction sources received a very high proportion of indifferent respondents. The outstanding item concerned schools, 41% of the respondents claiming indifference to the kinds of schools in the neighborhood. Only households with children of school age or younger children were seriously concerned with the neighborhood schools. Households whose need for school had passed or who did not contemplate residence in the area when their children would need schooling contributed the bulk of the indifferent households. Only four other sources received significant amounts of indifferent responses: street noises, nearness to friends and relatives, travel to work, and nearness to church. Three of these four refer to distance factors. Apparently there are parts of the population to whom this is a matter of little concern.

If the content of the seven most frequently given sources of complaints are considered, five out of the seven refer to characteristics of the structure or dwelling unit itself (e.g., amount of room and closets), one refers to characteristics of the surrounding environment (street noises), and one refers to the location of the dwelling unit in relation to significant social relationships (nearness to friends and relatives). Apparently, the character of the particular dwelling unit itself is more important as a source of felt dissatisfaction than the other characteristics of the dwelling such as its distance from important activities or its milieu. Particularly striking are the relatively infrequent complaints about the "journey to work" or about the schools, factors which have played a somewhat prominent role in the discussions of city planners and housing experts.

The complaints about various aspects of housing were all positively interrelated. If a household complained about one aspect of housing, it was more likely to have complained about each of the other aspects than if it were satisfied with that aspect. Behind the complaints with specific aspects seem to be several general areas of satisfaction or dissatisfaction. In fact, the 14 aspects upon analysis resolved into six "dimensions" of satisfaction, each consisting of various combinations of the 14 specific aspects.[10] The six dimensions abstracted were labeled according to what seemed to be the common content of the complaints included in that dimension, as follows:

Dwelling Unit Space:	composed of complaints about the amount of space within the dwelling
Utilities:	complaints about facilities of the dwelling unit, e.g., closets and heating
Distance Complaints:	composed of complaints about the dwelling's location with regard to work, school, shopping, and so on
Physical Environment:	composed of complaints about the physical aspects of the dwelling's immediate environment, e.g., open space, street noise, and air and sunlight
Social Environment:	complaints about the "kind" of people in the neighborhood, nearness to significant others, and so on
Housing Costs:	complaints about the rent or maintenance costs of the dwelling.

Each household was given a score for each of the complaints indexes. The score was composed of the number of complaints it registered to each of the questions which define each of the indexes. Thus, a family which complained about the three aspects of dwelling unit space received a score of three on the Dwelling Unit Space Index.

Table 5.11 shows how each of these indexes is related to inclinations
toward mobility. The proportion wanting to move among households with
different complaints scores are shown. The indexes in this table are arranged
roughly in the order of their potency in producing desires for moving.[11] Thus
the complaint index most strongly related to mobility inclinations is the

TABLE 5.11 Complaints Indexes and Mobility Inclinations

A. Dwelling Unit Space Complaints Index

	No Complaints	One Complaint	Two or More Complaints
Proportion wanting to move	31%	61%	86%
100% equals	(516)	(218)	(168)

B. Utilities Complaints Index

	No Complaints	One Complaint	Two Complaints
Proportion wanting to move	33%	64%	84%
100% equals	(544)	(275)	(93)

C. Social Environment Complaints Index

	No Complaints	One Complaint	Two Complaints
Proportion wanting to move	41%	59%	89%
100% equals	(691)	(166)	(45)

D. Physical Environment Complaints Index

	No Complaints	One Complaint	Two or More Complaints
Proportion wanting to move	34%	53%	80%
100% equals	(502)	(252)	(148)

E. Costs Complaints

	No Complaints	One Complaint
Proportion wanting to move	44%	67%
100% equals	(775)	(134)

F. Neighborhood Location Complaints

	No Complaints	One Complaint	Two or More Complaints
Proportion wanting to move	44%	64%	54%
100% equals	(650)	(171)	(81)

Dwelling Unit Space Index, and the index least related to wanting to move is the Distance Complaints Index.

Each complaint index shows a fairly high relationship to residential mobility desires. The more complaints a family registered, the more likely it was to want to move. There is, however, one striking exception to this pattern: the Neighborhood Location Complaints Index shows a very weak and irregular relationship to mobility potential.

The poor showing of the Location Complaints Index was a complete reversal of expectations. Previous literature on residential mobility and migration laid heavy stress on residential mobility as a mechanism whereby households minimize their distances from place of employment, service institutions, and persons who play a large part in their lives. Particularly stressed was the role played by the "journey to work" in mobility. In this study, little weight can be given to these location factors despite the fact that the study areas are quite variously situated within Philadelphia.

Perhaps the stress laid upon the journey to work expresses the former importance of this factor in days when mass transportation was relatively poorly developed and more expensive (relative to the wages and salaries of the period). Today's well-developed mass transportation networks and extensively diffused car ownership may make accessibility a minor consideration compared to a generation ago. Dissatisfaction with the distance between job and homes can be easily lessened by car ownership and a residential shift avoided.[12]

THE COMBINED COMPLAINTS INDEX

Although five of the six complaints indexes each have a strong relationship to residential mobility, even stronger relationships can be found when these indexes are considered simultaneously. For example, in Table 5.12, the

TABLE 5.12 Dwelling Unit Space Complaints,
Physical Environment Complaints and Mobility
Inclinations

	(Percentages Are Proportions Wanting To Move)		
		Dwelling Unit Space Complaints	
Physical Environment Complaints	*None*	*One*	*Two or More*
None	26%	50%	72%
100% equals	(317)	(100)	(142)
One	36%	56%	80%
100% equals	(114)	(76)	(66)
Two or More	70%	77%	88%
100% equals	(43)	(46)	(66)

combined effect is shown of the Dwelling Unit Space Complaints Index and the Physical Environment Complaints Index. The percentages in this table increase across each row from left to right and down each column. Each type of complaint has an independent effect on mobility inclinations. The more complaints a family registers in one dimension, the more it wants to move, regardless of the number of complaints it has registered in the other dimension. The spread of percentages is very large, ranging from 26% wanting to move among those who register no complaints on either index to 86% wanting to move among those who register the highest number of complaints on both indexes.

Note that the Space Complaints Index has a greater effect on mobility inclinations than the Physical Environment Complaints Index. The percentages across the rows have a greater spread than the percentages down each column.

Some of the complaints indexes were found on analysis to add little to the relationship to mobility inclinations shown by other indexes. Table 5.13 shows that the Utilities Complaints Index does not show much relationship to mobility inclinations when it is considered together with the Dwelling Unit Space Complaints Index. Comparing the percentages in each column, it can be seen that, once the level of dwelling space complaints is held constant, households are not very much more likely to want to move if they also register complaints about the dwelling utilities.

Four of the six complaints indexes were found to be related independently to wanting to move.[13] This finding suggested that an overall complaints index could be formed whose relationship to mobility inclinations would be very strong. Accordingly, the Combined Complaints Index was formed by adding together each of the complaints registered by each household with regard to each of the four complaints dimensions.

The relationship of the Combined Complaints Index to mobility desires is shown in Table 5.14. The correlation is a particularly strong one. Among those registering no complaints, about one in five families want to move; among those with the highest number of complaints, about four out of five

TABLE 5.13 Dwelling Unit Space Complaints,
Utilities Complaints and Mobility Inclinations

| | *(Percentages Are Proportions Wanting To Move)* | | |
| | | *Dwelling Unit Space Complaints* | |
Utilities Complaints	*None*	*One*	*Two or More*
None	29%	59%	91%
100% equals	(484)	(60)	(13)
One or More	59%	58%	91%
100% equals	(44)	(162)	(161)

TABLE 5.14   Combined Complaints Index and
Mobility Inclinations

	Number of Complaints						
	0	1	2	3	4	5	6 or more
PROPORTION							
WANTING TO MOVE	22%	43%	43%	52%	74%	73%	82%
100% equals	(304)	(160)	(94)	(52)	(149)	(119)	(28)

want to move. Note that the greatest jump in desire to move occurs between those families with no complaints and those with one complaint. A slight degree of dissatisfaction brings about a considerable increase in mobility inclination.

The households' evaluations of their dwelling units and neighborhoods as satisfactory or not is strongly related to their desires to move. The relationship is almost as strong as the relationship shown between mobility inclinations and Mobility Potential in a previous section.

Yet this correlation is not perfect. There are still many families whose mobility inclinations seem to be out of line with the satisfaction or dissatisfaction which they feel concerning their homes. Obviously other factors must also play a role.

INCONGRUENCIES BETWEEN COMPLAINTS AND INCLINATIONS

The strong relationship between complaints and moving desires has been noted in Table 5.14. There are, however, many households who are quite satisfied, yet desire to move. There are also many families who desire to remain although they are quite dissatisfied. What brings about a desire to move in the absence of complaints? What prevents the crystallization of moving desires in the presence of dissatisfaction?

To attempt to answer these questions, the households have been classified into four groups:[14]

Type I   —satisfied stayers: households with few complaints and no desire to move
Type II —satisfied movers: households with few complaints but who want to move
Type III—dissatisfied movers: households with many complaints and who want to move
Type IV—dissatisfied stayers: households with many complaints but with no desire to move.

Now let us consider some of the characteristics of these four categories which may help in indicating why the relationship between mobility inclinations and complaints is not higher than it is. One factor which turns out to be of considerable importance is the tenure status of the household: whether it is a renter or an owner.

Table 5.15 indicates the proportion of households of each type who are renters. It can be seen that there are strikingly more renting households among satisfied movers than among satisfied stayers. Owners apparently keep their inclinations in line with their complaints, particularly when their complaints are few. Renters, on the other hand, seem somewhat freer in this regard, and they make up a plurality of the families who have a higher inclination to move than their level of satisfaction seems to warrant.

Comparing dissatisfied stayers with dissatisfied movers, many more renters can be found among the second type than among the first. Two out of three dissatisfied movers are renters; only one out of three dissatisfied stayers rent their homes. Dissatisfied owners apparently do not crystallize moving desires out of their dissatisfactions as easily as renters do.

In short, renters often express a moving inclination when they are satisfied, and overwhelmingly so when they are dissatisfied. Owners rarely express a desire to move when satisfied and also when dissatisfied seem reluctant to crystallize the dissatisfaction into a desire to move.

The difference in behavior shown between renters and owners illustrates the different relationships owners and renters have to the dwelling units they occupy. By and large, a renter's felt dissatisfactions can best be met by obtaining other quarters without the relevant objectionable features. Owners, however, are more often able to reduce their complaints by modifying the dwelling itself. Closets can be built, rooms converted, extensions made to the building, and so on. Tenants occupy inflexible dwellings, their adjustments must usually be made by moving to another. Owners can be more flexible in modifying their homes to suit the changes in their needs.

Of course owners cannot satisfy all their complaints through the modification of their homes. Some of the sources of dissatisfaction lie outside the unit itself, as in the case of complaints about the neighborhood's physical aspects

TABLE 5.15   Tenure Status and Deviance Between
Complaints and Inclinations

| Mobility Inclinations | Complaints | |
	Satisfied	Dissatisfied
Stayer	(I) 39% renters (377)	(III) 34% renters (269)
Mover	(II) 63% renters (206)	(IV) 68% renters (164)

or its social composition.[15] The relationship between the complaints index and desires to move, therefore, still holds for owners even though it does not reach the strength of the correlation shown for renters.

UNFRUITFUL APPROACHES–FRIENDSHIP PATTERNS AND MOBILITY DESIRES

In designing the questionnaires used in interviews with the families studied, many items of information were obtained which were felt to be related to mobility inclinations. Some of these items were found to be especially important and have found their way into either the Mobility Potential Index or the complaints index. Other kinds of data turned out to be largely irrelevant, even though initially we had strong convictions of their importance. We have already seen that the journey to work, considered to be of considerable importance in much of the literature on mobility, turned out to be largely irrelevant.

Other kinds of data, the importance of which was much written about, also turned out to be relatively unfruitful. It was found, for example, that annual family income had practically no relationship to mobility inclinations, once Mobility Potential was taken into account. Many other supposedly obvious factors, such as previous mobility, occupation, and such, were also discarded because they did not help to discriminate between families wanting to move and those wanting to stay.

One such unfruitful variable will be treated in some detail in this section, primarily because of the attention given to it in the literature on residential mobility. Some writers[16] have made the claim that mobility is lessened when households within an area have developed strong interpersonal ties. The data of this study does not lend any support to this generalization.

In Table 5.16, families are classified according to the location of their best friends and "most well-liked" relatives. In the upper half of this table, where the locations of the respondents' best friends are considered, it can be seen that there is practically no difference in mobility inclination between renters whose best friends are located in the immediate vicinity and renters whose best friends are located at large in the city. Having one's best friends in the neighborhood in which one resides does not make for stronger desires to remain in that neighborhood. Owners show a little more sensitivity in this respect: Those who have their best friends located primarily outside the neighborhood are somewhat more likely to want to move. It should be noted that this percentage difference (42% as compared with 32%), although statistically significant, is not very large at all. By and large, it makes little difference in so far as mobility potential is concerned whether or not the household is integrated into the neighborhood in the sense of having close friends living nearby.

In the lower half of Table 5.16, the same information is presented concerning the respondents' closest relatives. No particular pattern of relationship can be discerned. Persons whose closest relatives are located nearby in the neighborhood are not particularly less likely to move than persons whose relatives are residing at some distance. This finding holds both for renters and owners.

The development of close personal relationships within the local area apparently is not a deterrent to mobility. It apparently does not matter too much to a household where its significant personal relationships are. Yet we saw in Chapter 3 that in the two stable areas, friendships tended to be closer physically than in the two mobile areas. Apparently the closer location of personal relationships is a *consequence* of stability rather than a cause. Persons develop close personal ties in a neighborhood as a consequence of living there over a period of time, but proximity to friends and relatives has little effect on their desires to move or remain.

TABLE 5.16 Location of Close Friends and Relatives as Affecting Desires to Move

I. Location of Best Friends

		Friends Mostly
	Local	*Metropolitan and Cosmopolitan*
Proportion desiring to move		
Renters	61%	62%
100% equals	(264)	(164)
Owners	32%	42%
100% equals	(277)	(123)

II. Location of Closest Relatives:

		Relatives Mostly	
	Local	*Metropolitan*[*]	*Cosmopolitan*[*]
Proportion desiring to move			
Renters	60%	69%	53%
100% equals	(130)	(177)	(141)
Owners	32%	32%	36%
100% equals	(214)	(143)	(53)

[*]A respondent's relatives were classified as "Cosmopolitan" if the majority of them lived outside of Philadelphia, and classified as "Metropolitan" if a majority lived outside of the same ward as the respondent, but still within the limits of Philadelphia.

POTENTIAL, COMPLAINTS, AND MOBILITY INCLINATIONS

The Mobility Potential Index expresses the extent to which a household's characteristics dispose it toward wanting to move. Its usefulness as a predictor of mobility inclinations lies in the way it expresses the housing needs of families. The complaints index expresses the way in which a household regards its housing as either satisfactory or not. The latter's relationship to mobility inclinations is apparently generated by families' desires to reduce their levels of housing dissatisfaction.

It would seem that these two indexes should be very highly interrelated. In part, a family's complaints—whether great or small—are a function of its needs. The greater the needs, the more likely it is to find its housing wanting. In part, a family's complaints are a function of the kind of housing it occupies, particularly the way in which its housing satisfies the needs that are generated by its characteristics.

Yet the actual relationship between these two indexes is not extremely high. In Table 5.17 we can see that families with high mobility potential are more likely to be dissatisfied than persons with low potential scores. But the differences are not very great.

On further consideration, however, this relatively low relationship can be seen to be quite understandable and only an apparent paradox. It must be remembered that potential is measured without regard to the family's present housing situation. Thus, even after a household has made all attempts to bring its housing into line with its needs and has satisfied those needs as much as it can, it will still manifest a high potential score. Under such circumstances, of course, its complaints will be rather small. Complaints, then, represent the interaction between needs and a particular situation. When needs are met— whatever strength the needs may have—complaints are low; while even the minimal needs of older, smaller households may be poorly satisfied by their present housing. Some households with low potential scores will manifest

TABLE 5.17 The Mobility Potential Index and the
Combined Complaints Index

Combined Complaints Score	Mobility Potential Score				
	0	1	2	3	4 and 5
0	45%	35%	35%	34%	22%
1	22	19	20	12	14
2 and 3	14	18	14	18	15
4	8	15	15	25	21
5 and 6	12	14	16	10	28
100% equals	(170)	(136)	(193)	(194)	(190)

high complaint scores because they are in a particularly poor housing situation. Conversely, some households with large potential scores will manifest few complaints because they have managed to satisfy the needs generated in their present housing.

In the long run, needs and housing tend to come into line with each other. There is a "strain to consistency" between a household's composition, its housing philosophy, and its housing behavior. At any particular point of time, however, large groups of households will be found in the anomalous situation of having greater needs than their present housing can satisfy; hence the generally positive but low correlation between mobility potential and complaints. Potential, it should be noted further, is not a static measure—households grow in size and age—families are therefore always "growing out" of their housing, thus reducing the relationship between potential and complaints.

A family's Complaints Score and its Mobility Potential Score together should afford a very good prediction of its inclinations toward mobility. It has been shown that each score is related to mobility desires, and also that the scores are not interchangeable. Table 5.18 presents the empirical evidence.

The relationships shown in this table are *extremely strong*. Among those with few complaints and low potential scores (upper left-hand corner) only 11% desire to move. In contrast, 93% of the households with high scores on both accounts want to move (lower right-hand corner).

Note that with increasing scores on either index, mobility inclinations increase. The percentages in the table rise, almost without exception, from left to right along the rows and from top to bottom along the columns.

As Table 5.18 indicates, knowing a family's complaints and certain of its characteristics enables a fairly accurate[17] prediction of whether that family

TABLE 5.18   Combined Effect of Mobility Potential Index and Complaints Index on Mobility Inclinations

| | *(Percentages shown are proportions wanting to move)* | | | |
| | | Complaints Index Score | | |
Mobility Potential Score	0	1–2	3–4	5 or More
0–1	11%	34%	56%	47%
100% equals	(122)	(88)	(56)	(40)
2–3	21%	40%	67%	80%
100% equals	(131)	(108)	(95)	(50)
4 or more	60%	70%	87%	93%
100% equals	(42)	(46)	(53)	(55)

wants to move from its present abode. Accurate predictions of mobility inclinations can be made in 75% of the households, using the data shown.

Although this correlation is much higher than one usually finds in social research, a perfect relationship is by no means often attained. It is important to point out, at this juncture, how one might refine these relationships still further. One way is to look at how these relationships obtain in different subpopulations of households. To illustrate how this may be accomplished, Table 5.19 considers, in abridged form, the relationships between mobility potential, complaints, and wanting to move, separately for renters and owners. The top half of this table refers to renters; the bottom half to owners.

Among renters, it can be seen from the fact that the proportion desiring to move increases with both increasing potential and increasing complaints, that both complaints and potential contribute about equally to the arousal of

TABLE 5.19   Potential,
Complaints and Mobility
Desires: Renters and Owners[*]

(Percentages are proportions wanting to move)

RENTERS ONLY

Mobility Potential	Complaints	
	Few	Many
Low	36%	54%
100% equals	(131)	(73)
High	53%	88%
100% equals	(120)	(136)

OWNERS ONLY

Mobility Potential	Complaints	
	Few	Many
Low	21%	54%
100% equals	(187)	(73)
High	21%	61%
100% equals	(99)	(67)

[*]Households were classified as having few complaints and low potential if they fell into the cells marked "I" in the scheme shown below; as few complaints and high potential if in cells marked "IV; as "many complaints and low potential" if in cells marked "II", and as "many complaints and high potential" if in cells marked "III".

Potential Score	Complaints Score			
	0	1–2	3–4	5 and more
0–1	I	I	I	II
2–3	IV	I	III	II
4 or more	IV	IV	III	III

mobility inclinations. This suggests that perhaps there are important complaint areas which may have been missed in this survey.[18] It is hard to imagine potential converting itself directly into wanting to move without expressing itself in some variety of felt dissatisfaction.

Among owners, as shown in the bottom half of the table, quite a different pattern is presented. It can be seen here that complaints play a far more important role in producing desires to move than the sorts of household characteristics which went into the Mobility Potential Index. Among owners with few complaints, there is no difference in the proportions wanting to move for families with low or high Potential Scores. Families with high complaint scores, however, show about the same proportions wanting to move, regardless of the Mobility Potential Score which they may have. For owners, then, the desire to move is primarily a function of the experienced dissatisfaction with housing.

Analyses such as reported here point the way to further knowledge about mobility desires. The addition of still other factors, the study of special kinds of households, will specify further how the characteristics of a household, its attitudes toward its dwelling, and other factors unite to generate inclinations toward mobility.

SUMMARY AND CONCLUSIONS

The analysis presented in this chapter was designed to demonstrate how predictive schemes may be built from interview materials and to point out the *kinds* of data which are helpful in explaining why some households are mobile and some households are stable.

Two indexes were constructed. The Mobility Potential Index, a simple combination of household size, age, and tenure preference, measured attributes of households independent of the housing occupied. A Combined Complaints Index, a combination of households' evaluations of their dwellings and neighborhoods, measured the extent to which each household was satisfied with the way in which its residence met its perceived housing needs. Each index was found to correlate highly, and to about the same degree, with mobility inclination. Moreover, when the indexes were considered together, they were able to discriminate extremely well between potentially mobile and potentially stable households.

The methodological point demonstrated is that simple indexes can be good predictors of mobility inclination. The data going into each of the indexes were easy to obtain, and the construction of the indexes was of the simplest kind.

From a substantive point of view, the kinds of data which went into these indexes have greatly illuminated the basic character of residential mobility. It is fairly well demonstrated that residential mobility is primarily a matter of the interaction of households with particular housing needs, with particular dwellings which do or do not meet these needs. Residential mobility consists of the adjustive reactions of households to their housing needs.

It is not likely that the findings presented here concerning family life cycle will be contradicted in other studies. However, life cycle as a variable may certainly be elaborated much further than the two elements—age and size— considered here. More detailed consideration of the compositions of households would probably add more depth and elaboration to the relationships we have shown.

A household's housing philosophy also plays an important role. This study only considered tenure preference as an index of housing philosophy. Obviously this variable can be elaborated further: Households vary according to the way in which they view the function of housing; they differ in the extent to which they are willing to compromise other needs to satisfy their housing desires; and so on. The elaboration of housing philosophy is another way in which the findings shown in this study can be built upon.

A household's complaints about its residence and neighborhood were also shown to be highly related to mobility. Particularly important were those complaints referring to the characteristics of the dwelling unit. In contrast, the environment of the residence and its location in space did not seem to be particularly relevant.

The complaints studied were gross attributes of dwelling units. Space complaints, for example, could be broken up into quite a number of subcomplaints, for example, space as the number and size of bedrooms, space as the size of kitchens, and so on. The importance of attitudes toward the dwelling unit has been demonstrated in this study. Now it is up to the architect and the housing expert to construct finer complaint indexes to discriminate those specific aspects of housing whose presence or absence affects mobility inclination.

Finally, we have seen how small a role was played by friendships in the neighborhood as deterrents to mobility. At least for these four areas, households do not cling to a neighborhood because their friends or relatives live there. Friendships and their locations are independent of mobility inclination. But, they are related to the mobility of an area in the sense that the more stable the area, the more likely a household is to establish ties in a neighborhood, but the existence or absence of such ties does not affect a household's desires to remain or move.

NOTES

1. In Philadelphia at the time of the field work phase of this study (October-November 1950), the housing market was still tight enough to justify the fear that many households might answer such a question in terms of their actual expectations about moving. By wording the question in this form, it was hoped that answers would reflect desires, free and clear of restrictions on moving imposed by the then-serious housing shortage.

2. See note to Table 3.10, Chapter 3, for a fuller explanation of the household typology.

3. Although not reported in this monograph, an attempt was made to analyze the difference between households which had experienced different amounts of mobility in their life histories. No differences of any significance, other than tenure status, were found. Rich or poor families, families of different occupational rank, and families of different compositions all were found to have experienced about the same number of moves, once age and tenure status had been held constant.

4. The structure of and rationale underlying the construction of this index have very strong resemblances to other indexes used in quite different areas of behavior. For example, in a study of voting behavior in a national election, Paul F. Lazarsfeld and his associates constructed an Index of Political Predispositions which expressed the way in which certain positional attributes of an individual predisposed him to vote for one or the other of the two political parties (see Paul F. Lazarsfeld, Bernard Berelson, and Hazel Gaudet, *The People's Choice*, Columbia University Press, 1948).

5. The way in which each family's score was computed is explained in the note to Table 5.7.

6. Households scoring either four or five are large, young households. Apparently having both these predisposing characteristics considerably outweighs having only one.

7. An attempt was made through an analysis of these data to see whether the presence of children counted more than the presence of adults in generating inclinations toward mobility. Unfortunately, not enough cases of households of equal size but differing in composition were found in the sample to make the crucial comparisons statistically sensitive. The findings were, however, that little difference could be found between the influence of the presence of additional adults and that of the presence of children.

8. Note, in addition, that larger households tend to be more complaining about space. A comparison of the base figures (shown in parentheses) show that the larger the household, the more likely it is to have a complaint about space within the dwelling unit.

9. Any list of possible sources of complaints might go wide of the goal of adequate coverage of significant areas. To obtain some measure of the adequacy of this list's coverage of complaint sources, an additional "free answer" question was asked at the end of the list, "Is there anything else you don't like about this place?" Only 34% of the respondents had anything additional to report and many of the complaints made in answer to this additional question were repetitions of complaints registered in the answer to specific questions. Of the 372 respondents who did register additional complaints (not repetitions of the previously registered complaints), the significant complaints were as follows:

Dwelling Unit design complaints (e.g. kitchen too small, poor fixtures
in bathroom, poor layout of apartment, etc.)   26%

Complaints about structure (total structure in which dwelling unit

is located, including location on block, exposure orientation, lack
of garage, etc.)   21%

Undesirable land uses in neighborhood (complaints about stores,
factories, railroads)   12%

Complaints about the landlord (not enough services, too much
supervision of activities, etc.)   24%

Future research into housing complaints might profitably investigate these four possible
important areas of housing complaints in addition to those which were found of
importance in this study.

10. The analysis undertaken is described in the Appendix. The interrelationships
among the 14 questions were analyzed using the methods of Latent Structure Analysis.
The complaints which were combined into the several dimensions are given below:

Dimension	*Component Complaints*
Dwelling unit space	Amount of room, privacy, and closet space
Utilities	Closet space and heating equipment
Distance	Travel to work, nearness to church, nearness to friends and relatives, shopping facilities
Housing costs	Rent or maintenance
Neighborhood physical structure	Street noises, air and sunlight, open space about the house
Neighborhood social environment	Kind of people in the neighborhood and nearness to friends and relatives.

The complaints indexes constructed represent the number of complaints given to the
questions which make up a particular dimension.

11. This rank order should not be interpreted as showing strong differences among
the several complaints indexes. The first four indexes in Table 5.11 all have about the
same relationship to mobility inclinations, with differences among these indexes in this
respect being very slight. For example, if the difference in percentage points between the
lowest and highest score groups are considered for each index, we can see that only slight
differences between the first four indexes emerge:

Difference between lowest and highest percentage in Table 5.11

Dwelling Unit Space Index	55%
Utilities Index	51%
Social Environment Index	48%
Physical Environment Index	46%
Cost Index	23%
Location Index	10%

12. The data on car ownership within the four study areas bolsters this interpretation. Although the socio-economic level of Oak Lane, a relatively inaccessible area, is
about the same as that of West Philadelphia, three out of four living in that area own
cars, compared with fewer than one out of every two in West Philadelphia. The same
pattern holds for the two low status areas: Kensington, more inaccessible than Central

City, shows a car ownership level of one out of three while the latter has a ratio of one in four.

	Oak Lane	West Phila.	Kensington	Central City
Proportion of families owning cars	76%	44%	34%	25%
100% equals	(215)	(283)	(213)	(206)

13. The complaints indexes found to be independently related were as follows: Dwelling Unit Space Complaints, Physical Environment Complaints, Cost Complaints, and Social Environment Complaints. Independence was tested by seeing whether an index had a relationship to mobility desires when each of the other indexes was held constant. This was accomplished by constructing sets of tables similar to 5.12 and 5.13. Under this criterion the Utilities Complaints Index and the Location Complaints Index were omitted in the construction of the Combined Complaints Index.

14. The scheme by which households were classified as belonging to one or another of the four types is presented below:

Classification Scheme for Deviant Case Analysis

Mobility Inclinations	*Complaints Score*						
	0	1	2	3	4	5	⩾6
Anxious to stay	I	I	I	I	IV	IV	IV
	(187)	(57)	(35)	(15)	(25)	(3)	(2)
Stay but not anxious	II	I	I	I	III	IV	IV
	(48)	(34)	(18)	(10)	(16)	(14)	(3)
Move but not anxious	II	II	I	III	III	III	IV
	(50)	(42)	(21)	(14)	(56)	(23)	(2)
Anxious to move	II	II	II	III	III	III	III
	(18)	(27)	(20)	(13)	(62)	(64)	(21)

In this table, each cell represents one of the 24 combinations of scores on the Combined Complaints Index and mobility inclinations. The roman numbers indicate to which types households classified in each cell were allocated. The arabic numerals in parentheses indicate the number of cases to be found in each of the cells.

15. In Chapter 8 it will be shown that many owners cite as important reasons for leaving their former home factors which relate to the old neighborhood's social environment and physical structure.

16. See especially Robert W. Kennedy "Sociopsychological Problems of Housing Design" in Festinger, Leon, Schacter, Stanley and Back, Kurt, *Social Pressures in Informal Groups,* Harper & Bros., New York 1950. Kennedy cites some findings which indicate that a housing project wherein the residents are integrated into a satisfactory interpersonal life achieve more approval from the residents than another housing project—objectively better off with regard to housing—where interpersonal ties among residents did not develop.

17. If each cell in Table 5.18 is predicted as wanting to move or wanting to stay according to whether a majority of the households in that cell want to move or want to stay, only 25% of the households would be classified incorrectly. For example, if the households in the extreme upper left-hand cell are predicted as wanting to stay, only 13 households (11% of 122) will be predicted incorrectly. If the same calculations are made for each cell, it will be found that 233 families would be incorrectly predicted, leading to accurate predictions in 75% of the cases.

18. See Note 9 of this chapter for some of the neglected complaint areas reported by the respondents.

Chapter 6

MOBILITY AS PROCESS

INTRODUCTION

Wanting to move may be viewed as the initial step in a sequence leading eventually to the act of moving itself. Sometimes the sequence takes place over a short time period. In other cases, each stage may occupy a considerable length of time, and may even never eventuate in a residential shift.

Desire is not always followed by the desired activity, as everyone has experienced. The gap between desire and its fulfillment varies with the kind of desires involved. When someone tells us he is thirsty, we usually expect that he will shortly make some move toward getting a drink. The gap between desire and behavior is small in this case because the individual usually controls most of the relevant aspects of his life situation. In contrast, if someone says he wants to go to Europe, we do not ordinarily expect him to be leaving the next day. Going to Europe involves a series of preparatory acts—saving money, obtaining a passport, and such—and the consummation of the desire must be postponed until these intervening acts are performed. To predict whether someone is going to go to Europe within a short time span, it is necessary to know more than just whether or not he wants to go. More confident predictions can be made if his specific plans are known, whether he has saved money, and so on.

To predict whether or not a family will move, we need to know whether mobility is more like the act of going to Europe or more like the act of drinking water. In other words, can we predict whether a household will move when we know only whether it wants to or not? Or, do we need to have additional information?

Before a family can move, it ordinarily must manifest more than the desire to do so. Moving resembles more the act of going to Europe since it usually entails a series of preparatory acts—obtaining a new dwelling, arranging for the transfer of possessions, and so on. The number and complexity of these preparatory acts varies with the kind of household and the nature of its tenure: it is very easy for a single person, living in a furnished room, to move; moving becomes a relatively complicated affair for home owners who have accumulated a great many possessions.

Wanting to move is not ordinarily followed by an immediate residential shift. At any one point in time, it is to be expected that more families are inclined to move than the actual level of turnover would apparently indicate. Mobility desire, therefore, are not the best predictor of moving.

Better predictions can be made, however, if one ascertains whether or not mobility desires have crystallized into intentions. A family's mobility intentions—whether it expects to move within the near future—can serve as an index of whether a family is at a stage close to the act of moving itself. *Mobility intention and its relationship to mobility behavior is therefore a central topic in the pages to follow.*

This chapter presents statistical data on the mobility process. The relationships between wanting to move, intending to move, and moving itself are studied as they manifested themselves during the eight months' field work phase of this project. There are four major questions which will be raised in this connection:

(1) Under what conditions are mobility desires crystallized into moving intentions?

(2) What are the factors which facilitate the carrying out of an intention to move?

(3) How well can mobility behavior be predicted from a family's intentions and desires?

(4) What are the factors that upset the relationship between intentions and behavior? What precipitates a stable household into moving? What prevents a household from carrying out its intention?

The answers to these questions are intended to throw light on residential mobility as a process. But they also serve another crucial function. In the previous chapter, the discussion of mobility inclinations was based on the explicit assumption that wanting to move and moving itself were so closely related that whatever we found out about mobility desires would also hold for mobility behavior. Hence the analysis in this chapter is intended to validate and justify the findings of the previous one.

HOW MOBILITY INTENTIONS WERE MEASURED

A family may want to move without feeling that it will undertake a shift in the very near future. Planning for the actual move may be postponed for a variety of reasons: Jack of sufficient resources at the time, preoccupation with other matters, and so on. Conversely, families whose wishes are for stability may expect that circumstances will make moving necessary.

Expectations and inclinations will be related but there is good reason to expect that they will *not* be identical. In measuring both the desire to move and expectations concerning moving, an attempt was made to separate the two as much as possible. Desires were defined to the respondent as the wish to move or remain, regardless of realistic expectations.[1] In measuring mobility intentions, in contrast, each family was asked to predict its own behavior over the 10-month period following the initial interview. The exact wording of the question employed was as follows: "Now about your plans. As things look now, do you think that in 10 months—by next summer—you will still be living here, that there is a fifty-fifty chance of your moving, or that you will definitely move out by that time?"

Table 6.1 contains the mobility intentions of the families studied in this research, along with their mobility desires. Mobility intentions run far behind the expressed desires to move. Three out of four families expected to be at the same dwelling; 8% definitely expected to move; another 14% claimed to have a fifty-fifty chance of moving.

HOW MOBILITY INTENTIONS ARE FORMED

Many more families want to move than actually intend to do so. Common sense indicates that, by and large, wanting to move and intending to do so should go hand in hand. But the character of the relationship between wishes and intentions is important enough to investigate in some detail. To understand residential mobility as a process, we need to know how the desire to move is transformed into the intention to do so. What are the factors that translate the wish into the intention? What precipitates behavior when the wish is not present?

The desire to move and the intention to move may be viewed as successive steps in a sequence whose last stage is the move itself. This viewpoint implies

TABLE 6.1   Mobility Intentions and Mobility Desires

Mobility Intentions		Mobility Desires	
Expects to stay on	77%	Anxious to stay	36%
50-50 chance of moving	14	Stay but not anxious	16
Definitely Moving	8	Move but not anxious	23
Don't know	1	Anxious to move	25
100% equals	(924)	100% equals	(924)

that a special kind of relationship exists between desire and intention: Wanting to stay and intending to stay should be virtually synonymous. But wanting to move does not necessarily imply the intention to do so. The convverse, however, should apply: Virtually everyone intending to move should want to do so. In other words, given a family's mobility desires, it should be easier to predict whether it intends to stay than whether it intends to move.

By and large, Table 6.2 supports this expected relationship. Practically everyone who is anxious to stay intends to do so. In contrast, of those anxious to move, only one in four is planning to move, and another one in three claims to have a fifty-fifty chance of moving. It can also be seen that about six out of every seven persons planning to move were anxious to do so.[2]

There is another point of interest in Table 6.2. The proportions intending to move do not increase uniformly as the desire to move increases. The greatest difference occurs between those who want to move, but who are not particularly anxious to do so, and those who are anxious to do so. This indicates that there is apparently some sort of threshold relationship between desires and plans. The desire to move must go above a particular level before moving intentions begin to crystallize.

There are two types of households whose mobility desires and mobility plans seem to be "out of joint." A very large number of households desired to move but were not planning to do so. These, one may assume, are the households in an early stage of the sequence leading to a residential shift. Their deviance is quite understandable. The other type of household, those desiring to stay but planning to move, comprise less than half a dozen cases. The expectation was that these cases should be few in number. Yet their existence still needs some explanation. One reasons for their presence is that some moves are involuntary, in the sense of being forced on the household either by other persons or events, or required by decisions made by the

TABLE 6.2   Mobility Desires and Mobility Intentions

Mobility Intentions	Mobility Desires			
	Anxious to stay	Stay but not anxious	Move but not anxious	Anxious to move
Plans to stay	97%	86%	82%	40%
Fifty-fifty chance of moving	2	12	15	33
Definitely moving	1	2	3	27
100% equals	(340)	(137)	(191)	(224)

household regarding nonhousing matters. The clearest cases of forced moves are those occasioned by evictions, the destruction of the dwelling unit by fire, job changes where the new place of work is outside of commuting range, and changes in marital status. Some of the satisfied households planning to move are undoubtedly forced moves of these types.[3]

Some of the households desiring to move have developed plans for doing so; some have not. In order to understand the dynamics of residential mobility, it is necessary to consider what factors play a role in the crystallization of plans from desire. Some of the factors which we found in the previous chapter to play a very large role in the formation of mobility potential will help in providing an explanation. We found that the Mobility Potential Index—consisting of measures of certain qualities of each household, e.g., its size, age, and such —and the household's dissatisfaction with certain aspects of its dwelling as expressed in a complaints index had very strong relationships to mobility desires. Each of these indexes by themselves and taken together have a very strong effect on whether or not a household desiring to move will have formulated mobility plans.

Table 6.3 shows how the complaints index and the Disposition Index help to explain why some households desiring to move crystallize those desires

TABLE 6.3   Potential, Complaints, Desires and Intentions

I. Proportion Planning to Move* Among Those Desiring to Stay

	Complaints Index			
Potential Score	*0*	*1–2*	*3–4*	*5–6*
0, 1	6%	5%	8%	0%
100% equals	(108)	(58)	(25)	(20)
2, 3	2%	8%	9%	10%
100% equals	(102)	(65)	(31)	(10)
4, 5	19%	7%	**	**
100% equals	(16)	(14)	(7)	(4)

II. Proportion Planning to Move* Among Those Desiring to Move

	Complaints Index			
Potential Score	*0*	*1–2*	*3–4*	*5–6*
0, 1	14%	26%	23%	28%
100% equals	(14)	(30)	(30)	(18)
2, 3	41%	37%	30%	43%
100% equals	(27)	(43)	(64)	(39)
4, 5	26%	48%	59%	80%
100% equals	(25)	(31)	(46)	(51)

*The percentages in this table are the proportions within each sub-group who either definitely planned to move or who claimed to have a "fifty-fifty" chance of moving.
**Too few cases to present percentages.

into intentions and why some do not. (This table is divided into two parts: In the upper half of the table the relationship between the indexes and mobility plans are shown *only* for those households desiring to stay. In the lower half of the table, the same relationships are shown *only* for those desiring to move.) Among those who desire to stay, the scores on the two indexes show a very weak relationship to mobility plans. Among those desiring to move, the Complaints Index and the Disposition Index show a strong relationship to mobility plans.

If a family does not desire to move, it will ordinarily not intend to do so, no matter how dissatisfied it may be with the dwelling or how many characteristics predisposing it to move it may have. However, if the household has already crystallized desires to move, the existence of either a high Potential Score or a high Complaints Score tends to crystallize mobility intentions. *We find that the same factors which help to understand why some households desire to move, also help to understand why some households translate these desires to move into mobility plans.*

HOW MOBILITY BEHAVIOR WAS MEASURED

One of the major features of the present study is that it attempts to go beyond the families' verbal expressions of desires for mobility and their intentions, to actual behavior itself. Mobility behavior can therefore serve as an important check on whether the analysis presented up to this point has a sufficient degree of validity.

Mobility behavior can be studied because its measurement is a fairly simple matter. Mobility involves spatial movement and whether or not a family has moved can be easily ascertained by returning at periodic intervals to its dwelling unit and noting whether or not the same family still occupies it.[4]

Mobility behavior was measured[5] in this study by returning after eight months to the homes occupied by the 924 households at the time they were initially interviewed. If a dwelling was still occupied by the family, it was classified as remaining on. If another family occupied the dwelling, or if it was unoccupied, the family was classified as having moved.

Information on the present occupants of the 924 dwellings was obtained from either the present occupants themselves or from neighbors or landlords. In most cases the evidence was quite clear. In a few cases, especially when interviewers were unable to talk directly with present occupants, the evidence on moving is less strong. The outcome of the check survey is shown in Table 6.4.

Thirteen percent[6] of the families were found to have moved when the interviewers returned to their dwellings in the check survey. By comparison with Table 6.1, presented earlier, it can be seen that the amount of moving in

Table 6.4   Mobility Behavior

Stayers		87%
Including --		
Certain cases	82%	
Uncertain*	5	
Movers		
Including --		
Certain cases	11%	
Uncertain*	2	
100% equals		(910)
Ambiguous cases**		(12)
Not contacted		(2)

*A case was classified as "uncertain" if the household occupying a dwelling unit could not be contacted and other informants were unsure of the information which they gave to the interviewer. Thus if the occupants of a neighboring dwelling unit told an interviewer that he was "pretty sure", but not completely certain, that the present occupants of that dwelling unit had moved in *since* November 1950 (date of initial interview with households), the case was classified as an "uncertain" mover.

**The twelve "ambiguous" cases comprise all cases in which the present occupants claim occupancy going back before November 1950 but information from the initial interview indicates that the family initially interviewed had different characteristics than the family contacted in the check survey. Such cases occurred primarily in rooming houses where precise identification of dwelling units was difficult.

this period was certainly considerable less than the proportion of families who reported themselves as anxious to move (25%), but slightly higher than the percentage who definitely expected to move (8%).

THE DETERMINANTS OF MOBILITY BEHAVIOR

The results of the check survey can now be used to serve as a validation measure of the analysis presented in the previous chapter. It was shown that a family's desire to move was a function of its structure and its attitudes toward the housing it occupied. How closely related are these factors to actual moving behavior?

Before the data answering this important question are presented, it is helpful to consider how close these relationships must be in order to furnish a validation for the analysis presented earlier. It cannot be expected, for example, that mobility desires and behavior will be identical. Before a family can translate the desire to move into the actual move itself, a series of intervening events ordinarily must occur. Hence, at any one time the number desiring to move will usually considerably outnumber those who actually will move shortly thereafter. The time period between the measurement of mobility desires, Mobility Potential and Complaints, and the check survey was but eight months. Over a longer time period, perhaps, one might anticipate that the correspondence with behavior should be high: For such a short period, all that can be hoped for is some degree of relationship, but not one that is extremely high.

The findings of the check survey are presented in Table 6.5. Each of the three intensively studied variables has a consistent and fairly strong effect on mobility behavior. Four percent of the families who are anxious to stay moved; among those who were anxious to move, more than eight times that number (33%) did so. Similar relationships are shown for both the Mobility Potential Index and the Complaints Score; the higher the scores on each of these two variables, the more likely the household was to move.

The relationships in Table 6.5 are high enough to lend support to the validity of the analysis presented in the previous chapter. The same factors which determine whether or not a family wants to move will also predict, but to a lesser degree, whether or not it actually will move in the near future.

Because a family's intentions measure whether it is close to the point of moving itself, a much higher relationship can be anticipated between intentions and moving behavior. The findings of the check survey bear out this expectation. Table 6.6 indicates that among those who planned to stay, 96% actually did so. Eighty percent of the households definitely expecting to move were found to have done so. Among families rating themselves as having an even chance of moving, 26% moved.

The relationship is extremely high. The overwhelming majority of the households who planned to move or who planned to stay carried out their intentions.[7] In other words, a family's reported intentions about moving can be taken as a good indicator of how that family will actually behave.

Some of the families, however, carried out their intentions and some did not. The carrying out of moving intentions is not a chance event. Certain kinds of families are much more likely than others to follow through on their plans. Although the direct relationships between moving and either the complaints or the potential index are not very high, these two measures play a very important role in explaining why intentions are sometimes carried out and sometimes not.

Table 6.7 shows that among families intending to move, the higher the potential or complaints scores, the more likely the family is to carry out that intention.[8] The increase percentage-wise is very high: Among families with low potential scores, only one in four carry out their intentions to move;

Table 6.5 Mobility Inclinations, Potential, Complaints
and Behavior

I. Inclinations and Behavior

	Anxious To Stay	*Stay But Not Anxious*	*Move But Not Anxious*	*Anxious To Move*
Proportion moved	4%	9%	11%	33%
100% equals	(341)	(141)	(204)	(224)

II. Potential and Behavior

	Mobility Potential Score				
	0	*1*	*2*	*3*	*4 and 5*
Proportion moved	5%	8%	10%	13%	31%
100% equals	(168)	(140)	(186)	(193)	(193)

III. Complaints and Behavior

	Complaints Score			
	0	*1–2*	*3–4*	*5 or more*
Proportion moved	8%	10%	16%	26%
100% equals	(304)	(251)	(207)	(145)

TABLE 6.6 Intentions and Behavior

Actual Behavior	*Planned to Stay*	*50–50 Chance of Moving*	*Definitely Expected to Move*
Moved	4%	26%	80%
Remained	96%	74%	20%
100% equals	(698)	(129)	(74)

among similar families with high potential scores, one out of every two families carries out its intentions. Note, however, that neither index has much effect on the carrying out of intentions to remain. No matter how low their scores on either index, households intending to remain are just about equally likely to stay. *In other words, the same factors which explain why families intend to move, also help to explain why some families are more likely to carry out their intentions.*

The findings of this section answer in a positive way some of the major questions which might be raised concerning the use of interview methods in the study of residential mobility. Interviews, and the kind of data collected by them, can afford more than an exercise in the analysis of verbal reports. *It has been shown here that the actual behavior of the families interviewed conforms closely with their verbalized desires and intentions.* If one knows

TABLE 6.7   Mobility Potential, Complaints, and Fulfillment
of Intentions

Mobility Intentions and Behavior	Mobility Potential Score		
	0 & 1	2 & 3	4 & 5
Proportion actually remained of those intending to stay	96%	97%	90%
100% equals	(265)	(296)	(98)
Proportion actually moved of those intending to move*	26%	42%	51%
100% equals	(31)	(73)	(96)

Mobility Intentions and Behavior	Combined Complaints Score			
	0	1 & 2	3 & 4	5 & 6
Proportion actually remained of those intending to stay	94%	97%	95%	94%
100% equals	(255)	(192)	(140)	(72)
Proportion actually moved of those intending to move*	35%	40%	45%	52%
100% equals	(34)	(48)	(57)	(63)

*In order to obtain enough cases to make this analysis, the category "intending to move" contains both families with definite expectations of moving and families who gave themselves an even chance of moving.

certain crucial characteristics of a family, its desires, and its intentions, the prediction of its mobility behavior can be made with considerable accuracy.

This finding is, of course, of crucial importance to the analysis undertaken in the previous chapter. *The families who want to move are to an acceptable extent the same families who actually move.* The analysis of what kinds of families are inclined toward mobility has been given an underpinning of validity. We can be more confident that the knowledge gained in that analysis is not just the result of an academic exercise but of considerable practical importance.

HOW ACCURATELY CAN BEHAVIOR BE PREDICTED FROM INTENTIONS?

The accuracy of prediction afforded by the relationship between intentions and mobility behavior can be expressed more precisely if phrased in quantitative terms. How many mistakes in prediction of behavior would be made if mobility intentions are used as the basis of prediction?

Two types of prediction can be made about mobility behavior: First, a prediction can be advanced concerning the *amount* of moving that will take place over a given period. Here the problem is how much moving will take place? Will X% of the households move? How close to the actual percentage of moving can a prediction come based on mobility intentions?

The second type of prediction concerns the mobility of individual households. Can mobility intentions afford an accurate prediction of *which* households will move and *which* will remain? How many errors of prediction will result?

The two types of prediction are somewhat related. If we are able to predict with great accuracy how individual households will move, we are thereby enabled to predict with accuracy how much mobility there will be. However, it is possible to predict the amount of mobility accurately even though the accuracy of prediction for individual families is quite poor.

How accurately can mobility intentions predict the *amount* of mobility? Thirteen percent of the families actually moved; how close can we come to this figure using mobility intentions? The scheme which follows shows how such predictions can be made:

Intentions	*Percent*	*Prediction*	
		Stay	*Move*
Expect to stay	77%	77%	None
50-50 chance of moving	14%	7%	7%
Definitely moving	8%	None	8%
Total predicted:		Stay: 84%	Move 15%
		Actually Moved:	13%

Note that all of the families who expected to stay are predicted to stay; half of those claiming to have an even chance of moving are predicted to move; and all of those expecting to move are predicted to do so. The amount of mobility thereby predicted is 15%, somewhat higher than the 13% who actually moved.

Intentions, in this case, somewhat overpredict the *amount* of mobility. But when it is recalled that the households were asked their intentions concerning a 10-month period and that the check survey took place after only 8 months, the accuracy of prediction can be seen to be quite high. For most purposes, the *amount* of residential turnover is quite correctly predicted from mobility intentions.[9]

Most of the error in this prediction is caused by the fact that although we predict that half of the families claiming an even chance of moving would move, only 26% did so. Had the check survey occurred a few months later, it is reasonable to assume that more of these households would have realized their anticipated moving.

How accurately can the behavior of individual households be anticipated? If we take each household's intentions and predict from this information whether it will move or not, how many errors will be made? The scheme for this prediction follows:

Intentions	Prediction and Behavior*				Errors
	Move-Moved	Move-Stayed	Stay-Moved	Stay-Stayed	
Expect to stay (698)	— —	— —	(32)	666	(32)
50-50 chance of moving (130)	17	(48)	(17)	48	(65)
Expect to move (74)	55	(19)		— —	(19)
Total Errors		(67)	(49)		(116)

Proportionate error (116/902) = 12.9%

*Circled figures indicate errors of prediction

All of the households whose intentions were to stay were predicted to stay. Thirty-two of these households actually moved, so that 32 errors are recorded. Half of the households claiming an even chance of moving are predicted to move and half are predicted to stay. Thirty-four of these 129 families actually moved. Assuming that these 34 are distributed evenly between those we predicted to stay and those predicted to move, 65 additional errors are recorded. All families expecting to move were predicted to do so. But of these 74 families, 19 actually remained in their homes, contributing another 19 prediction errors. The total number of errors, 116, divided by the total number of predictions, 902, yields a proportionate error of 12.9% or conversely an accuracy of 87.1%. *In other words, by employing a household's mobility intentions, accurate predictions of moving behavior can be achieved in about 9 out of 10 cases.*[10]

Both the amount of moving and the moving of individual households can be accurately predicted by their intentions. The success of this prediction suggests a possible practical use of surveys as devices for estimating the future mobility of an urban area.[11]

DEVIATIONS FROM MOBILITY INTENTIONS

A household's intentions in most cases coincided with its subsequent behavior. Households whose plans did not jibe with behavior were a small minority: 32 cases of "unexpected movers"—households planning to stay but who actually moved; and 19 cases of "unexpected stayers" whose plans for moving were not carried out. These deviant cases consist of households whose behavior is yet to be accounted for. Their existence indicates that the analysis presented up to this point has omitted some of the factors which play a role in residential mobility.

One large class of factors has been completely neglected in the analysis. We have been primarily concerned with the household itself, considering the family abstracted from the larger context which is its environment. Certain household characteristics—age, size, and so on—and certain attitudinal variables—dissatisfactions, mobility desires, and so on—have been the factors which received greatest emphasis in the search for the causes of mobility behavior. Obviously, residential shifts involve more than just households. For one thing, the housing market defines the moving opportunities available to a household and opportunities must be available before a household can complete its moving plans. Other "outside" factors are also involved. The actions of landlords, for example, can change the intended stability of a household by forcing a move.

In other words, there is more to mobility than just the desire to move, or complaints about the dwelling, or the size of the families involved. In order that a family may move, it has to obtain a new home. The state of the housing market, especially that segment in which the household is interested, could either facilitate or impede the fruition of moving plans.

Events which are not related to housing may also affect mobility. The break-up of a household through death, divorce, or marriage of its members may force a move against both desires and intentions to remain. The occupational sphere also impinges on mobility. If the head of the house obtains a job far from the old abode, a move may be forced even against complete satisfaction with the old home.

The analysis of deviant cases[12] of unexpected movers and unexpected stayers will provide clues to how such factors upset the expected relationship between intentions and behavior. Special interviews were undertaken with deviant cases in a search for the causes which forced these households to abandon or postpone the completion of their plans. The analysis of these cases will provide further insights into the dynamics of residential mobility.

Sixteen unexpected stayers and a like number of unexpected movers were interviewed shortly after the check survey had revealed which households fell into these categories. With so few cases, only a qualitative analysis is possible. At certain points statistical evidence drawing on the whole sample will be used to bolster qualitative evidence.

Unexpected movers and unexpected stayers will be treated separately in this analysis. As we shall see below, different factors account for each of these two deviant types, and the factors relating to one often show little relation to the other.

UNEXPECTED MOVERS

Households which had planned to stay but actually moved were somewhat difficult to interview. More than a third had left no address behind them to which they could be traced. Others had moved out of the Philadelphia metropolitan area or were very hard to locate at their new addresses. For these reasons, only half, 16 of the 32 unexpected movers, were finally reached and interviewed.[13]

Unstructured interviews with each of the 16 unexpected movers obtained a detailed account of the reasons for and the circumstances surrounding the move. Upon analysis, the 16 households were finally classified as in Table 6.8. In eight cases the move was "triggered" by the unexpected discovery of a better dwelling. These were primarily cases where a basic predisposition to move was suddenly precipitated into action by housing "windfalls." Seven of the eight were anxious to move as of the November interview.[14]

In most cases the new abode was not sought for actively but brought to the attention of the household by some outside agency.[15] A typical comment from these windfall cases is paraphrased as follows:

We were always crowded in the old place but we never thought we could get a better place for the price. So we put up with it as best we could. Then my sister-in-law told us about the people moving out in the apartment next to hers. We went right over and got this place. It's about the same rent, but we have another bedroom.

Statistical analysis bears out the importance of this type of unexpected mover who, as it were, bypassed the planning stage.[16] Table 6.9 indicates that the more a household wanted to move, the more likely it was to depart from its intentions to stay.

Certain further characteristics of these families help to round out their collective portrait. All rented their old abodes and are now renting new

TABLE 6.8   Reasons for
Unexpected Moves

Windfall Moves	8
Forced Moves	6
Including:	
Dwelling destruction	(1)
Divorce	(1)
Family financial shift	(1)
Breadwinner job losses	(3)
Family size change	1
Dwelling unit change	1

places. Most of the households are young, and they are smaller than average. In addition, they tend to be in the lower income range—the average annual income being approximately $2,500.

The statistical evidence from the sample as a whole supports the interview material. Table 6.10 indicates that the poorer the household, the smaller its size, and the younger the age of the household head, the greater the frequency of unexpected movers.

The overall interpretation of these cases of windfall movers may now be stated: these are young, small, poor households, free from ties of owning, dissatisfied with their old abodes, but reconciled to remaining where they are. When opportunities presented themselves, their predispositions to move crystallized into immediate action. It may also be the case that housing opportunities consisting of small dwellings, cheap in price, were more avail-

TABLE 6.9   Mobility Desires and Unexpected Moves

	Mobility Desires			
	Anxious To Stay	Stay But Not Anxious	Move But Not Anxious	Anxious To Move
Unexpected Movers				
(proportion moved among those planning to stay)	2%	4%	6%	9%
100% equals	(331)	(124)	(163)	(85)

TABLE 6.10   Age, Size, Income and Unexpected Moves

I.	Age of Household Head			
		Under 35	35–44	45 and over
	Unexpected movers	8%	6%	3%
	100% equals	(112)	(249)	(318)
II.	Annual Household Income			
		Under $3,000	$3,000–4,999	$5,000 and over
	Unexpected movers	17%	4%	2%
	100% equals	(229)	(250)	(157)
III.	Size of Household			
		Under 3 Persons	3 Persons	4 or more
	Unexpected movers	6%	4%	3%
	100% equals	(375)	(145)	(185)

able than housing opportunities of a different variety. The greater availability of such housing increases the chance encounter with a windfall.

Returning to Table 6.8, the group of unexpected movers next in size are the six households classified as forced movers. In one case, the family's old dwelling was destroyed by fire. In another case, divorce put an end to the household itself. In still another case, the household moved to help parents by sharing the expenses of maintaining the latter's home. In all these cases, the move was forced by the impingement of outside circumstances.

Among the forced moves were also classified three households who were forced to move because unemployment made a move to a cheaper rental necessary. All three of these cases consisted of single, older males in marginal, low-income occupations who moved to cheaper rooms when they suffered a period of unemployment. Their isolation from family ties and the low income of their occupations left them no kinship or financial cushions to fall back upon when unemployment struck. All three cases had indicated a desire to remain on in their old rooms. A quotation from one of the interviews dramatically illustrates this analysis, "My eyes went back on me. I lost my job and I couldn't afford to pay that much room rent." In two of these three cases, the persons were evicted for nonpayment of rent.

These three cases help to explain why income has such a strong effect on the incidence of unexpected movers (see Table 6.10). Their low income plus the low income of the windfall movers explains why poorer households are particularly likely to depart from their plans to remain on in their homes.

Two further cases of unexpected moves remain to be discussed. One high-income household, expressing a desire to move when interviewed in November 1950, told our interviewer that the move was decided upon after the birth of a child raised the family size to five persons. The initial predisposition to move was apparently crystallized into action in this fashion. In most ways, this family with its high income, large size, and home ownership is atypical of the larger group of unexpected movers.

The remaining case, also atypical, is that of an elderly single woman who lived in a furnished room. At the time we first interviewed her, she expressed a desire to stay on. She moved, she said, because "some noisy neighbors moved next door, so I moved right here, across the street, to get away from them." Her move represents a case whose moving decision was precipitated directly by a change in the characteristics of her dwelling unit. She bypassed many stages in the "ideal" moving sequence, moving directly from complaints to behavior.

 The general interpretation of these cases of unexpected movers seems to be along the following lines: Two major types of unexpected movers were found, windfall movers and forced movers. Windfall movers are cases whose desire to move is precipitated into action by the appearance of an unanticipated opportunity to improve their housing. Forced movers are cases which, while desiring to stay, are brought to move by the pressures of events unconnected with housing. Both types are characterized by low incomes, by renting rather than owning, and by their smaller than average size. By inference, these are families not very attached to their particular homes and easily precipitated into moving when events occur which either offer better housing opportunities or force a curtailment in housing expenditures.

UNEXPECTED STAYERS

When each household's intentions and behavior are matched, 19 households are found whose intentions to move were not carried out, 1 household was found to have moved after the check survey was conducted, 1 refused to be interviewed, and the other was repeatedly not at home.

Table 6.11 is based on detailed interviews and presents a classification of these reasons into two main types: Plan Changers and Blocked Movers. Plan Changers are households who cancelled their intentions of moving; Blocked Movers are households still intending to move but whose move could not be carried out.

Two households turned out to be Plan Changers. In one case, a widow who intended to move from her large apartment, remained on when she remarried. The change in marital status brought her housing needs into line with her housing accommodations. In the second case, repairs made by the landlord to the apartment occupied removed the source of the household's dissatisfaction with the dwelling. The household, now satisfied, remained on.

TABLE 6.11   Reasons for
Unexpected Stayers

PLAN CHANGERS	
(Now plan to stay)	2
Including:	
Marital status change	(1)
Dwelling unit change	(1)
BLOCKED MOVERS	
(Still plan to move but	
move postponed)	13
Including:	
Suitable housing could	
not be found	(8)
Purchased house could	
not be occupied	(4)
Old house could not	
be sold	(1)
DISAGREEMENT WITHIN	
FAMILY ON PLANS	1

The most frequent type of unexpected stayers comprised the Blocked Movers. These were all households whose intentions to move remained but who each failed in one way or another to implement these intentions. Their failures can be explained as a consequence both of their housing needs and the state of the housing market.

Let us consider, first of all, the eight households which could not find suitable housing to which to move. Their most striking characteristic is their large size. Six of the eight are households containing 5 or more persons, with one household containing 11. Furthermore, six of these eight are seeking rental housing. Their inability to find suitable accommodations on the housing market for families of their sizes is expressed in the following quotations.

If I could find an apartment where they took children, I would move there. They will take two children, but I have four and that is out.

We can't get any place for five children. Those we can get are $80 - $90 a month. You have to buy a house to be able to move from here and we can't afford it.

Statistical evidence, based upon the entire sample, corroborates these findings: 40% of the households containing five or more persons were unable to carry out their intentions to move as compared with about 15% for small families.

It should be noted that it is not the lack of financial resources which hinders these families from finding new abodes. These families have considerably above average incomes. Rather, it is the amount of income in relation to family size which places these families at relative disadvantage. The amount which they can allocate to housing is not sufficient to buy housing adequate for their size.

Four of the remaining cases of Blocked Movers illustrate another effect of the state of the housing market in early 1951. All four families had already

TABLE 6.12   Household Size and Unexpected Stayers

	Household Size		
	1, 2 Persons	3 Persons	4 or More Persons
Unexpected stayers			
(proportion who remained among those planning to move)	15%	16%	40%
100% equals	(40)	(19)	(25)

purchased new homes but for one reason or another were unable to move into them. In three cases, builders were not keeping to their construction schedules. In another case, the family hesitated to move because their new home was in the path of a projected express highway.

In a final case of Blocked Move, the family could not move because it could find no purchaser for its old home. Its desire to move and intention to move remained firm and the household anticipated moving as soon as the present home was sold.

One final case of unexpected stayer remains to be explained. In this case, there is some question of whether our initial classification of this household as intending to move was correct. In the initial contact, the respondent, the male household head, told our interviewer of the household's intention to move. The next interview, this time conducted with the "woman of the house," revealed a long-standing disagreement between the two, with the wife intending to remain.

Unexpected stayers tended on the whole to be households of relatively high income. The eight cases who could not find suitable housing were cases of large households of higher than average income. The four cases whose moves were complete except for the physical transfer were all homeowners and were relatively well off. This income level of Blocked Movers is reflected statistically in Table 6.13.

Households which turned out to be unexpected stayers were, on the whole, held back from the fulfillment of their intentions by their inability to find new housing or their inability to occupy housing already chosen. The scarcity of opportunities for large families of moderate income prevented such families from realizing their plans. Families waiting to occupy new homes which they had already purchased also formed a large contingent in this group of unexpected stayers.

MOBILITY VIEWED AS PROCESS

At this point, it is now possible to combine the findings concerning households mobility into an overall view of residential mobility from the process viewpoint. All the factors—Mobility Potential, Housing Complaints,

TABLE 6.13   Annual Income and Unexpected Stayers

	Under $3,000	$3,000–4,999	$5,000 and Over
Unexpected Stayers	17%	26%	35%
100% equals	(18)	(35)	(17)

mobility desires, intentions, and behavior—fit together in a logical order which explains how and why households undertake residential shifts.

The process has its starting point in each household's structure and housing values. Households vary in their housing needs. The greatest demands are placed on housing among young, large, renting families whose housing values place a premium on home ownership. These are the families who are most likely to want to move and to be dissatisfied with their present housing. The Mobility Potential Index expressed the way in which these household characteristics were present in each family.

Needs, whether heavy or light, can be satisfied by a family's dwelling or can be frustrated by its deficiencies. The way in which a household's housing needs are satisfied by its dwelling is another important determinant of mobility desires. The more complaints a family had—as measured by the complaints index—the more likely it was to desire to move. When unsatisfied, needs lead to a rise in the desire to move.

Taken together, a household's needs and housing satisfaction determine what its level of motivation for moving is. The greater the need (its Mobility Potential Score) and the greater its dissatisfaction (the Complaints Score), the more likely it is to want to move.

Households differ in the extent to which its needs and dissatisfactions express themselves in mobility desires. Because of the flexibility in modifying their dwellings to suit their needs which home owners enjoy, and because owning involves a financial commitment to the dwelling, families owning their homes are less likely to want to move, given the same needs and dissatisfaction as renters.

When needs and dissatisfactions are particularly strong, families wanting to move crystallize a moving intention. Action is started toward obtaining a new home. It is important to note that it is among the households with particularly high Potential and Complaints Scores that the inclination to move is most likely to convert into an intention to move.

Once a firm intention has been established, a move is ordinarily accomplished. (We find that those families whose needs and dissatisfaction are strongest are also those who are most likely to carry out their intentions.) Occasionally some families whose desire to move is great but who have not yet formed moving intentions are precipitated into moving by the discovery of an unusual housing opportunity. Such windfalls are more likely to be taken advantage of by renters than owners because the latter's commitment to their dwellings is less flexible.

Some families' moving intentions are frustrated because the housing market presents few opportunities. Especially large families of moderate or low per-capita incomes, for example, find it difficult to carry out their intentions because suitable housing is difficult to find on the market.

Residential mobility as an urban phenomenon is to be viewed as the process whereby families bring their housing into line with their needs. Needs change as the family goes through its life cycle and housing varies considerably in its ability to satisfy the changing family needs. The gap between needs and the inflexibility of urban housing in meeting these needs produce the residential turnover so evident in urban America.

The relationship between family life cycle and housing needs also shows itself in the fact that most of the moves undertaken by households throughout their lifetime cluster in the first decade. During the first 10 years of its existence, the typical family undergoes its greatest period of growth. Young, large households are most likely to be those which have experienced the greatest growth in the shortest period of time and, hence, those whose housing is most out of line with needs.

Housing also varies in its ability to meet the changes brought about by life cycle shifts. Large dwellings can accommodate the different housing needs of the entire life cycle range; overfulfillment of needs is hardly as frustrating as underfulfillment. Owned units are also more flexible in this respect because of the greater control which can be exercised by the owner over his costs and his freedom in modifying his dwelling by alteration. Hence we find that it is the renting family which is most often precipitated into mobility by the pressure of its housing needs.

NOTES

1. The wording of the question measuring mobility desires was; ' Now I would like to ask you a few questions about what you would *like* to do and what you *plan* to do—If there were no housing shortage, would you like to stay on here or would you like to move from this place?''

2. Seventy-four persons were definitely planning to move, of whom 66 desired to move. The remaining 8 cases desired to stay.

3. In Chapter 8 we will see that the incidence of these forced changes is actually quite high, constituting a fairly large proportion of the recent residential shifts undertaken by households studied.

4. The ease with which measurement of behavior was accomplished contrasts sharply with most other kinds of behavior of concern to the social researcher. For example, in the study of political behavior, only the individual's own report of his vote is available. In other areas, the behavior in question is either so private or complex that measurement may never be accomplished.

5. Another device, of potential utility, was employed as an additional technique for the measurement of mobility. Each household was sent a letter by second class mail, enclosing a short questionnaire to be returned by the household. The envelope enclosing the questionnaire had instructions to the postmaster to notify the sender in case the addressee had moved. In practically every case where the household had moved, the

postoffice returned to our office a notice to that effect. The fees charged by the postoffice for such a service are so small that a running inventory of an area's mobility may be kept by periodic mailings to households at a relatively slight cost.

6. Cases in which interviewers' judgment concerning the household's moving was uncertain will not be treated separately from other cases in the remainder of this chapter. Each household will be classified as a stayer or mover according to the preponderance of the evidence in each case.

7. The strength of this relationship is particularly impressive when it is remembered that the households were asked to predict their own behavior over a 10-month period, while the check survey took place but eight months later. As will be shown later, some of the discrepancies of prediction occur because households which had intended to move had not yet been able to do so, but undoubtedly would do so within a short period of time.

8. This finding has a generality going beyond the field of residential mobility. In studies of vote behavior, it has been found that the same factors which correlate with how a person intends to vote also correlate with the carrying out of those intentions. For example, it has been found that well-to-do persons tend to favor Republican candidates while less privileged citizens favor Democratic candidates. However, rich Democrats are much less likely to carry this preference into the voting booth than are poor Democrats. Similarly, poor Republicans are less likely to end up voting for the Republican candidate than are rich Republicans, even though they both have earlier expressed preferences for the Republican candidates. See S. Martin Lipset and Paul F. Lazarsfeld "The Social Psychology of Political Behavior" in Gardner Lindsey (Ed.) *Handbook of Social Psychology*, Addison-Wesley Press Cambridge, 1954.

9. For rough estimations of the differences between subareas of a city over short periods of time, the accuracy of this prediction may be sufficient. For example, if applied to the four areas included in this study, the correspondence between prediction and performance is as follows:

	Oak Lane (Stable- High SES)	West Phila. (Mobile- High SES)	Kensington (Stable- Low SES)	Central City (Mobile- Low SES)
Predicted Mobility	6%	20%	6%	28%
Actual Mobility	4%	14%	4%	32%

The predictions and the actual mobility rank the four areas in the same way. In three out of four areas, the predictions overestimated mobility, and in the fourth the prediction underestimated mobility.

10. Another way of looking at the predictive ability of intentions is to consider how much better a prediction of behavior is afforded by intentions over the operations of chance alone. The maximum inaccuracy that could be made with the predictive scheme shown above would occur if there were no relationship between intentions and behavior. In that event, each of the columns in Table 6.6 would indicate that 13% had moved regardless of their intentions. Under these conditions, the predictive scheme would make errors in 30% of the households. The 13% inaccuracy afforded by the strong relationship between intentions and behavior should therefore be viewed against this maximum inaccuracy of 30%.

11. It should be noted, however, that the accuracy reported here obtains only for the time period studied. Predictions over a longer or shorter period may afford quite different degrees of accuracy. The degree of inaccuracy introduced by lengthening or shortening the time period is quite difficult to anticipate. On the one hand, the longer the time period, the greater the chance that families with intentions of moving will find

the opportunity to do so. However, a longer time period will also mean that household characteristics will change—particularly families may add members—and some households will develop and carry through intentions which were not evident at the beginning of the period. Furthermore, the congeries of events that force moving in the absence of desire and postpone moving even under strong motivation have a greater chance of making an appearance. It may very well be the case that the accuracy of prediction afforded by reported intentions for different time periods is a curvilinear function of time, rising to maximum at some point and thereafter declining.

12. For a detailed discussion of the major functions of deviant case analysis, see Patricia L. Kendall and Katherine M. Wolf "The Analysis of Deviant Cases in Communications Research" in Paul F. Lazarsfeld and Frank Stanton (Eds.) *Communications Research* 1948-1949, Harper and Bros., 1949.

13. The results of our attempts to interview the unexpected movers are as follows:

Unexpected Movers

Interviewed	16
Could not be located	12
Repeatedly not at home	2
Refused interview	1
Moved outside Philadelphia	1
Total	32

14. The exception was a household which moved to another apartment in the same apartment house. The family was satisfied with its previous apartment but when another apartment with more space and on a lower floor was offered to them by their landlord, they felt that this opportunity was worth taking advantage of. From the point of view of the family itself, this was not really considered a move.

15. In one case the household was brought to the planning stage by the survey itself. The respondent, complaining of his inability to pay the rents for larger apartments then on the market, was advised by the interviewer to apply to the Philadelphia public housing authority. The respondent's application was approved and when reinterviewed in his new apartment in a low-cost housing development, he expressed considerable approval of housing surveys.

16. The statistical evidence used from time to time in this section involves the entire group of deviant cases—not just those interviewed—and is based on information collected in the main survey.

PART IV
MOVING DECISIONS

Chapter 7

THE METHOD OF REASON ANALYSIS[1]

INTRODUCTION

The enormous complexity of human behavior appears to baffle understanding. The slightest human act can be viewed as the end link in a causal chain leading further and further into the actor's past. However, the complexity is overpowering only if an ultimate understanding is desired. Fortunately, for the most practical purposes, human behavior is sufficiently understood by considering only the more proximate causes of behavior.

Early childhood events may be of great concern to the psychoanalyst seeking to understand enduring patterns of personality. In everyday life, we usually find we can understand each other's actions without going very deeply into personality structure. This is particularly true where relatively superficial areas of behavior are concerned.

If a friend tells us that he has taken a great liking to a new television program, he can usually identify the features which attracted him so much. Why he liked those features may require a deep knowledge of his personality. But, the attractions of the program to this person can be studied without an understanding of the needs which those attractions met. In the same way, the voter who shifts allegiance from one candidate to another, the shopper who changes brands, and the family which has shifted residences can tell the researcher enough about his behavior to yield worthwhile information about such actions.

When asked why it has moved, a family might tell us that its old three-room apartment was too small for a growing family of five. This information tells us that a need for more space impelled the family to look for a more commodious dwelling. If we are interested in the relationship between family size, dwelling size, and moving, such information can help us to assess this relationship.

Reason analysis begins with the explanation which respondents themselves give for their actions, but its distinctive characteristic as a research operation lies in the *assessment* of the relative importance of the reasons given by respondents as forces bringing about the actions under study.[2]

Reason analysis, as a research operation, is particularly suited to actions which involve short-term changes in behavior. It makes little sense to ask a person why he votes for the Democratic Party if we know that this has been his party affiliation over the past 20 years. The reasons for his affiliation are probably buried among the many past events of his youth. However, if he has just shifted to the Democrats from the Republicans, the reasons he gives—perhaps in terms of the different qualities of candidates running for office or in terms of things read or heard—can enable us to interpret his voting shift. *Reason analysis is particularly applicable to human actions which involve a conscious choice among alternatives and which result in a change in the actor's behavior.*

As a type of human action, residential mobility seems particularly suited for study by this method. Moving decisions are usually undertaken by a family in a self-conscious manner. The pros and cons of leaving the old dwelling are weighed and the comparative attractions of new housing opportunities are ordinarily given some consideration. Most families are therefore capable of giving useful accounts of what seemed to them to be the more cogent reasons for their moves.

Since reason analysis is a somewhat unconventional research method, the remainder of this chapter is devoted to a detailed exposition of its application to mobility. The two major problems which will be dealt with are as follows:

(1) What interviewing procedures must be used to get reasons? How does one go about obtaining accounts of moves from respondents?

(2) How can the reasons be assessed? How can one judge whether one reason plays a more important role than another in bringing about a residential shift?

INTERVIEWING PROBLEMS IN REASON ANALYSIS[3]

The field operation involved in reason analysis consists essentially in asking respondents why they moved. Although this might seem to be a simple enough question, actually it is not feasible to ask it directly. A general "why" question usually produces a congeries of answers, each kind of answer corresponding to a different interpretation of the general "why" question by the respondent. There are many ways to answer such a general question: Some respondents will answer in terms of the event which "triggered" the move; others will tell us why they moved *here*; still others will tell us about changes that took place within their households, and so on.

Perhaps the best way to illustrate the inadequacies of the general "why" question is to present what happens when such a question is asked. In Table 7.1 drawn from another study[4] of residential mobility, we present a list of answers to the question, "Why did you happen to move?" Some of the respondents answered the question as if it referred to the house *to* which they had moved (category G). Others answered in terms of the house *from* which they had moved (categories A, C, D, and partly F).

The answers in Table 7.1 have been rearranged below according to different interpretations of the general "why" question.

Most of the new general classifications (marked by Roman numerals in Table 7.2) correspond to variant interpretations of the general why question. Some respondents assumed that the interviewer wanted to know what was wrong with his former home; others, that the interviewer wanted to know what was so attractive about the new house, and so on.

Category III (Decision Not Respondent's) includes responses which indicated that the respondent did not make the decision to move out himself but that he was forced out of his old home by events which were beyond his control, e.g., destruction of dwelling unit, eviction, and so on. The respondent, in effect, has said that he understands the question to refer to his old home, but that the question cannot apply to him since he did not make the decision to move himself.

Note that in Table 7.2 a new response category has been added to each of the main categories to indicate the proportion of persons who did not employ a particular mode of response in answering the question. Thus we find that 54% of the respondents did not refer to the characteristics of the old home, 74% did not refer to the new home, and so on through each of the four sets of categories.

The difficulty in interpreting a set of reason frequencies as shown in either table lies in the fact that the high proportion of no answers to each of the

TABLE 7.1   Reasons Given in Answer to "Why Did You Happen to Move?"

A.	"To secure better quarters or live in a better location"	18%
B.	"To build or purchase a home"	16
C.	"More space required"	13
D.	"Rents too high or house too large"	12
E.	"House sold, repaired, renovated, occupied by owner"	10
F.	"House in need of repairs, burnt or torn down"	3
G.	"Closer to location where employed"	10
H.	"Marriage"	5

TABLE 7.2   Answer Categories Classified by the Frame
of Reference Employed by the Respondent

I.	CHARACTERISTICS OF THE FORMER HOME:*	
	A. Better quarters or better location (i.e. unsatisfactory former home)	18%
	B. More space required	13
	C. Rents too high or house too large	12
	F. (In part) House in need of repairs	3
	Not answered in terms of former home	54%
II.	CHARACTERISTICS OF NEW HOME:	
	G. Closer to location where employed	10%
	H. To build or purchase home	16
	Not answered in terms of new home	74%
III.	DECISION IS NOT RESPONDENT'S:	
	E. House sold, repaired, renovated occupied by owner	10%
	F. (In part) House burnt or torn down	3
	No information as to decision maker	87%
IV.	CHANGES IN HOUSING NEEDS:	
	H. Marriage	5%
	No information about changes in needs	95%

*Note that the categories included under I are not mutually exclusive. "Better quarters" might mean quarters which are lower in rent, larger or smaller in size, and so on. Hence, many of the cases included in this general omnibus category might have been more properly placed in some of the more specific categories.

classifications means that a large number of facts necessary for the interpretation of residential shifts is missing. Certainly, the fact that a respondent answered in terms of the new home does not mean that his move did not involve important dissatisfactions with his old home, and the fact that he interpreted the question in that fashion may only mean, at best, that he gave more emphasis to the attractions of the new than to his complaints about the old home.

The analysis of residential shifts obviously requires information on each move under most of the categories of Table 7.2. We need to know not only what the respondent found attractive enough about his new place to move into it but also what complaints led him to contemplate moving, and so on.

The difficulties in the interpretation of such reason frequencies point up the necessity for having an a priori frame of reference outlining the kinds of data considered necessary for the interpretation of residential shifts and the necessity of collecting from respondents information on all the relevant points.

Such frames of reference might be thought of an analogous to a book-keeper's account books with their columns and boxes indicating the data needed for the proper accounting of funds, and may therefore be called accounting schemes. An accounting scheme for a particular research operation specifies in detail the kinds of information it is necessary to obtain from the respondent in order to adequately account for the respondent's actions.[5]

AN ACCOUNTING SCHEME FOR RESIDENTIAL MOBILITY

Where do the elements of an accounting scheme come from? How does one go about setting up a scheme for a particular reason analysis? In part, the scheme derives from the structure of the actions under study and, in part, from the purposes for which the study was designed.

The structure of the action under study itself conditions the accounting scheme, because it must be made to fit the experience of the actor as he sees his actions. For example, it makes little sense to ask an evicted family what were their complaints about their old home, since their complaints obviously played but a minor role in bringing about their move.

The purpose of the study specifies to what aspects of the total situation the attention of the actor should be directed. Thus, if we were interested primarily in what precipitated a dissatisfied household into a move, the interviewing program would lay heavy stress on events which "trigger" moves.

A utilitarian motive guided the selection of the elements to be included in the accounting scheme. It was felt that the most useful kind of data would be that which lends itself easiest to modification and control in the setting of housing policies. For this reason, the accounting scheme stresses the families' attitudes toward their old homes and the attractions they felt from their new places. The sources of such attitudes could, it was felt, be modified in setting new policies in the construction of housing units.

Four major elements are included within the accounting scheme to be used. Each move is considered as accounted for by the family's complaints about its old home, by the sorts of things it looked for in a new home, the way in which its new home outranked its competitor's attractions, and by the way in which the family went about looking for a new home. The elements of the accounting scheme are outlined below:

(1) complaints: unsatisfactory features of the previous dwellings which impelled the family to leave
(2) specifications: attributes of a new home which the family was particularly desirous of obtaining
(3) attractions: features of the new home which made that dwelling more desirable than other dwellings considered

(4) information sources: means by which the new dwelling was brought to the family's attention.

These four major categories formed the accounting scheme around which the interview was built. For our purposes, a residential shift was adequately explained when data on all four topics was obtained from the household involved.[6]

FITTING THE ACCOUNTING SCHEME TO EXPERIENCE

The accounting scheme was built primarily to account for moves of a certain type. The assumption underlying the scheme is that a household initially starts out with some sort of complaint, decides to move, has definite ideas about the kind of dwelling unit it wants, and finally makes a choice among several dwellings according to their relative merits. However, not all families go through all of the experiences assumed by the accounting scheme.

First of all, some households move without ever going through a period of dissatisfaction. Some moves are forced upon the household by the pressure of events beyond their control; by the destruction of their old home by fire, by eviction, by the sudden loss of income, and such. Other households bypass the complaints stage because their moves are undertaken as a necessary consequence of decisions made in some nonhousing matter. Most marriages and divorces involve moves on the part of at least one of the partners. Some job shifts, especially when the new job is located beyond commuting range of the old dwelling unit, can "force" a household to move.

Obviously, in cases where the move is forced or undertaken as a necessary consequence of some other decision made by the household, it makes little sense to ask a family about its complaints. The interviewing procedure has to be modified to sort out such households from families which go through a complaints stage.

In much the same way, some families do not experience their search for a new home as a choice among alternatives. Their new home may be the only one which presented itself to them. It makes little sense in such cases to collect data on the attractions category in the accounting scheme.

Such considerations lead to a typology of moves built according to the way in which the move involves each of the elements of the accounting scheme, as follows:

MOVE TYPE	INVOLVING			
	Com-plaints?	Specifi-cations?	Attrac-tions?	Information Sources?
I. Full Moves	Yes	Yes	Yes	Yes
II. Dissatisfied, No Choice Moves	Yes	Yes	No	Yes
III. Forced, Full Choice Moves	No	Yes	Yes	Yes
IV. Forced, No Choice Moves	No	Yes	No	Yes

Full moves are moves for which all elements of the accounting scheme are relevant. In each of the other types, either complaints or attractions or both are bypassed because the household was either forced to move out of its old dwelling and/or did not have a set of alternative homes from which to choose. Note that every move is assumed to have involved both specifications and information sources.

The interview used sorted out households into one of these types and collected only relevant information. The analysis that will be presented in the next two chapters will concern, at each stage, only those cases which are relevant for the topic under discussion. Thus, the analysis of complaints will exclude all forced moves (Types III and IV). The analysis of attractions will be concerned only with families which had more than one new dwelling to choose from (Types I and III). Note, however, that all the families will be involved in the analysis of specifications and information sources.

THE ASSESSMENT OF REASONS

It is easy enough to find out from each household what its complaints were about its previous home. It is much more difficult to assess the importance of such attitudes in bringing about the move. In fact, this assessment probably cannot be done with complete accuracy or certainty. What can be done, however, is to make approximations which are as close as possible to this ideal. In other words, we can make judgments about which factors are *most likely* to have played an important role in a move, even though we probably cannot be absolutely certain in every case.

The first step in making such assessments is to find out whether or not a particular type of complaint or attraction was present in each case of moving. Certainly, before a complaint about space can play a role, it must have been present. The "coverage" of a complaint—whether or not it was present in a move—defines the necessary but insufficient condition for assessing the importance of that complaint in bringing about the decision to move.

Coverage, however, needs to be supplemented by some way of characterizing its "impact"—the degree to which it was effective in bringing about the move. In this study, the impact is defined as the family's own judgment of the importance of a factor. Thus, a complaint about the landlord is considered to have had an impact if the family involved rated that complaint as an important factor in its decision to move. The impact of attractions was judged in a similar fashion.

Although impact and coverage are by definition related, they are somewhat independent. Thus, one particular type of complaint may have a high coverage and a low impact while another type may have a low coverage but a high impact. In other words, some complaints may be present in a very large number of cases, yet be rated as important by only a small number of families. Another complaint type may be present in a few cases, yet be rated as important in almost every case where it is present. Some types of factors are more "effective" than others because they play an important role in a greater proportion of the cases in which they are present. The assessment procedure allows each type of complaint or attraction to be judged according to three measures:

(1) Coverage: The extent to which complaint or attraction is present among movers. Thus, the coverage of a complaint would be the proportion of movers who said they had a complaint of that sort about their old homes.

(2) Impact: The extent to which a factor (complaint or attraction) is rated as important by movers. Thus the "impact" of an attraction is the proportion of families who say that they were primarily attracted to their new dwelling by that attraction.

(3) Effectiveness: The extent to which a factor, when present, is regarded as having an impact. Thus the effectiveness of a complaint is the proportion of families who register complaints of that sort. Expressed in another way, the effectiveness of a complaint may be defined as

$$\text{Effectiveness} = \frac{\text{Impact}}{\text{Coverage}}.$$

The specific ways in which impact and coverage were measured will be described more fully as each of the elements of the accounting scheme is presented.[7]

THE BASIC DATA

Memories are fallible. If one is asked to reconstruct the features of an event that has occurred even moments before, it is to be expected that the reconstruction be partial and modified. The distortions and omissions tend to increase the further into the past memory is asked to go. It was felt that households which had been long-term residents in their homes would be unlikely to give an accurate picture of their motivations for moving and the reasons for choosing their present homes. For this reason, the analysis to be presented here has been confined to families who had moved into their present homes within the five-year period preceding the interview survey.

A little less than half (48%) of the families were found to be "recent arrivals."[8] To these families was administered a special set of questions designed around the accounting scheme described earlier. These detailed interviews, taking as long as a half an hour, obtained the basic data on complaints, specification, attractions, and information sources which will be the focus of our attention in the next two chapters.

NOTES

1. The author owes much for whatever merit this section has to the advice and patient guidance of Professor Paul F. Lazarsfeld, whose writings, furthermore, provide the methodological basis for this approach. Whatever shortcomings this section may have stems primarily from the author's inability to profit from his help.

2. For a thorough methodological discussion of the rationale behind reason analysis, see Paul F. Lazarsfeld "The Analysis of Reasons as a Research Operation," *Sociometry,* 1942.

3. The general argument employed in this section is adapted from Paul F. Lazarsfeld "The Art of Asking Why," *National Marketing Review,* Vol 1, No. 1, Summer 1935.

4. Adapted from a nationwide survey of housing satisfactions and dissatisfactions by Melville C. Branch, *Urban Planning and Public Opinion,* Bureau of Urban Research, Princeton, 1942. The reasons given are abridged from a longer table. The survey was undertaken on a nationwide scale and covered four city-size groups in six regions of the United States. Other studies presenting comparable tables are as follows: Betty Tableman, *Intra-Community Migration in the Flint Metropolitan District,* Institute for Human Adjustment, University of Michigan, 1948, (mimeo.); Mary Schauffler, *The Suburbs of Cleveland,* Unpublished doctoral dissertation, University of Chicago, 1941; Citizens Housing Council of New York, *Why Do Tenants Move?* New York, (mimeo.); Milwaukee County Regional Planning Dept., *Residential Development in the Unincorporated-Areas of Milwaukee County,* Milwaukee, 1946 (mimeo.).

5. What is meant by accounting schemes in this discussion has a close kinship, if not identity, with what other discussions have termed "conceptual schemes," "conceptual models," and such. A good example of an accounting scheme in the field of general psychology is contained in Edward C. Tolman's article "A Psychological Model" (in

Talcott Parsons and Edward A. Shils, *Toward a General Theory of Action,* Harvard Univ. Press, 1951). Tolman in this article specifies a framework of variables in terms of which behavior in general may be explained. The difference between such conceptual models and accounting schemes lies primarily in their level of generality rather than in any difference in logical structure. The accounting scheme which is employed here for residential shifts is applicable primarily to such actions and not to actions in general, while the efforts of Tolman are directed primarily to the construction of a generalized accounting scheme applicable to behavior in general.

6. It is *not* maintained here that these four categories completely exhaust all aspects of a move. One can, for example, be interested in the question of why complaints arise. In that case, the accounting scheme would search for changes in the household or dwelling unit which changed the dwelling from a place which met the needs of the family to one which did not. Or, one may be interested in the timing of the move: Why did a move take place at the time it did? In that case, the accounting scheme would probably include data on factors or events which retarded or facilitated the transformation of complaints into moving behavior.

7. The terms *coverage* and *impact* are borrowed from the fields of communications and advertising research. In fact, the assessment procedure employed here was first applied to the study of marketing behavior. The brand shifts undertaken by a sample of housewives was studied by Paul F. Lazarsfeld and his associates in order to assess the relative importance of mass media and personal contacts in their changes of cosmetics and grocery products (see Katz, Elihu and Lazarsfeld, Paul F. *Personal Influence,* The Free Press, 1955).

8. Of the 444, 290 or 65% were previously renters and 35% (154) were previously owners. The distribution of recent movers among the four study areas was as follows: Oak Lane, 21%; Central City, 30%; Kensington, 16%; West Philadelphia, 33%. The bulk of the households had moved in since January 1949, so that the span of time between the move and the interview was less than two years in more than half the cases. The distribution by date of move is as follows: January 1950 or later, 31%; January 1949-December 1949, 21%; January 1948-December 1948, 17%; January 1947-December 1947, 16%; January 1945-December 1946, 15%.

Chapter 8

THE ROLE OF COMPLAINTS IN THE DECISION TO MOVE

INTRODUCTION

The decision to move is the first stage in a residential shift. Sometimes, as will be shown in detail, the decision is not made by the mover; in other cases the decision to move is a by-product of some other decision. In most cases, however, families voluntarily leave their homes and do so for reasons which are directly related to housing. Our problem in this chapter is to study *voluntary* moves, and particularly to see what households found in their old homes to be sufficiently inadequate to warrant a search for a new home. What were the complaints involved? Which complaints are particularly effective in bringing about a move?

Complaints about the old dwelling were chosen to be the focal point of our analysis of the first stage of moving because there were several purposes that could be served by this emphasis. First of all, it was felt that complaints, because they could be related to specific aspects of dwellings and their environments, would yield data of a more directly practical nature. This analysis would enable a highlighting of the elements of housing and neighborhoods which might be modified in an effort to control residential mobility. If we could point to the things which were most important to the families as they made up their minds to abandon their old dwellings, perhaps we would be making some progress in the direction of eventual control over mobility.

Second, the analysis of mobility inclinations, presented in Chapter 5, rested heavily on the study of complaints as they were related to the desire to move. A parallel emphasis in the retrospective analysis would allow a check on the results. Our analysis of the relative importance of complaints of different sorts would gain considerable strength if confirmed by another method.

Finally, the moves which were studied in the previous section all concerned dwellings within the four study areas and are, to an unknown degree, conditioned by the nature of the housing to be found within them. But, the previous residences of the households were located in most cases outside the study areas and, for that reason, form a more heterogeneous group of dwellings. *The analysis of the roles played by complaints in moves from this more varied set of dwelling can therefore enlarge the bases for the generalization of our findings.* If we find that the analysis to be presented in this chapter confirms our previous results, we can be more sure about the generality of our findings.

FORCED MOVES

Some of the households were precipitated into a move and bypassed the first stage of the typical residential shift. Some moves are involuntary and are forced upon the household by the pressure of events beyond its control. Other moves are the consequences of decisions which are unrelated to housing. Obviously, in such cases the roles played by complaints are minimal. The major reasons for moving in such cases are unrelated to the characteristics of the former dwelling.

We will not consider forced moves in the analysis of complaints, but will consider them separately and return to these cases later in the next chapter where the search for a new home is taken up.

The number of forced moves was unexpectedly large, constituting 39% of the recent movers (see Table 8.1). Although it is doubtful that this figure is representative of all residential shifts in American urban areas, the possibility that a significant portion of the high level of residential mobility is composed of such forced moves should be seriously considered.

More than half of the forced moves were imposed upon families by events completely outside of their control. Evictions, physical destruction of dwellings, and severe income losses accounted for 23% of the moves studied. Many of the evictions were caused by the withdrawal of rental units from the rental market. The destruction of dwellings was in every case the result of fire. The severe income losses were occasioned either by the sickness or death of the major breadwinner of a family.

Some of the forced moves were classified as such because they involved long-distance (more than 50 miles) migration. Such moves are ordinarily motivated not by the search for a new dwelling but by the search for a new job or other opportunities. After all, most housing needs can be met by the variety of housing types than can be found within a 50-mile radius (at least in the highly urbanized northeastern United States). Moves going beyond that distance are probably motivated by considerations other than a search for housing.

Another 4% of the moves involved cases in which the previous abode was only occupied as a temporary expedient pending the finding of more suitable housing. Many of these cases consisted of young, newly married couples doubled-up with parental families. For these families, the decision to move had been made before they had taken up their abode in their previous dwellings. The roles played by complaints were particularly difficult to pin down because the rejection of their dwellings was almost total.

Changes in marital status made up the bulk of the remainder. Their shifts were not undertaken for the sake of changing dwellings so much as necessary consequences of their marital status changes. Newly formed families and newly broken families made moves because of their changes in status and, hence, their complaints about their previous dwellings were largely irrelevant.

In a few cases, moves were made because the families involved had inherited their new homes. In these cases, complaints were irrelevant to their moves and such moves can be accounted for almost entirely by the attractions of their new homes.

The forced moves, comprising 39% of all moves, will not be considered any further in this chapter. For an understanding of the reasons behind these moves, complaints about the old place are, by and large, not particularly important. It is only among the voluntary movers—the 61% who had a clear choice between staying and moving—that complaints could have played a role. These 273 cases of voluntary movers will be our concern during the remainder of this chapter.

THE ASSESSMENT PROCEDURE

For those families which had voluntarily left their former homes, the analysis will attempt to assess what role various types of complaints played in

TABLE 8.1   Classification
of Recent Moves

FREE CHOICE MOVES	61%
FORCED MOVES	39
Including:	
Involuntary moves: (evictions, dwelling destruction, severe income losses)	23%
Inter-city Migration	8
Previous dwelling occupied temporarily	4
Newly married	3
Others (mainly recently divorced)	1
100% equals	(444)

their decisions to move. To accomplish this purpose, it is necessary to ascertain two basic things about each move: Whether or not a particular type of complaint about its former home was held by the family, and whether the complaint was an important reason for leaving. In other words, the analysis will attempt to present, for each complaint type, the following information:

(1) The coverage of a complaint: the proportion of households which had complaints of that type

(2) The impact of a complaint: the proportion of households who undertook moves because of that complaint.

What were the methods used to obtain this information? The collection of coverage and impact data for each of the major complaints was accomplished by the use of three types of questions. First, each respondent was asked what might be called a stimulus question: "What was it that made you think of moving out?" The rationale behind the employment of this question was that it would start the respondent thinking of the things that prompted his initial desire to move.[1] The respondent was, of course, free to answer this question in any fashion he chose. If he mentioned a particular complaint, however, this was an indication of the importance of the complaint in the genesis of his family's move.

The next item type, called "exposure" questions, was designed to obtain the coverage of a complaint. These questions asked in a straightforward manner whether or not the respondent was dissatisfied with some feature of his former home. For example, with regard to complaints about space in his old home, we asked: "Did you have too much room, enough room, or too little room in your old place?"

Finally, after a series of exposure questions had alerted the respondent to the frame of reference of complaints, an "assessment" question was asked, as follows: "Now, you've mentioned several reasons why you and your family moved from your former place. Which of these would you say were the most important reasons?" The importance of the assessment question is fairly obvious. The respondent himself is asked to make a judgment about the impact of a particular complaint.

Let us consider first of all how the answers to these three questions appear for a particular type of complaint—the costs of the former dwelling unit. The proportions complaining about costs in answer to each of the three question types is shown in table 8.2. Note that the questions have been arranged in a sequence according to their "diagnostic" ability in assessing the "cause" of a move. Least diagnostic is, of course, the exposure question, in response to which 26% of the households registered complaints. Next in diagnostic ability is the "stimulus" question which obtained complaints from 18% of the households. Most important, diagnostically, is the assessment question. Here we find that 12% registered a complaint.

Similar distributions can be shown for each of the complaint categories which we shall study in detail in the body of this chapter.[2] More households are *exposed* to a complaint than consider that complaint a *stimulus* to their move or than consider that complaint an *important* motive for their move. The existence of such uniformities lends some credence to our use of the questions.

How shall we use these questions to classify the households according to whether or not a particular complaint was effective in bringing about the move? Certainly the clearest case is where the household explicitly states that a particular complaint was the most important thing in causing it to move. These are cases which come closest to the ideal of primary complaints.

Some respondents mention a particular complaint spontaneously in response to the stimulus question but do not mention that complaint as one of the important causes of moving. Apparently the complaint brought the notion of moving to mind, but it was not the important reason for the move. In these cases, we shall consider that the complaint played a "contributory" role.

Next, we have households which mention being exposed to a particular complaint but do not rate that complaint as being an important reason for their move, nor do they mention the complaint as a stimulus to the desire to move. These are cases where the complaint was *ineffective* in bringing about the move.

Finally, we have households which were not exposed to the complaint in question. These are households, along with the previous group mentioned, to whom a particular kind of complaint was irrelevant to their moving decision.[3]

Recapitulating the classification in outline form, the three questions allow us to separate respondents into four groups:

(1) Primary complaint (Impact): respondent mentions a particular type of complaint as being an important reason for his move

TABLE 8.2   Complaints About Costs

	Proportion Registering Complaints
Exposure question	26%–Coverage
Stimulus question	18%
Assessment question	12%–Impact
100% equals	(273)

(2) Contributory complaint: respondent does not rate the complaint as important but mentions that the complaint was the thing which started him thinking about moving

(3) Ineffective complaint: respondent acknowledges complaint but does not rate it as of any importance in the move

(4) No complaint: respondent was satisfied with the previous home in this regard.

It should be noted that it is necessary to have an exposure question in order to present the classification discussed above. The important complaints had to be anticipated in advance and built into the questionnaire. It is, of course, difficult without considerable previous experience and exploratory work to anticipate every conceivable variety of complaint which might be encountered. For this reason, the analysis in this chapter will be restricted to just a few out of the wide variety of complaints which the respondents mentioned spontaneously.

Three complaint categories will be considered: complaints about space or room, complaints about neighborhoods, and complaints about costs (rent or maintenance). These are obviously broadly conceived categories. Under the concept of neighborhood, we have considered such diverse aspects of the surrounding environment as its social composition, features of land use in the neighborhood, and the neighborhood's location with regard to transportation and services. For many purposes it might appear profitable to break these broad categories down into more specific components. For the purpose of illustrating analytical procedures, such broad classifications will suffice.

THE ASSESSMENT RATINGS

The assessment ratings for the three major complaint types—space, neighborhood, and costs—are shown in Table 8.3. The coverage of the three complaints varies considerably. Almost two out of three families complained

TABLE 8.3   Complaints Assessment Ratings

	Ratings			
	Primary Complaints (Impact)	Contributory Complaints	Ineffective Complaints	Total Coverage
Space Complaints	45%	8%	11%	64%
Neighborhood Complaints	14%	8%	7%	29%
Cost Complaints	12%	7%	13%	32%

that their previous homes had too little or too much space. Three out of 10 complained about the old neighborhood. Thirty-two percent complained about the old dwelling's costs.

The "impact" ratings of the three complaint types—the proportion of families who rated a complaint as of primary importance in its move—show the overwhelming importance of space complaints as a primary factor in decisions to move. Almost half (45%) of the families cited their complaints with the space in their old abodes as the primary reason for moving.

Considerably fewer households pointed to the neighborhood or costs as important reasons for leaving their former houses. The impact rating of neighborhood complaints was 14% and for costs complaints was 12%.

Note that the assessment procedure is accomplished separately for each type of complaint. In other words, the households are first classified according to the role that space complaints played in their moves, then according to neighborhood complaints, and so on. In some cases, more than one type of complaint was rated[4] as having an impact, although such cases were very few in number.

The heavy importance of space complaints is consistent with the findings presented previously concerning the determinants of mobility desires.[5] It was shown that complaints about dwelling space was an extremely important factor in explaining why households want to move. The more complaints a household registered concerning the space within its home, the more it was likely to be anxious to move. The results presented in Table 8.3 indicate that when families are asked about the moves they have undertaken in the past, space complaints also loom very large as primary factors in their decision to move.

It should be noted that the importance of complaints about the neighborhood and about costs is also consistent with previous findings. It was shown in an earlier chapter that complaints about the neighborhood ranked higher than complaints about costs as a determinant of mobility desires. In Table 8.3 we see that as far as impact is concerned, the same order results from retrospective accounts of previous moves (see Note 5).

The impact of a factor is in part a function of its coverage. The more complaints of a particular type there are, the more likely this complaint type is to be mentioned as a primary reason for moving. The relative effectiveness of a complaint, therefore, has to be judged apart from the coverage. In order to adjust for a coverage, an Index of Effectiveness was formed which expresses the proportion of all complaints which were effective:

$$\text{Index of Effectiveness} = \frac{\text{Impact (Primary Complaints)}}{\text{Coverage (Total Complaints)}}.$$

The values of the index for the three complains are presented in Table 8.4. Space complaints, with an index value of .70, turns out to be the most effective of the three, followed by neighborhood complaints (.48) and costs complaints (.38). Note that although the coverage of neighborhood complaints and costs complaints is about the same, their effectiveness differs somewhat. This is due to the fact that while costs complaints has slightly larger coverage, it also has a slightly smaller impact.

The three complaint types considered so far account for about two-thirds of the 273 voluntary moves. What were the important factors in the remaining cases? Since it is essential that an "exposure" question be built into an interview before an assessment can be made, only those complaint types for which an exposure question was available can be given assessment ratings. However, the remaining cases can also yield valuable information since the important complaints cited by such cases can be used as guides for future research.

In Table 8.5 the 89 cases are considered in which space, costs, or neighborhood complaints did not play a role. This table contains the complaints which these families rated as important in their moves.

Three important complaint types appear in Table 8.5.[6] In about one out of four cases, the primary complaint registered by the family concerned the way in which their old homes were designed. This category covered all aspects of a dwelling except its dimensions, e.g., whether it had a bathroom or not, how

TABLE 8.4   Effectiveness
Ratings of Complaints

Complaint	Effectiveness Index
Space	.70
Neighborhood	.48
Costs	.38

TABLE 8.5   Complaints Rated as
Important in Cases Where Space,
Costs or Neighborhood Did Not
Play a Role

Dwelling unit design complaints (no privacy, no kitchen, etc.)	26%
Complaints about the landlord	19%
Complaints about persons in the former households (e.g. couldn't get along with my sister-in-law)	18%
Other and vague complaints	37%
100% equals	(89)

much light there was, the kitchen fixtures, and such. Another one in five households complained about the landlord who owned their former home. Most of these complaints centered about the landlord's refusal to render services to which the families felt entitled. The third important complaint type concerned interpersonal matters. These were households which moved because their previous dwelling involved living with in-laws, relatives, or other persons with whom relationships were not very good. These three categories point out ways in which accounting models in future research may be amplified to cover aspects of housing which were neglected in this study.

THE VALIDITY OF ASSESSMENT

Behind the employment of the assessment procedure described in this chapter lies the assumption that families can correctly assess the role that various complaints played in their moving decisions. Are the families' assessments and memories free from distortion?

The ideal data for a validation study would involve tracing families as they go through the various stages of moving, recording what their complaints are at various points and noting carefully the things which go into their decisions. Obviously, even if this sort of research design were feasible, nothing of the sort has been attempted in this study. However, another way of approaching the validity of the assessment procedure is to see whether the data obtained is consistent with other information known about the households.

For example, we would expect to find that the impact of space complaints should vary with the objectively available amount of space within the former home. A good index of available space is the number of rooms, considered in relation to the number of persons in the household. Table 8.6 classifies households according to their size and the amount of room in the previous home. Only very rough categories of family and dwelling size are used since the number of cases rapidly dwindles when finer classifications are employed.

TABLE 8.6   Objective Space Pressure and Space Assessment

Dwelling Unit	Proportion of Primary Space Complaints Household Size		
	1-2 Persons	3 Persons	4 or More
1-2½ rooms	45%	52%	54%
100% equals	(45)	(21)	(13)
3-4 rooms	41%	41%	60%
100% equals	(68)	(24)	(40)
5 or more rooms	41%	35%	35%
100% equals	(68)	(20)	(40)

Objectively measured space pressure and the number of primary space complaints shows a positive relationship. For a given family size, the smaller the dwelling unit, the more likely the household is to cite space complaints as a primary reason why it left its former home. Similarly for a given dwelling size, the smaller the household, the less likely the family is to cite space complaints as having had an impact on its moving decision. However, the relationships described in this table are not very strong.[7]

There is a plausible reason why space pressure and the assessment of space complaints do not show a particularly high relationship. In an earlier analysis of mobility desires, it was shown that family size had to be considered along with the age of the family in interpreting the relationship of family size to mobility desires. Young, large households living in small dwellings were the most likely to want to move. It was these households, we reasoned, which had most likely experienced an increase in family size. Perhaps it is *change* in the relationships between space and family size which generates the impact of space complaints and not just the amount of space alone.

This explanation is consistent with the findings shown in Table 8.7. Families are classified in this table into those families which have recently experienced a change in their size and those families which have not gone through this experience recently. When size changes had been experienced, 90% of the families complained about the space within their former homes. When change was not experienced, the corresponding percentage was only 51%. The impact of space complaints shows a similar difference: Where changes in size had occurred, the impact of space complaints was 71%; where such changes had not occurred, the impact was only 33%. Note, however, that the effectiveness of space complaints did not change substantially.

The amount of space available to the family in its old home is apparently not as important as the experience of shifts in the relationship between this

TABLE 8.7   Space Complaints and Changes in Household Size[*]

Space Complaint Assessment	Change in Household Size	No Change in Household Size
Impact (Primary Complaint)	71%	33%
Contributory Complaints	9	6
Ineffective Complaints	10	12
Coverage (Total Cases with Complaints)	90%	51%
100% equals	(86)	(178)
Index of Effectiveness	.78	.65

*Households were classified according to the answers to the following question: "Were there any changes in the number of persons living with you?"

space and the size of the family. A family living in a dwelling with a particular amount of space becomes accommodated to that space over time. When the family expands, the space is then experienced as inadequate. Such family size changes are most likely to occur to families which are under 10 years old; hence, the strong tendency for most of a household's moves to be accomplished during the early years of its existence.

The findings of this section provide some positive evidence for the validity of the assessment procedure.[8] Families are consistent in their accounts of their past moves. The greater the family size and the smaller the dwelling, the more likely are space complaints to be assessed as important factors in bringing about residential shifts. Furthermore, when a change in the relationship between family size and dwelling size had occurred, space complaints, as would be expected, played a particularly strong role.

COMPONENTS OF NEIGHBORHOOD COMPLAINTS

Complaints about the neighborhood cover a considerable range of specific aspects of the former place. Some families were concerned primarily about the social composition of the old neighborhood, others were concerned with its physical aspects—location, presence of obnoxious land uses, and so on. Table 8.8 presents a breakdown of the different aspects of the neighborhoods which the families cited as deficiencies.

The largest number of complaints—almost half of all neighborhood complaints—concerned neighborhood social composition. One out of 5 families were concerned with the physical structure of the neighborhood. Another 1 in 10 considered the services of their old places to be deficient.

What is the relative effectiveness of these different aspects of the old neighborhood as important reasons for moving? Since there were only 75 cases of complaints about the neighborhood, it is only possible to compare social composition complaints with other types of complaints; not enough cases of service and physical structure complaints are available to make a separation in these respects worthwhile.

TABLE 8.8   Types of
Neighborhood Complaints

Social Composition	49%
Physical Structure	23
Services	13
Other Aspects	15
100% equals	(75)

TABLE 8.9* Relative Effectiveness of Different Types
of Neighborhood Complaints

	Primary Complaints	Contributory Complaints	Ineffective Complaints	100% Equals
Social Composition Complaints	60%	16%	24%	(37)
Services and Physical Structure Complaints	24%	38%	38%	(26)

*Note that this table has a different structure than previous assessment tables. The basis for the percentages presented are the total number of complaints registered. Thus, 60% *of the complaints registered* about the social composition were rated as primary.

Complaints about the neighborhood's social composition were much more effective in bringing about residential shifts than all other types of complaints about the neighborhood.[9] When other types of neighborhood complaints were present, they tended to play a contributory rather than a primary role.

What gives rise to a complaint about the neighborhood? Is it that the neighborhood changes as physical structures deteriorate or new social groups take up residence? Or, is it the case that the neighborhood remains constant while the needs of the family change and make a neighborhood unsuitable to its new status? Some insight into the answers to these questions can be obtained from the data presented in Table 8.10.

TABLE 8.10 Sources* of
Neighborhood Complaints

Types of Changes	
Qualitative Family Changes	18%
Neighborhood Changes	20
Job Location Shifts	5
No discernible change	57
100% equals	(79)

*The classification of moves presented here is based on a qualitative analysis of the answers to all the open-ended questions. Wherever a spontaneous answer led to some inference as to whether the respondent had changed his attitudes towards the neighborhood, an attempt was made to classify him into one or another of the change groups. Undoubtedly, a much better way of accomplishing this classification would have been to ask questions directly concerning whether or not a change was experienced. For this reason, the number of changes reported in this table is probably underestimated.

The data in Table 8.10 are based upon spontaneous mentions of changes by the households studied. Undoubtedly, these represent those shifts in which changes were most salient to the families. In many cases where no discernible change occurred, it is probably the case that such changes also occurred but that they did not play an important role.[10] Despite the limitations of the evidence, it can be seen that neighborhood complaints have their sources as frequently in changes that take place in the family as in changes that take place in the neighborhood itself.

In other words, a neighborhood can be viewed as unsatisfactory in two ways. First, as a family goes through its life cycle, its needs for a particular kind of social environment, location, and services change, making a previously satisfactory neighborhood less so. Second, neighborhoods can change as new types of land use establish themselves, new social groups enter as residents, and old services and physical structures change.

TENURE STATUS AND COMPLAINTS

Whether a family owns or rents its dwelling has turned out to be an important datum throughout this report. Tenure status, in part, indicates the kind of dwelling inhabited by the family. Owned dwellings tend on the whole to be larger and more spacious than rental units. But, more important than size alone, tenure represents the control a family has over its housing. Owners are freer to modify their dwelling to fit in with their needs. Their costs are not entirely fixed. An owner may expend a great deal on his home by constant improvements and painstaking maintenance or he may forego improvements and let maintenance slip. A renter's housing costs are fixed by his landlord. Owners may, within limits, enlarge the amount of space within their homes, or change the configuration of that space to fit their needs. Renters may only rarely change their apartments in any radical way.

The differences involved in renting versus owning show up in the different assessment ratings given to the three complaint types. Owners and renters can be found to be particularly sensitive to those aspects of their former dwellings over which they had little control. Owners exercise little control over the characteristics of their neighborhood. Renters, in contrast, have little control over their costs. Owners are particularly sensitive to their complaints about their former neighborhoods; renters show a correspondingly high sensitivity to costs complaints. Table 8.11 presents the relevant data.

Renters and owners were about equally sensitive to space complaints. However, when renters were dissatisfied with space, they were slightly more likely than owners to cite such a complaint as a primary reason for their move, as indicated by the higher value of the Effectiveness Index for renters as compared with owners.

Owners, on the other hand, show a considerably greater sensitivity to unsatisfactory aspects of their former neighborhoods. Three out of five owners were dissatisfied in this respect, as compared with only one of four renters. Furthermore, of those owners who complained about their neighborhood, almost every one cited that as either a primary reason for leaving or as at least contributory to their desire to leave. Only two out of three of the renters cited neighborhood complaints as either a primary or contributory reason for their move. This is reflected in differences in the Index of Effect: A value of .58 is recorded for owners as compared with only .44 for renters.

The opposite pattern is shown for costs complaints. Here it is the renters with their fixed rent charges who complain more frequently about costs and

TABLE 8.11   Previous Tenure Status[*]
and Assessment

		Previous Tenure Status	
		Owners	Renters
I.	Space Complaints		
	Primary Complaints	42%	44%
	Contributory Complaints	13	6
	Ineffective Complaints	11	12
	Coverage	66	62
	Index of Effect	.64	.71
II.	Neighborhood Complaints		
	Primary Complaints	35%	12%
	Contributory Complaints	22	6
	Ineffective Complaints	3	9
	Coverage	60	27
	Index of Effect	.58	.44
III.	Costs Complaints		
	Primary Complaints	5%	16%
	Contributory Complaints	8	8
	Ineffective Complaints	11	14
	Coverage	24	38
	Index of Effect	.21	.42
	100% equals	(37)	(197)

[*]This table refers only to households who rented or owned their previous homes. There were 39 households which had been "doubled up" with other families in their former homes. These cases are *not* treated in this table.

who cite these costs as a primary reason for their move. The Index of Effect values for renters and owners, respectively, is .42 and .21. Costs are twice as effective for renters than for owners.

The flexibility of owning is shown in the relative insensitivity of owners to the space and costs of their former dwellings. Owners can adjust their costs within limits; renters have fixed charges. Renters, with smaller dwellings and limited control, find the space within their homes relatively fixed, and hence are more sensitive to the space and cost deficiencies of their homes.

SUMMARY AND CONCLUSIONS

In this chapter the method of reason analysis is applied to the study of the roles played by complaints in moving decisions. The findings provide additional confirmation for the thesis that residential mobility is integrally related to the changes undergone by a family as it passes through its life cycle.

The analysis of complaints could only be accomplished with three out of five of the households studied. The remaining households had been forced out of their former homes by the pressure of outside events. One out of five had moved primarily because of evictions, threatened or actual, or because the old home had been destroyed. The remaining households had been forced to move because moving was implied by other decisions made by the households—job transfers involving long distances and so on.

For the moves undertaken voluntarily, a new method of analysis was able to assess the importance of the roles played by different kinds of dissatisfactions with the former home. It was found that almost half of the families had as the primary reason for their move their reported dissatisfaction with the amount of room afforded by their former dwelling. Another one in four households had as its primary complaint some feature connected with their old neighborhoods or concerning the costs of the former home.

It was shown that effective space complaints arose with particularly great frequency when families have recently experienced shifts in family size. The connection between mobility and life cycle changes, demonstrated previously in Chapter 5, received considerable support from this finding. Moving, then, is seen as the reaction of the family to shifts in its housing needs occasioned by the changes in family composition accompanying the life cycle process.

Renters and owners differed significantly in the impact which various complaints had upon their decisions to move. Renters were especially sensitive to those aspects of rental dwellings which are fixed and outside tenant control—costs and space. Owners showed less sensitivity to these complaints due to the flexibility of owned units in meeting these pressures. Owners, in contrast, showed more sensitivity to aspects of former neighborhoods.

NOTES

1. This question followed another question directed at bringing the respondent back to the point at which the desire to move first entered his mind: "When did you first think of moving out of your former place?"

2. See Note 3, this chapter, for one complaint category for which such a distribution was not obtained and the reasons for the deviation from expectation.

3. Actually, there are eight possible response combinations to the three questions employed, and the classification given here is a reduction of these patterns according to a particular scheme. The full response patterns are as follows (a plus sign indicates that a respondent has mentioned a particular complaint in answer to the question indicated by the column heading):

Type Combination	Assess- ment Item	Stimulus Item	Exposure Item	Complaints about Landlord (Previous renters only)
A	+	+	+	6
B	+	−	+	0
C	+	+	−	(8)
D	+	−	−	(5)
E	−	+	+	5
F	−	+	−	(22)
G	−	−	+	8
H	−	−	−	143
			Total	(197)

According to the classification scheme used, response combinations A, B, C, and D have been classified as "primary complaints," E and F as "contributory complaints," G as "ineffective complaints" and H as "no complaints."

It can be seen that certain of the response patterns are "contradictory." For example, patterns C, D, and F represent cases where the respondent does not acknowledge exposure to a complaint but rates that complaint as of some degree of effectiveness. If the classification is to make sense, the number of such cases should be very small. Errors of measurement arising out of interviewing and processing inevitably lead to a few such "contradictory" cases. In the tables presented in the text, the number of such cases was very small.

But what happens when the number of such cases is relatively large? In the last column of the table in this note, the distribution of previous renters with regard to complaints about their landlords is shown. The contradictory cases are represented by the parenthetical numbers in this table. Most of them seem to be caused by an unfortunate misunderstanding of our exposure question, "Did you get along with your previous landlord?" The respondent interpreted the question to mean disputes of a personal nature. As one respondent put it, "We got along all right, but he never wanted to fix up the place or give us enough heat." The intended meaning of the exposure question was to cover any aspect of the dwelling unit which was customarily the landlord's obligation to provide. An unfortunate question wording necessitated dropping the analysis of complaints about landlord from the presentation in this chapter.

The experience with landlord complaints points up the necessity for clearly specifying what exposure questions are meant to cover. The respondents' view of a particular stimulus may not coincide with the investigator's definition; and the incongruence between the two may often, as in the case above, vitiate the research efforts.

4. The overlap among the three complaint types was as follows: (1) both space and costs rated as contributory or primary, 19 cases; (2) both space and neighborhood rated as contributory or primary, 23 cases; and (3) both costs and neighborhood rated as contributory or primary, 6 cases.

5. These findings are presented in Chapter 5.

6. The category "Other and vague complaints" comprises cases in which the families' complaints were either vague and unidentifiable or covered a wide range of miscellany. Some examples of miscellaneous complaints were complaints about vermin, the lack of cleanliness in furnished rooms, and so on.

7. It should be noted that a similar lack of congruence was found in Chapter 5. There we noted that while space complaints were associated with the density within the dwelling unit, the association between the two factors was not perfect and there were many households of the same size and occupying homes of the same size who differed radically in their satisfaction with the amount of space.

8. Attempts to assess the validity of the analysis of the other types of complaints could not be undertaken because appropriate data were not available in the survey.

9. This finding is consistent with that of Chapter 5, where it was shown that complaints about the social composition of neighborhoods showed a stronger relationship to mobility desires than complaints about neighborhood physical structure.

10. Where a change could be discerned, it was much more likely that the neighborhood complaint played a very strong role in bringing about a shift. The assessment ratings for complaints associated with a change and complaints not associated with a change was as follows:

	Primary Complaints	*Contributory Complaints*	*Ineffective Complaints*	*100% Equals*
Change associated complaint	71%	20%	9%	(35)
Complaint not involving change	32%	31%	37%	(45)

Chapter 9

THE CHOICE OF A NEW DWELLING

INTRODUCTION

Up to this point the analysis has attempted to account for the reasons why the households moved out of their previous homes. It still remains to explain how they selected the places the interviewers found them occupying in November 1950. To complete the analysis, it is necessary to consider other portions of the accounting scheme relating to the factors that brought them to their present homes.

The accounting scheme, as outlined in Chapter 7, specifies three types of information which are needed to account for the households' choices of new homes. Each household is viewed as facing its choice with a certain set of *specifications* in mind, employing certain *sources of information* to obtain knowledge about available housing opportunities, and choosing a particular dwelling because of its *attractions*. This chapter tries to account for the households' choices of new homes by raising the following questions:

(1) What were the important features—*specifications*—each family had in mind as it looked for a new place in which to live?

(2) What were the *information sources*—newspaper, real estate agents, and such—which it employed in this search? Which were the most effective sources of information?

(3) What was it about their final choice which particularly attracted the family to it? *What were the most important attractions?* Are there certain features which a family was likely to pass over in favor of other, more important, attractions?

In the previous chapter, the analysis was restricted to those moves which were judged to be voluntarily undertaken by the families under study. Whether a family's move is voluntary or forced is somewhat irrelevant to its choice of a new place in which to live. The analysis presented in this chapter can therefore focus on the full set of 444 recent movers.

SPECIFICATIONS

When a would-be car purchaser looks for an automobile, he generally has a set of criteria in mind against which the cars offered to him for purchase can be compared. He wants to purchase a car within a certain price range, which has certain features which he desires—perhaps, whitewall tires or an automatic shift. Often these criteria can be summarized in a brand name or in the year of manufacture. If he is a particularly discriminating shopper, he may consult publications which describe features he should look for or which evaluate different automobile brands.

The family seeking to rent or purchase housing faces this activity in very much the same way. Of course, housing, with the exception of some prefabricated units, is much less standardized than are automobiles. The features of dwelling units are usually found in greatly varied combinations, and specifications cannot be summarized by a brand name or the year of construction. The heterogeneity of housing units forces a household to pick out specific features of a new place which are deemed particularly important to obtain.

Specifications will vary from family to family. Some households will be mainly interested in a house within a particular locality; others will be interested primarily in units of a particular size, and so on. We can expect that such specifications will have some correspondence with the needs felt by the families as expressed in their life cycle position, experience with different housing, and so on.

The array of specifications of importance to the families as they looked for their new homes is presented in Table 9.1. The data consist of answers to a question asking each household what were the important things they had in mind when they were looking for a place.

From the analysis of complaints presented in the previous section, it can easily be anticipated that space requirements would occupy a prominent position among specifications. Half of the respondents indicated that they had particular space dimensions in mind when looking for their new place. Just as important in point of view of frequency was a factor which had received much less attention as a complaint source, namely, dwelling unit design. Half of the respondents indicated that they had some particular type of dwelling unit in mind.

Next in importance as criteria looked for in the families' new dwellings were particular locations. About one fourth of the households were looking for new homes in specific localities within Philadelphia. They had particular neighborhoods in mind to which they desired to move. Unfortunately, the

TABLE 9.1   Specifications*

I. Specific Dwelling Unit Attributes:	
Particular space dimensions	51%
Particular design requirements (heating, layout, utilities)	50
Costs (rent, maintenance, or purchase price)	19
Other dwelling unit attributes	16
II. Specific Neighborhood Attributes:	
Social Composition	6%
Location	26
Other Neighborhood Attributes	9
III. Other Considerations	5
IV. Vague Considerations	13
V. None ("looking for anything")	5
100% equals	(444)

*The specific wording of the question which elicited the reasons in this table was as follows: "What were the important things you had in mind about a place when you were looking around?"

"Other dwelling unit attributes" included such qualities as cleanliness (mainly referring to furnished units), details of construction (frame, brick, detached, attached), and so on.

"Other considerations" consisted primarily of "availability," e.g. "I needed a place right away and I would have taken anything that was available."

"Vague considerations" included such responses as "a better apartment," "a nicer neighborhood," etc. In part, the large number of vague responses indicates poor interviewing since such responses should ideally be followed with probes to bring out specific details. But, in large part, the high proportion of such responses indicates the difficulty respondents felt in verbalizing such matters.

interviewers did not attempt to find out what the specific aspects were of the neighborhoods to which the families were attracted. It is probably the case, however, that most of these households were interested in particular localities because these neighborhoods symbolized an especially desired "social climate," rather than some aspect of accessibility either to friends or their jobs.

Running fourth in importance were considerations of costs: 19% of the households stated that the costs of their new places were of particular importance to them.

The percentages in Table 9.1 add up to considerably more than 100%, indicating that many respondents had more than one criterion in mind when looking for a new place in which to live. Indeed, the modal number of specifications was two. Usually, the respondent had a particular kind of dwelling unit in mind and also some ideas about the kind of neighborhood desired.

The bulk of the specifications concerned the dwelling unit itself. People were looking for a particular kind of apartment or house and were much less frequently concerned with its social environment.

TACIT ASSUMPTIONS IN SPECIFICATIONS

Although the specifications acknowledged by the households cover a fairly wide range of criteria of choice, it can easily be seen that this information is not complete. What was uppermost in their minds appear in Table 9.1; but other criteria were employed which only appear as tacit assumptions.

Certain features of the dwellings they were looking for are so completely taken for granted that they are not mentioned as specifications. To cite an extreme example, not one of the families stated that they were looking for a house or an apartment which had a bathroom. Bathrooms are such an essential feature of dwellings that units which did not have one would have been automatically rejected.

There are undoubtedly other tacit assumptions which, while not as dramatic as the case cited above, certainly enter into the determination of which dwelling a household will choose. Tacit assumptions, for example, are held concerning the location of the dwelling. Not all areas of the city are considered, only those within some range of acceptability.

Tacit assumptions are also held concerning whether the family will seek its new home on the rental or purchase markets. Few families picked renting or owning as a specification, yet virtually every household held such a specification. The search within one or the other market effectively excludes a considerable range of housing opportunities, yet this is rarely mentioned as an explicit specification by the families.

TABLE 9.2   Tenure* Sought by Households

	Present Renters	Present Owners
Sought only to buy	–	75%
Sought only to rent	89%	–
Sought either to buy or rent	11	25
100% equals	(290)	(154)

*Data from a question asking, "Did you look only for a place to rent or a place to own?"

Table 9.2 shows the importance of tenure as a specification which orients the household to either the rental or the purchase markets. Nine out of 10 families presently renting sought only within the rental market for their new places. Three out of four of the owners sought only within the purchase market. Yet practically none of the households *spontaneously* mentioned tenure as a specification for their new homes.

Other tacit assumptions were probably held concerning almost every one of the categories under which specifications were tabulated in Table 9.1. Households were in all likelihood searching for dwellings within a restricted costs range, within particular areas of the city, and so on. The specifications mentioned by the household only cover those which are most salient to it, but not the entire range held.

What is the significance of a salient response? Why are some of the criteria mentioned and some ignored? Most of the things which one takes for granted in a dwelling unit tend to become tacit assumptions. Thus, it is pretty much taken for granted that a dwelling will have a bathroom, gas or electric stoves rather than coal burning ranges, and so on. Things which tend to be mentioned, on the other hand, are the important ways in which homes differ—the number of rooms, their layout, location and such. Incidentally, the things which are sought specifically today may be the tacit assumptions of tomorrow. For example, practically every urban dwelling now has some sort of mechanical refrigeration; 20 years ago a refrigerator may have been a major specification.

The importance of tacit assumptions points up some of the major interviewing problems involved in reason analysis. Before one can effectively interview about complaints, specifications, or attractions, it is necessary to spell out the possible responses in advance, making sure that the respondent is always reminded that tacit assumptions are also relevant in the accounts of their moves.[1]

COMPLAINTS AND SPECIFICATIONS

If a family has complained about some aspect of its former home, it is to be expected that this same aspect should loom large as a specification for the new place. For example, if a household had complained about the costs of its former home, it should cite costs as one of the primary yardsticks against which the suitability of the new place would be judged.

Although this expectation seems quite reasonable, there are several other considerations which enter in to obscure the expected relationship. One major qualification concerns persons who did not make a particular complaint. It cannot be argued, for example, that because a household was not pressed for space in its old home, space would not be a major specification for a new place. In order to *avoid* the development of a complaint in the new place, it must be of a sufficient size. Hence, we should expect that since space is such an important feature of dwellings, space requirements should be a major criterion for most households.

Table 9.3 indicates that when a household cited a particular aspect of its former dwelling as a complaint, it also tended to cite that aspect as a specification employed in looking for its new home. For example, two out of three families who had complained about the space in their old home cite space requirements as an important specification for their new homes. Fewer than half of the other households cite space as a specification. The difference between "complainers" and "noncomplainers" holds up for each of the three dwelling features: space, costs, and neighborhood.

The appearance of a housing feature as a specification also has a relationship to the needs of a household. The stronger the need for space, the more likely a family is to specify space as a requirement for its new space. In Table 9.4, it can be seen that the smaller a family, the less likely it is to cite space as a requirement. The biggest difference in this table is shown between households composed of only one person and all other households. Space becomes

TABLE 9.3   Complaints and Specifications

I.   Space:

	Proportion Citing Space as a Specification Among	
	Those Citing Space as Complaint*	All Other Households
	64%	46%
100% equals	(123)	(321)

II.   Costs:

	Proportion Citing Costs as a Specification	
	Among Those Citing Costs as a Complaint*	Among All Other Households
	38%	17%
100% equals	(34)	(410)

III.   Neighborhood:

	Proportion Citing Neighborhood as a Specification	
	Among Those Citing Neighborhood as a Complaint*	Among All Other Households
	68%	35%
100% equals	(40)	(404)

*These are cases in which a complaint was registered about the former place regardless of the role played by the complaint in bringing about the move.

TABLE 9.4   Household Size and Space Specifications

	Number of Persons				
	1	*2*	*3*	*4*	*5 or more*
Proportion citing space as a specification	28%	50%	53%	55%	63%
100% equals	(65)	(134)	(98)	(86)	(51)

important primarily for households beyond the minimum size and then increases more slowly as the size of the family increases.

In other words, dissatisfactions with the old dwelling tend to sharpen felt requirements for the new place. The needs of the family also tend to highlight what its specifications for a new place will be. The stronger the need for a particular feature, the more likely that feature is to be an important requirement.

INFORMATION SOURCES

Between the household and the housing market intervene the channels of information. Before moving plans can be translated into action, a household must somehow become informed of the existence of at least one vacancy[2] which meets the criteria set forth by its specifications.

The sources of information which may be employed cover a wide range. Some are sources expressly dedicated to the task of bringing household and housing together. Newspapers carry advertising listing both rental and purchase housing. Real estate brokers act as middlemen between the housing market and the households.

There are also informal channels of information. Friends and relatives may be employed to widen the areas of knowledge. Active first-hand searching, involving walking or riding about residential neighborhoods, is also often employed.

The channels we have described so far require that the household take active steps to employ them. The newspaper ads have to be read, the real estate agent has to be talked to, friends asked to help, and so on. Often, however, information about housing vacancies is brought to the household without active seeking on its part. An acquaintance may casually mention a vacancy in her apartment house. A local storekeeper might comment on the fact that one of his customers is about to move.[3]

The roles played by the different information sources may be studied by the same method used to study complaints. Some sources are employed more frequently than others; sources vary in their "coverage." Information channels also vary in their effectiveness. Some channels are more productive than others: their "impacts" vary.

In other words, assessment ratings may be given to information sources in the same way that they were given to complaints. The frequency with which different channels of information were used by the families defines their "coverages." The cases in which a particular source of information was instrumental in bringing a new place to the attention of a household define the "impact" of that source.

The various information channels were not employed with equal frequency. In Table 9.5, the first column indicates the "coverage" of each of the channels. (The other two columns will be discussed later on.) Most frequently employed are newspapers: 63% of our households looked at newspapers when they were searching for a new dwelling unit. Three out of five employed personal contacts, asking friends and relatives to inform them of any vacancy which came to their attention. Direct searching and real estate agents were employed by about half of the families.

Of course some households are apprised of housing opportunities without any expenditure of effort on their part. Something comes to their attention without their doing anything about it; 31% had one or more such "windfalls."[4]

A channel of information may be employed to no avail and, as we shall see, many efforts at finding a place are without results. The second column of Table 9.5, entitled "Impact," presents the proportion of respondents who actually found the places they now inhabit through each of the five channels of information. "Impact," then, represents the proportion of effectively employed information channels. The impact of personal contacts is the

TABLE 9.5   Assessment Ratings of Information Sources

Information Source	Coverage* (Proportion Using Source)	Impact* (Proportion Effective Use)	Index of Effectiveness
Newspaper	63%	18%	.29
Personal contact	62%	47%	.76
Walking or riding around	57%	19%	.33
Real estate agents	50%	14%	.28
Windfall	31%	25%	.81

*100% in this table is the 444 cases of recent movers.

The coverage of each channel was ascertained by asking the respondents questions concerning each of the channels along such lines as the following:
    "Did you read newspaper ads?"
    "Did you ask people you know?"

The "impact" of the channels was obtained from answers to the following question:
    "You told me what you did in looking for a place in general.
    Now would you tell me how you found this particular place?"

highest of all five channels: 47% of the households found their present dwelling unit through personal contacts.

Next in importance are windfalls: 25% of the households found their present dwelling units in this fashion. Walking or riding around is next in importance, followed by the newspapers and real estate agents.

The impact of a medium is, of course, not independent of its coverage. A channel can have a great impact and a small exposure, indicating each exposure is very effective. Or the other situation may prevail: A channel may have a great exposure but a small impact, indicating that the effectiveness of such a channel is very slight. In order to show each channel's effectiveness, we have computed Indexes of Effectiveness which are presented in the final column of Table 9.5. Each impact proportion was divided by its corresponding coverage, giving the proportion of effective exposures of the total amount of exposure.

As may be expected, windfalls are most effective, with an index value of .81. Next in importance are personal contacts with .76. The index values for the remaining channels ranged between .28 and .33.

Apparently the most effective means of obtaining a new dwelling unit are personal contacts. Real estate agents and newspapers, although commonly employed, have a high proportion of fallow results. Windfalls are not, of course, a means which can be "employed"; windfalls can only "happen."

The effectiveness of a source of information varies somewhat with the kind of dwelling desired by the household. Real estate agents are much more frequently and effectively employed by persons seeking to purchase homes. Newspapers are also much more frequently employed and more effective for seekers on the purchase rather than the rental markets.

Conversely, rental units were more effectively sought through personal contact and direct search than through agents or newspapers. In addition, the cheaper the rental, the more informal the means by which the unit was found. In other words, lower status renter households tended to find their new places through personal contacts and direct search, while upper status persons used the newspapers and real estate agents more frequently and more effectively.

The coverage and impact of different information sources also differed according to the location of the housing in one or another of the four study areas. The most frequently employed and most effective means of looking for a new place in Central City—the low status, mobile area—was direct searching by walking or riding through the area. Most of the new places in that area were found by looking for vacancy signs posted in ground floor windows or asking door to door.

Friends or relatives were most effectively employed in Kensington—the low status, stable area. A large number of the households moving into that area had found their new places in that fashion.

Real estate agents and newspapers were better sources of information for the households which had moved into West Philadelphia and Oak Lane—the two high status study areas. Real estate agents were particularly important for the newly constructed purchase units in the stable, high status Oak Lane area.

The apparent preference of low status families for the more informal information sources may be more realistically a function of the kinds of dwellings handled by real estate agents or advertised in newspapers. Low-priced rental or purchase housing may not be listed as often with agents or advertised in newspapers.

RESTRICTION OF THE RANGE OF CHOICE

A family's specifications determine what kinds of dwellings fall within the range of acceptability. Homes which meet the criteria set down are, by this token, "eligible" for renting or purchase. However, it often turned out to be the case that only one dwelling unit was found within this range of accept-ability. Some families were able to consider several places within their acceptability ranges; others had their choice limited to only one place.

A little more than two out of every five households indicated that they considered just one place—the one to which they moved. The range of choice available is, in part, a function of the state of the housing market.[5] In a period of housing shortage it is likely that the range of choice is limited. In addition, some parts of the housing market are more restricted than others. Rental housing, in great demand at the time of this survey was undertaken, had a more limited market than purchase housing. Two out of three prospec-tive purchasers considered several places; only one out of every two renters were in that fortunate position, as Table 9.6 indicates.

The accounting scheme which underlies the analysis presented here, defines "attractions" as the comparative advantages of the home chosen over all other dwellings considered. Obviously, this restricts the analysis of attrac-tions to those families considering more than one place to which to move. The assessment of "attractions" is therefore limited to the 247 cases where households made choices among several possibilities.

TABLE 9.6   Number of Places Looked At

	Renters	Owners
Just one place	48%	33%
Several places	52	67
100% equals	(289)	(148)

THE ASSESSMENT OF ATTRACTIONS

While a person's specifications—as we have employed the term—indicated what will be acceptable in the way of new housing, it may often turn out that the information sources employed present at least several possibilities within this "acceptable" range. What are the factors which enter at this point, to determine the selection among the acceptable array of possibilities?

"Attractions," as we shall call those specific features of the dwelling unit which played a role in this level of choice, need not necessarily be the same as specifications. By the time the household has come to the point of choosing a particular dwelling unit, the alternatives before it have generally been found to meet the major requirements of the household. Elements which we found to be subsidiary among specifications may now achieve a more prominent position as guides to the choice.

In fact, this seems to be the case. Things which seemed of considerable importance when considered as specifications play a minor role as attractions, while minor specifications become major attractions. The empirical evidence on this point is contained in Table 9.7.

The most frequently cited attraction was ' costs," with 60% of the households responding in this context. The reader may recall that costs played a relatively minor role among specifications. Apparently, when two or more generally acceptable dwelling units are considered, the cheaper one is chosen. Costs enter in as a major consideration at the level where choices are made between units which are equivalent in more important respects.

TABLE 9.7   Attractions of Present Dwelling Over
Others Considered*

Attractions	Portion Rating Present Dwelling as Better than Others Considered
Costs	60%
Outside appearance	50%
Transportation to work	42%
Neighborhood reputation	38%
Number of rooms	37%
Kind of people in neighborhood	31%
Nearness to friends	31%
Nearness to relatives	29%
Schools	28%
Open space or garden	28%
Garage or parking space	19%

*Responses to the question, "Compared to the second-best place you looked at, would you say this place was better or worse with regard to . . .?

Space, which played so important a role as far as specifications were concerned, now appears to be subordinated to such things as the "outside appearance" of the dwelling, and its accessibility to the place of employment of the family's breadwinner. Neighborhood reputation also plays a fairly important role equaling that of dwelling unit space.

The findings presented in Table 9.7, however, only indicate the proportion of chosen dwellings which were "better" in certain respects than the other candidates considered. From this information, we cannot tell whether an attraction was effective or not. In other words, before judgments about the relative importance of these attractions can be made, it is necessary to subject the data to an assessment analysis.

In order to make assessment ratings, it is necessary to know in how many cases an attraction was present—its "coverage"—and in how many cases this presence was the "clinching" factor in the choice—its "impact." The two items of information we seek are as follows:

I. *The Coverage of an Attraction:* the number of households exposed to a particular attraction, i.e., whose chosen dwelling unit was better with respect to that particular attribute

II. *The Impact of an Attraction:* the number of households whose choice was *determined* by a particular attraction.

The coverage of each attraction was ascertained by asking the following question (*Exposure Item*): "Compared to the second best place you looked at, would you say this place was better or worse with regard to (number of rooms, outside appearance, etc.)?" A checklist of 11 attributes followed this question and each respondent rated his home as either "better," "the same," or "worse" in each respect. (The 11 attributes along with the proportion rated as "better" are shown in Table 9.7.)

The impact of each attribute was ascertained from the following item: (*Assessment Item*) "Why was this place picked, over all the other places you looked at?" For each of four major attractions each case was then classified as to whether it fell into one or another of the following types:

(1) *Primary Attraction* (Impact Cases): all cases in which the family cites a particular attraction as being the reason why that house was chosen over all others

(2) *Ineffective Attractions*: all cases in which the new place was rated as being more attractive than the others which were considered, but in which that particular attraction was not considered as the reason for the choice of the dwelling.

The reader may recall that, in the assessment of complaints, an intermediate category called "contributory" effectiveness was employed. Such a classification was made possible by the existence of a third item, which enabled the separation of complaints into three categories: "primary" complaints, "contributory" complaints, and "ineffective" complaints. The absence of a third item in the assessment of attractions means that the category "ineffective attractions" undoubtedly contains some cases in which a particular attraction did play a supporting role in determining the household's choice.

Assessment ratings were computed for four of the major attractions—costs, space, location, and neighborhood social composition. The ratings are presented in Table 9.8.

In terms of coverage, the most important attraction was costs: 60% of the dwelling units chosen were better in this respect than the other places looked at. Close to costs was location with 55% coverage. Trailing behind were space and neighborhood social composition with 36% and 31% coverage, respectively.

The rank order with regard to impact was somewhat different, however. Costs, with an impact of 42%, was clearly the most important of the attractions. Location (19%) and space (18%) with about the same impact, were obviously of secondary importance. Neighborhood social composition with its minute impact of 6% turned out to be a definitely minor attraction.

The Indexes of Effectiveness for these four attractions show costs to be of rather high effectiveness (.70). Next in effectiveness was space (.50), then location (.35). Trailing in last place was neighborhood social composition with an effectiveness index of .19.

The cost of a dwelling is thus the major "clinching" factor determining whether it is to be chosen over its competitors. A good location or a favorable social environment, on the other hand, tends to come along as a "bonus." They are not important factors in determining a choice, but such attractions tend to be achieved when the choice is made with reference to more

TABLE 9.8   The Assessment of Major Attractions[*]

	Costs	Space	Location[*]	Social Composition
Impact — Primary				
Attractions	42%	18%	19%	6%
Ineffective Attractions	18	18	36	2
Coverage	60%	36%	55%	31%
100% equals	(247)	(247)	(247)	(247)
Index of Effectiveness	.70	.50	.35	.19

[*]A "location" attraction was defined as a rating of the present dwelling as being better than the other considered with regard to either transportation to work, nearness to friends, or nearness to relatives, or any combination of the three.

"important" things. This is particularly the case with respect to the social composition of a dwelling's environment.

The space within a dwelling, when it is an issue in the choice between that abode and others, also turns out to be very important. Although most dwellings considered by a household are about the same with regard to space, those which have an edge in this respect turn out to be chosen fairly often.

DISREGARDED DEFECTS

Another way of approaching the general question of why the families chose their new abodes is to look for the faults which were most easily disregarded. What defects were the families most likely to overlook in their choice of a new place? For example, did the attraction of adequate space within the dwelling unit compensate for the dwelling's poor social environment or its poor outside appearance?

Each family was asked to rate its new place as either better than, the same as, or worse than the other places it considered. Features of a dwelling which were rated as "worse" than the other places considered can yield an insight into the kinds of defects which are most easily overlooked in the search for a new place. This information is given in Table 9.9.

Few of the dwellings were rated as defective with regard to any of the 11 features considered. Only "open space" about the dwelling received as much as one-quarter of the families rating their dwellings as worse in this respect. For all of the dwelling unit characteristics studied, the overwhelming majority of the respondents felt that their present homes were either the same as or better than the other places they considered.

TABLE 9.9   Features Rated as Being Worse Than in
Other Places Considered

Dwelling Feature	Proportion of households rating feature as worse than in other dwellings considered
Open Space or Garden	27%
Outside Appearance	22%
Nearness to Relatives	18%
Nearness to Friends	17%
Costs	17%
Number of Rooms	17%
Garage or Parking Space	12%
Transportation to Work	11%
Neighborhood Reputation	11%
Kind of People in Neighborhood	8%
Schools	8%

The two highest frequencies of mention as defects were "open space" and "outside appearance." These were the dwelling features which were most likely to be rated as "worse," and may be viewed as the features most easily disregarded in making a choice. Location factors, as expressed in nearness to friends or relatives, were next in order, along with costs and the number of rooms in the dwelling.

It was shown in the previous section that costs and the amount of space within the dwelling were assessed as playing strong roles in the process of choosing among attractions. Should we not then expect to find that these factors are least easily disregarded? However, we find that more than half of the features have received lower frequencies of ratings as "worse." Features which receive the lowest amount of worse mentions—garage, schools, kind of people in neighborhood—are primarily features which received very low mentions as being better in the dwelling chosen over other homes considered. These features apparently receive their low mention as being worse, because in general they are not considered very important. They are apparently not very salient features of homes.

THE COMPATIBILITY OF ATTRACTIONS

It is not always the case that dwellings are attractive in all respects. Very often the choice before the family involves what defects it is willing to accept in order to maximize the feature it is particularly desirous of obtaining. For example, in order to obtain a new place which is just right cost-wise, it may have to accept a home which is worse than other possibilities with regard to space, location, and so on.

When a family maximizes one particular aspect of its choice, what does it ordinarily have to give up? Is it possible to get a dwelling which is superior in many respects, or is it the case that when one chooses a home which is superior, say, in costs, it is likely to be inferior with respect to neighborhood reputation?

In order to measure the association between attractions and defects, we have computed an index of incompatibility showing the extent to which particular kinds of superior qualities tend to be associated with different kinds of defects. The reasoning behind this index is as follows: If two dwelling qualities are compatible, then when a choice is superior with respect to one quality, it should not be any more likely to be inferior with respect to the other quality than if it were not superior with respect to the first quality. On the other hand, if two qualities are incompatible, when the first is rated as superior, the second should tend to be rated as inferior.

Incompatibility Indexes are presented in Table 9.10 for a selected number of dwelling qualities. A greater value than 1.00 indicates that when a quality

TABLE 9.10   The Compatibility of Different Dwelling
Qualities: The Index of Incompatibility

Qualities as Inferior	Transportation	Neighborhood Reputation	Costs	Outside Appearance	Number of Rooms
		Qualities Rated as Superior			
Transportation	–	1.27	1.09	1.30	.73
Neighborhood Reputation	1.09	–	1.27	.55	.36
Costs	.82	.94	–	1.29	1.18
Outside Appearance	1.18	.68	1.46	–	.64
Number of Rooms	1.29	.82	1.18	.76	–

*An index value of greater than 1.00 indicates that the two qualities tend to be incompatible. A value less than 1.00 indicates compatibility.

indicated in the column heading is rated as superior, the quality listed in the row heading tends to be rated as inferior. Hence the two qualities tend to be incompatible—maximizing the first means accepting a dwelling which is inferior with respect to the seconds. An index value of less than 1.00 indicates that two dwelling qualities tend to be "positively" associated—when the quality represented in a column is rated as superior, the quality referred to in a row also tends to be superior to or at least as good as the other alternatives considered by the household.

For example, the value 1.29, found in the first column, indicates that a dwelling superior with regard to transportation tends to be inferior with respect to the number of rooms in the dwelling. In contrast, the value of .82 in the same column indicates that superior transportation is associated with lower costs. In other words, superior transportation tends to be *incompatible* with a superior number of rooms but *compatible* with lower costs.

Turning to the first column of Table 9.10, the values[7] of the Index of Incompatibility for the transportation aspect of the dwellings chosen indicate that superior transportation is compatible only with lower costs, and incompatible with a good neighborhood reputation, a better outside appearance of the dwelling, and the dwelling size. In other words, homes which maximize accessibility tend to be cheaper, of poor appearance, and small in size.

Maximizing neighborhood reputation—as shown in the second column—means that the family is likely to get a dwelling which is inferior transportation-wise. Outside appearance is particularly compatible with a superior neighborhood reputation. Dwellings superior in this respect also tend to be larger and slightly better cost-wise.[8]

Costs are the most incompatible quality. When costs are superior, the dwelling tends to be inferior in all the other respects considered (although the association with transportation defects is but very slight—index value of but

1.09). Lower costs are particularly incompatible with a superior outside appearance of the house.

A better outside appearance—as indicated in the fourth column—is associated with a better neighborhood reputation and a larger number of rooms, but also involves accepting a house which is inaccessible and smaller.

Finally, a dwelling which is superior in its space, tends to be also superior with regard to neighborhood reputation, outside appearance, and transportation. Space, however, tends to be incompatible with superior costs.

In other words, we seem to find the following associations: A house superior in its costs tends to be inferior in a large number of other ways. Houses which maximize outside appearance tend to be larger and located in a neighborhood with a good reputation. Accessible homes tend to be cheaper, smaller, of poorer appearance, and located in neighborhood with a poorer reputation.

SUMMARY OF FINDINGS

In this chapter we were concerned with how the households came to choose the particular dwelling units we found them occupying at the time of the household interview. Information was presented on three major points: "specifications," "information sources," and "attractions."

"Specifications," conceived of as the standards of judgment the households applied to housing in their research for a new place, showed a distribution of attributes very much like complaints. Space requirements were most important, followed by particular dwelling unit designs, and neighborhood location, in that order.

It was further shown that the importance of a particular specification followed objective indexes of family needs. Thus, the larger a family, the greater was the importance of space requirements as a standard against which particular housing opportunities were judged.

The households employed a variety of means for obtaining information about places to which to move. Newspapers, personal contacts, direct search, and real estate agents, in that order, were each employed by more than half of the families in their search for new homes. Some households were apprised of opportunities without active searching: In 3 out of 10 cases a "windfall" opportunity was brought to the families' attention.

Information sources varied in their effectiveness. A larger proportion of households found their present homes through personal contacts than through any other means.

Families seeking to own tended to rely heavily on newspapers and real estate agents while families seeking to rent preferred direct searching and personal contact.

Attractions, defined as the reasons why a particular unit was chosen over all the units considered, when compared to specifications, showed quite a different distribution. Costs were most important as an attraction, followed by space, neighborhood location, and neighborhood social composition.

The outstanding position of costs as attractions requires some explanation since this attribute of housing played a very small role as either a specification or a complaint. It is apparently the case that the more important attributes such as space requirements, neighborhood location, and so on are the primary criteria by which the choice is initially narrowed down to among just a few places. In deciding among places which are otherwise acceptable, the costs of the dwelling unit enter in as a decisive element. When the household is confronted with two or more dwelling units which are identifical with regard to space, design, and location, the cheaper is chosen.

NOTES

1. The role played by tacit assumptions has been documented in other studies as well. Prof. Paul F. Lazarsfeld's study of movie-going revealed that in giving an account of why they chose one rather than another movie, respondents consistently denied speaking to anyone about their choice although most went to the movies in question with at least one other person. It is inconceivable that conversation with their companion about the movie did not take place. Rather, the conversations that did occur were taken so much for granted that the respondents felt that the interviewer was asking about someone *other than* the movie-going companion.

2. Prospective vacancies are stressed here because vacancies alone do not give anywhere near a complete picture of the composition of the housing available to persons seeking accommodations. Many of the dwelling units which are on the market are not vacancies but only prospective vacancies. For example, for those of the households who were home owners, the status of their homes at the time they were first offered to them for purchase was as follows:

Occupied by former owner		33%
Occupied by tenant		27
Occupied by self as renter		4
Vacant		36
Including:		
New construction	69%	
Old construction	28	
No information	3	
100% equals		(417)

Most of the housing on the purchase market, as these households experienced it, were not vacancies. Only about one-third of the units were vacancies and most of these were new construction.

3. In Chapter 6 we saw that half of the cases of respondents who had not planned to move but actually did so had come upon opportunities in just this fashion. Apparently it happens rather often that the event which crystallizes a desire to move into action is the chance appearance of opportunities.

4. While such "windfalls" may be experienced as being completely unsolicited, it may very well be the case that a person lets it be known among his friends and acquaintances that he is searching for a new place and that the friend is alerted for information about opportunities. When an opportunity is discovered and the person apprised, it may only *appear* as a "windfall."

5. Many observers have noted that low income persons have a restricted outlook which limits the range of opportunities available to them in the way of educational services, medical or psychiatric help, and so on. It may be that the differences between renters and owners are accentuated by this restricted outlook, especially since families seeking rental units are, on the whole, of lower income than households seeking to own. See Genevieve Knupfer "Portrait of the Underdog" and Herbert Hyman "The Value Systems of Different Classes" in Reinhard Bendix and S. Martin Lipset *Class, Status, and Power,* The Free Press, Glencoe, Ill., 1953.

6. Assessment ratings for other kinds of attractions could not be accomplished because their impact was so minor. Thus the outside appearance of the dwelling turned out to be unimportant as far as impact was concerned, even though the coverage of this attraction, as shown in Table 9.7, was quite high.

7. The Compatibility Index for a given quality A with respect ao nother quality B was computed as follows:

$$\text{Index of Incompatibility of A with respect to B} = \frac{\text{Proportion rating chosen dwelling as defective with regard to B among all families whose choice was superior with respect to A}}{\text{Proportion reporting choice as defective with regard to B in entire sample}}$$

8. Note that the indexes for two qualities are not necessarily symmetrical. In other words, houses superior with regard to costs may also tend to be superior with regard to neighborhood reputation, while at the same time houses superior with regard to neighborhood reputation may tend to be inferior with regard to costs.

Chapter 10

AN OVERVIEW OF THE DECISION PROCESS

INTRODUCTION

The previous two chapters have presented step-by-step accounts of the decisions made by households in choosing their new homes. We tried to show the different kinds of considerations which play their parts as families first decide to move out of their old homes; then, as they go through the stage of looking over the housing market; and, finally, as they make a choice among the opportunities available to them.

The analysis presented has been of necessity somewhat atomized as each step was treated in detail, somewhat in isolation from the one which preceded it and that which followed. It is necessary now to weld the various segments into a more integrated whole, and this is the task to which this chapter is devoted.

THE ACCOUNTING SCHEME

The accounting scheme which has been employed as the guide to the analysis of moving decisions partitioned the moving process into several distinct steps. These various stages might be viewed as successive decision points, the outcome of each determining the course of events until the next decision point is reached.

The starting point of the moving process, for our purposes, is the decision to leave the old dwelling. Some households left voluntarily, others were forced to move by the pressure of other circumstances. Among those who left voluntarily, we sought the dissatisfactions which gave rise to their desire to leave. The analysis of complaints sought to assess the importance of different kinds of dissatisfactions.

The search for a new home is the next stage in the moving process. Families employ a variety of means, some formal and some informal, to gather information about actual or prospective vacancies. The search is also guided by whatever the households may have in mind as the especially desired features of the new place. The families are apprised of the moving opportunities open to them by the channels of information which they employ and the dwellings offered are judged according to specifications for a suitable abode. The task attempted by the analysis of this stage was to assess the differential use and effectiveness of the various information sources employed by the households and also to make an inventory of the kinds of criteria which went into specifications.

The final stage of the moving decision involves choosing from among the set of dwellings brought to the attention of the family. Of course, some families are not fortunate enough in their search for a new place to be faced with alternative opportunities. They manage to hear about only one new place and, finding that to be acceptable according to their criteria, decide to take it. Most families, however, look at several places before deciding on which is to be their new home. The final choice is analyzed in terms of the features of the dwelling which attracted them. The accounting scheme and its various elements can now be summarized in outline form as follows:

ACCOUNTING SCHEME FOR MOVING DECISIONS

Stage I *The Decision to* *Leave the Old Home*	*Stage II* *The Search for a New* *Place*	*Stage III* *The Choice Among* *Alternatives*
Reasons for leaving	A. *Channels of Information Employed*	*Reasons for Choice*
A. Decision forced by outside circumstances	a. Formal b. Informal	A. *Only one opportunity offered:* reasons presumed to be identifcal with specifications.
B. Decision made because of dissatisfaction with old place	B. *Specification* (Features desired in new home)	B. *Several Opportunities:* choice made because of comparative attractions of alternate opportunities

The results of the reason analysis will be summarized in the sections which follow according to what appears to be the modal family behavior in each of the three stages.

THE DECISION TO LEAVE

In looking back over their decisions to leave their old dwellings, two out of five households were found to have been either forced to leave their old homes or had left because a residential shift was implied in other decisions concerning their jobs or their marital statuses.

Among the three out of five whose moves were undertaken voluntarily, the most frequently encountered motive for the shift lay in dissatisfaction with the amount of room available in their old dwellings. Next in importance were complaints about the former place's environment, and last in importance were complaints about costs.

Space complaints were particularly effective in furnishing a motive for moving when the family had previously experienced a shift in its size, either through the addition of new members or through the subtractions that occur through death and marriage.

Typically, then, most moves are undertaken voluntarily and are motivated by the changes in family size which rendered the old dwelling's space inadequate to its requirements. The decision to move out is primarily a function of the changes in family composition which occur as a family goes through its life cycle.

THE SEARCH FOR A NEW HOME

Typically, a family employed several means to obtain knowledge about moving opportunities. The real estate sections of daily newspapers were most frequently consulted, but comparatively few families found their new places by this means. Personal contacts were also extensively used but with greater effectiveness. Many families asked friends and relatives to let them know when they heard of a prospective vacancy. Real estate agents, used infrequently by the majority of families, were particularly useful in searching for a place to purchase.

In looking for its new place, the modal family read newspapers and asked friends and relatives to pass on information to them. Typically, the new place was brought to the attention of renters through personal contacts. The typical owner found that consulting real estate agents was a more fruitful approach to the purchase market.

Only a very small proportion of families stated that they would take any dwelling offered to them. Most families were looking for particular kinds of places. Practically every family was looking for a new place of a particular size or design. Some families were searching only in particular sections or neighborhoods within the city. Others wanted homes near their relatives or friends or which had a congenial—to them—social composition. The modal family in its search for a new home was looking for a dwelling of a particular size and having certain essential design features.

THE CHOICE AMONG ALTERNATIVES

Half of the families made their choice of a new home after looking at only one possibility. They found this single opportunity close enough to their desires to take it without looking further. The other half of the families studied made their choices from among several alternative possibilities.

At this stage of the decision process, factors which appeared to play minor roles as either complaints or specifications took on greater importance as decision "clinching" factors. Typically, the choice among alternatives was made on the basis of the relative costs of the several dwellings offered. Other features which played important roles as attractions were the relative interior dimensions and locations of dwellings.

A decision in favor of the dwelling of lower cost generally meant a decision against a dwelling which was superior in many other respects—size, location, the amount of space about the home, and so on. The modal family, when faced with alternative dwellings to choose, picked the one lower in costs, and generally poorer with respect to its accessibility and outside appearance.

THE MODAL DECISION PROCESS

The modal family left its old home voluntarily, impelled by a recent change in its size which had rendered the size of its former place inadequate to its new composition. In searching for a new place, it looked through newspapers and asked friends and relatives to apprise it of prospective vacancies. Typically, the new home was brought to its attention by the personal contacts it had employed.

In judging whether the place brought to its attention was suitable, the average household applied standards involving the size and design of the dwelling. These two criteria were most frequently used as specifications against which places brought to their attention were judged.

The average family had an even chance of taking the first opportunity offered to it or of making a choice among several alternatives. When two or more places were considered, the ruling criterion was comparative costs. The cheaper place was typically chosen even if it meant abandoning other desirable features.

PART V
CONCLUSIONS

Chapter 11

CONCLUSIONS

INTRODUCTION

Because one of our major purposes has been to illustrate the application of certain methods to the study of residential mobility, our treatment of empirical findings has often suffered from being embedded in a more-than-ordinarily-detailed discussion. To correct this underplaying of our findings, and to bring them together into an overall interpretation, the first sections of this concluding chapter are devoted to answering the following questions: Why is there residential mobility? What can our findings tell us about the function served by mobility for the family? What functions do mobile areas serve in the city's total social structure?

This concluding chapter will also be devoted to another purpose as well. As an exploratory study employing new methods in a special design, this research owes an obligation to the future. In the later sections of this chapter, we will try to lay out what we believe to be the directions which further research into residential mobility might profitably take. We will also point up what we believe to be the major gaps and shortcomings in our own study.

AN INTERPRETATION OF RESIDENTIAL MOBILITY

The mobility which characterizes our urban places is made up of countless thousands of individual moves. Each individual move is not a random event but determined by a household's needs, dissatisfactions, and aspirations. There is an underlying social psychological "order" to the apparently restless milling about of our urban population.

The adequate understanding of mobility requires a knowledge of what moving means to individual households. What part does mobility play in family life? What are the needs, desires, and aspirations which mobility expresses?

An overall statement concerning the function of mobility for individual families can be abstracted from the findings of this study, "Mobility is the mechanism by which a family's housing is brought into adjustment to its housing needs."

What are the needs which must be met by housing? Housing needs are determined primarily by composition of the household. Families change as they go through a life cycle of growth and decline. Family size first rapidly increases as children are born in the early years of marriage. Housing needs change rapidly in these early years as space requirements quickly grow and as the family at the same time becomes more sensitive to the social and physical environment provided by the location of its dwelling. It is this period in a family's life cycle that its housing, because of the rapid change in its needs, is most likely to be out of adjustment with its requirements. The family during this early stage typically moves from smaller to larger dwellings, from mobile, familyless areas to areas where family living is the typical pattern of household existence.

Once through the life cycle stage in which family size manifests the most dramatic increase, housing needs tend to stabilize. Residential stability is also attained as successive moves takes the family into housing which closely matches these stable needs.

Finally, as children marry and leave the household, and as death puts an end to the basic marital relationship, household space requirements contract; the family is less sensitive to the social and physical environment of the dwelling. But the family's housing, chosen to fulfill the greater needs of the child-rearing stage, does not frustrate its housing requirement; rather it is now a matter of overfulfillment. Mobility is less often resorted to, at this point, to bring housing in line with family needs. It is easy to adjust, without moving, to a *surplus* of space, but difficult to adjust to a *shortage* of space.

The substantive findings stress space requirements as the most important of the needs generated by life cycle changes. But these are needs most easily observed and most readily articulated by a family. Life cycle changes also involve changes in other kinds of needs, more elusive to the observer. The ages of the household members and the social needs accompanying age grades are also important life cycle aspects which have housing implications. Residence determines what kinds of companions children will have, for a child's social "range" is sharply limited spatially. Residence also determines which school a child will attend. As children grow older and spend more of their time outside the dwelling, the qualities of the *exterior environment* of the home become more important to the family.

Residential mobility also plays a role in "vertical" social mobility. The location of a residence has a prestige value and is, to some degree, a determinant of personal contact potentials. Families moving up the "occupational ladder" are particularly sensitive to the social aspects of location and use residential mobility to bring their residences into line with their prestige needs. In the findings of this study, some of the households who were strongly dissatisfied with their housing's social environment were expressing the way in which their home no longer fitted in with their social aspirations.

The changes in needs generated by the life cycle changes become translated into residential mobility when the family dwelling does not satisfy the new needs. A home can either satisfy, frustrate, or overfulfill the housing needs a family may have. What are the most important qualities of dwellings as far as needs are concerned?

The findings of this study indicate that the space contained by a home is probably the most important dwelling quality. The larger the housing unit, the more it is able to accommodate the changing needs of the family. Small dwelling units severely frustrate the space requirements of families going through the rapid expansion of the early years of marriage. A large home may be satisfactory to small families: A surplus of space is not considered as a frustration. In other words, a large dwelling unit can fulfill the space needs of a family through many life cycle changes, while a small unit is congenial only to the earliest and final stages.

Space is not the only relevant quality of dwellings. The design of a unit also plays a role. The utilities of the dwelling, the layout of rooms, its orientation to other buildings, and so on, all are important. Units which allow a relatively flexible utilization of space accommodate easier to family size and age shifts. Designs which rigidly limit space utilization make mobility necessary as life cycle changes generate needs for more space and for different kinds of space uses.

The control which a family may exercise over the dwelling also conditions the way in which the home may be adapted to changing needs. When a family rents its home, its control over design, utilities, and costs are minimal. Rents are fixed and tenants are rarely encouraged to make changes in their abodes. In contrast, owners can change the designs of their homes to some extent through alterations. Costs can be manipulated to some degree: one can maintain a house lavishly, or expend just a bare minimum on its maintenance.

For these reasons, families living in large units and who own their homes, almost regardless of their life cycle position, contribute least to mobility. Large families renting small apartments are the most mobile of all households, especially when they are in the earliest life cycle stages.

THE FUNCTIONAL ROLE OF MOBILE AREAS

Mobility, as we have seen, is the mechanism which adjusts housing to housing needs. Different kinds of housing vary in their ability to accommodate the needs of families in the several stages of the life cycle. Some types of housing are suitable to a wide range of family types; other dwellings fit in only with the needs of a very limited variety of family types.

What is especially characteristic of mobile areas is the concentration of "limited purpose" dwellings to be found in such areas. The suburb, with its large owned units, provides the setting for minimal mobility and attracts families in the most stable of their life cycle stages. In contrast, because mobile areas offer small rental units with limited facilities for family living, they contain the housing least adjustable to the changes occurring to families in their life histories.

The small rental units characteristic of mobile areas—furnished rooms or apartments, "one-room-and-kitchenette" unfurnished apartments—are housing types congenial only to the familyless individual or the childless couple. Young unmarried adults, young couples without children, older couples whose children have married and left the family, old widows and widowers all find these small units suited to their housing needs.

Those households with children which are found in mobile areas tend to be either broken families whose precarious economic condition make cheap housing a premium, or young couples using the areas as only a waystation. Couples with children are therefore the most mobile of all households in mobile areas. Their residence in such areas is only a temporary expedient with their next destinations in other areas where dwellings are larger and the social environment more congenial to child raising.

Mobile areas perform an important function within the urban housing market. They provide rental dwellings for the "marginal" familyless urban dwellers. The young migrants from the hinterland, the aged, the broken families living on the edge of poverty all can find in the mobile areas the housing which fits their needs. Services catering to the familyless can also be found there: All-night delicatessens, restaurants, and "bachelor's" laundries take care of the needs of the familyless which are ordinarily provided for in family living.

In an urban society where the aged no longer fit into the family homestead and where thousands of migrants arrive in the city from the hinterland every year, mobile areas provide the housing once taken care of by a family system in which grandparents, parents, and unmarried children occupied the same dwelling.

Mobile areas are mobile because they provide housing for households in those life cycle stages which are particularly unstable. The young, single, migrants soon marry and take their places in the areas which provide for family living. Oldsters suffer the heaviest tolls of the death rate. The breadwinners of broken families work in marginal occupations and constantly adjust their housing to the fluctuations of an income frequently interrupted by unemployment. The families with children who do locate themselves in such areas do so primarily out of economic necessity and regard residence there as a temporary expedient to be abandoned as soon as opportunity presents itself.

The mobility of an area affects its social integration. Mobile areas contain ✗ population types of considerable heterogeneity. The gulf of interests and needs between the young unmarried and the old retired is especially great. The temporary character of residence makes it hard for persons to identify with each other and feel that they share common interests. The opportunities for friendship and association on an informal level seem slight in a situation of diverse population types and impermanency.

Organizational life suffers as well from mobility. Membership organiza- ✗ tions find the task of constant recruitment especially worrisome. Some adjust successfully to the problems presented by such areas but only by dint of considerable effort.

GUIDES TO FUTURE RESEARCHES

Every research is partly oriented to the future. It aspires to be a guide to the research which follows it, and hopes that future research will build on its successes and correct its failures. It is hoped that, with the aid of this report, future research into mobility will proceed on somewhat firmer ground.

Building on the work reported here, there are three directions which future research might take. Perhaps the most important involves the *extension* of the methods tested here to other populations. The four study areas whose residents have been studied are not a representative sample of any urban place. While it is unlikely that the findings reported here whould be changed markedly by the study of another, more representative population, some important modifications of these findings might result.

Future research might also take the form of more *intensive* research on those topics which have received only sketchy treatment in this study, or on variables which were only crudely measured. More refined work on the important characteristics of housing units is certainly in order.

Finally, future research may be devoted to *new* directions beyond those taken by the present study. For example, this research has not touched upon the spatial aspects of mobility, or sought to study the values involved in housing.

FUTURE RESEARCH EXTENSION

The population which this research studied was restricted by the fact that only residents within four small subareas of the city of Philadelphia were involved. This feature of the study design made it possible to make a very intensive study of crucial types of urban areas, but at the same time it restricted the generality of the findings. An essential task is to broaden the generality of these findings by studying more representative areas and populations.

The sample studied here is unrepresentative in two ways: First, it was restricted to only the four study areas. Households living in areas of medium mobility or in the middle ranges of socio-economic status were excluded. Second, areas containing large numbers of either Negroes or foreign-born whites were not considered as eligible for the sample. The few Negroes who were in the four study areas were not interviewed.

Areas with large proportions of Negroes or large numbers of foreign-born persons tend to be on the mobile side. All indications are that these groups have special housing problems and it may be the case that their mobility is responsive to the special restrictions which are placed on their housing opportunities.

For these reasons, it is important that the generality of the findings reported here be tested by studying more representative populations and special types of populations which were excluded by this study design.

FUTURE INTENSIVE RESEARCH

Another important direction which future research may profitably take is the elaboration of the relationships which have shown up with such strength in this study. Many of the variables which have been found to account for differences between mobile and stable households have been measured only crudely. Future research might try to refine the measurements we have made and attempt to specify why they are so effective in accounting for mobility.

For example, although family life cycle changes have been referred to many times throughout this report, this research has not gone much beyond defining life cycles in terms of family age and size. Life cycle stages can be more fruitfully approached by definitions of families of differing compositions—e.g., only adults, families with small children, and so on.

Many of the dwelling unit characteristics which played so large a role in the analysis of complaints were only crude measures of differences between dwellings. For example, very often one family in complaining about space may mean that it needed another bedroom while another family may be referring to a need for a larger living room.

The design aspects of dwelling units need to be given a more specific formulation. Homes differ in the way in which their designers have molded space into rooms, corridors, and so on. Two units with the same cubic volume may be quite differently regarded by the same family because one design may fulfill while the other frustrates its needs. What are the essential design aspects?

Further attention should be given to ways of objectively measuring a dwelling's relevant qualities. In this study the only "objective" aspect of dwelling units used was the number of rooms they contained. It is entirely possible to work out ways in which an investigator may characterize a dwelling according to volume, design, and other relevant attributes.

In presenting the results attained through reason analysis, it was shown that many of the things the households were looking for when they searched for new homes need to be made explicit. Many of the more crucial desired characteristics were held as tacit assumptions by the households.

The accounting scheme which guided the reason analysis could also be elaborated to take into account elements which were omitted in this study. For example, it is not possible to understand with the information contained in this study why the families ended up in homes located where they were. Certainly equivalent dwellings in other areas must have been also available. What are the mechanisms whereby a household only gets to know about dwellings available within relatively circumscribed areas of the city?

NEW DIRECTIONS FOR RESEARCH

The research reported here did not cover all of the important aspects of mobility. Some topics were deliberately omitted because the study design did not lend itself easily to analyses of that sort; other topics appeared to be of importance only during the course of the analysis of these data.

Perhaps the most seriously neglected aspect of mobility is its spatial patterning. For example, the reason analysis presented in Part III accounts for why the households moved and why they made particular choices in new dwellings, but does not account for the spatial patterning of those choices. Nor is the overall patterning of shifts within a city touched upon, except in the most tangential fashion. Of course, the spatial patterning of mobility has received considerable attention in previous studies. Particularly noteworthy in this regard has been the important formulation of Samuel A. Stouffer.[1] Few of these studies have considered the social psychological aspects of spatial patterning and this dimension might well deserve the attention of future research.

In this study we have treated households as if their conceptions of housing were identical. There is enough known about the value differences among the various social classes and ethnic groupings in America to suspect that housing means somewhat different things to different segments of the American public.[2] For example, among some groups, family life centers about the kitchen, where the family eats, listens to the radio or looks at television, and spends most of its time. In other groups, the center of family life may be the living room. Different kinds of housing requirements flow from these contrasting orientations to the dwelling. Other value differences undoubtedly have their housing implications and will explain the differences in sensitivity to housing displayed by different classes and subcultural groups.

Residential mobility is often the spatial expression of vertical social mobility. As families rise in social class position, they often change their residence to accord with their class destination. Inferential data on this aspect of mobility were shown in this study; more direct research is necessary to show the extent of this type of movement and its significance for the American social structure.

Much of the concern of this research was with the relatively recent mobility of households. We studied what the households were going to do in the near future, and also what they had done in the very recent past. An attempt to study the past mobility histories of the families in the sample turned out to be unfruitful. Despite our failure, this topic still remains of considerable importance. What are the differences between households which have been extremely stable in the past and those which have been extremely mobile? Does mobility have an effect upon families which have changed residences a more than usual amount? Are mobile people isolated people without social contacts? Does mobility at some particular life cycle stage have a deleterious effect upon the social adjustment of children?

NOTES

1. Samuel A. Stouffer "Intervening Opportunities: A Theory Relating Mobility and Distance," *Amer. Socio. Review,* V, No. 6, December 1940.

2. A noteworthy step in this direction is the following article on the variant meanings of home ownership: Irving Rosow "Home Ownership Motives," *Amer. Socio. Review,* XIII, 6, Dec. 1948.

APPENDIX

CONSTRUCTION OF COMPLAINTS INDEXES

The data on which the complaints indexes (used in Chapters 3 and 5) are based consist of the answers to 14 questions concerning the respondent's satisfaction with, dissatisfaction with, or indifference to different aspects of his dwelling unit. The texts of the questions were as follows: "Now, about this place, by and large, would you say you were satisfied with, dissatisfied with or doesn't it matter to you about. . . ."

Proportion
Dissatisfied

22%	The amount of room
12	The amount of privacy
33	The amount of closet space
16	The heating equipment
23	The street noises
15	The amount of air and sunlight
15	The rent (maintenance and carrying charges)
28	The amount of open space around the house.

"How about the location of this house (apartment)—are you satisfied with, dissatisfied with or doesn't it matter to you about. . . ."

6	The travel conditions to work
13	The kinds of schools around here
7	The kind of people around here
9	The shopping facilities
15	Nearness to church
15	Nearness to friends and relatives.

(100% equals 924)

The proportions of persons registering dissatisfaction (or "complaints") are given in the column of percentages to the right of each question. Note that in no case does a majority of the respondents complain about any one aspect of their dwellings: The highest percentage (33%) concerns closet space and the lowest (6%) concerns "travel conditions to work."[1]

In using this battery of questions, our purpose was to obtain a measure of the respondents' dissatisfaction with their homes and neighborhoods. We were also interested in whether different dimensions of dissatisfaction could be discerned and whether or not some dimensions of dissatisfaction were more important than others in generating mobility desires. We wanted to rank the respondents according to their degree of dissatisfaction and at the same time learn something about the separate elements which make up dissatisfaction with the dwelling.

In short, two problems concerned us in combining these responses: How to combine answers to the various questions so that different kinds of dissatisfaction could be measured and how these different kinds of dissatisfaction might be characterized.

The logic of the procedure employed was patterned after those of latent structure analysis, developed by Professor Paul F. Lazarsfeld of Columbia University.[2] Essentially, the procedure was to inspect the interrelationships among complaints. Complaints which were highly correlated with each other but poorly correlated with other complaints were grouped together into separate indexes. Complaints which did not clearly fall into one or another of these clusters were either dropped from consideration or left to form separate indexes by themselves. The resulting indexes were then each identified by the name which best seemed to characterize the common elements in the several complaints which were combined to make up the index.

The starting point of the index construction was a matrix showing the interrelationships between the 14 complaints included in the battery of questions. Each cell in this matrix (reproduced here as Table A1) contains a value[3] whose size and sign indicate the nature of the relationship between the complaints represented in the column and the row which intersect to form that cell.

The complaints are so arranged in Table A1 that the cross-products between complaints in adjacent columns tend to be higher than the cross-products between those complaints and other complaints shown in the tables. Boxes have been drawn around those groups of cross-products which indicate that the complaints included within those boxes are especially highly interrelated (in comparison with other cross-products involving those complaints). The reader is invited to inspect this arrangement to see for himself whether our judgments concerning the relative sizes of these cross-products are justified.

Note that two of the complaints (represented in the last two columns and rows)—costs and schools—are not fitted into any of the boxes superimposed upon the matrix. Complaints about schools, although showing a few high relationships with other complaints, were omitted from consideration as a

TABLE A1 Complaints Cross-Products Matrix

	Room	Privacy	Closet	Heating	Noise	Air	Open Space	People	Friends & Relatives	Travel	Church	Shopping	Costs	Schools
Room														
Privacy	0476													
Closet	0767	0373												
Heating	0279	0165	0393											
Noise	0262	0269	0327	0179										
Air	0279	0150	0330	0199	0211									
Open Space	0414	0293	0575	0256	0419	0458								
People	0282	0288	0222	0192	0376	0124	0201							
Friends & Rels.	0236	0133	0187	0203	0244	0180	0132	0303						
Travel	0059	0110	0040	0013	0035	0056	0111	0154	0161					
Church	0054	0031	0087	0015	0052	0007	0068	0032	0197	0110				
Shopping	0005	0041	0035	0016	-0017	-0030	0079	0013	0075	0154	0059			
Costs	0270	0129	0151	0136	0310	0091	0136	0158	0117	0079	0018	-0018		
Schools	0161	0103	0100	0122	0074	0034	0086	0151	0085	0050	0019	0016	0077	

component of the various indexes because it was relevant only for a rather limited segment of the sample—families with children of school age. The correlations of complaints about costs with other complaints turned out to be somewhat irregular. Accordingly, a judgment was made that this complaint defines a dimension by itself and was treated as a separate kind of complaint about housing.

Each cluster of highly interrelated complaints was judged to define a separate dimension of dissatisfaction. The resulting combinations, along with the designations we gave to them, are as follows:

    I: Dwelling Unit Space Complaints: Consisting of complaints about . . .
        Room
        Privacy
        Closet Space
   II: Utilities Complaints: Consisting of complaints about . . .
        Heating equipment
        Closet space
  III: Physical Environment Complaints: Consisting of complaints about . . .
        Air and sunlight
        Street noises
        Open space around the house
  IV: Social Environment Complaints: Consisting of complaints about . . .
        Kind of people around here
        Nearness to friends and relatives
    V: Distance Complaints: Consisting of complaints about . . .
        Nearness to friends and relatives
        Travel conditions to work
        Nearness to church
        Shopping facilities
  VI: Housing Costs Complaints; Consisting of complaints about . . .
        Rent or maintenance and carrying charges.

It should be noted that two complaints participate in more than one complaints index. "Closet space" participated in both "Space Complaints" and the "Utilities Complaints." "Nearness to friends and relatives" plays a part in both "Social Environment Complaints" and "Location Complaints." These are complaints which apparently participate in two dimensions of satisfaction. Their double participation is indicated by the high relationships which they have with each of the indexes in which they participate.

Once the dimensions were identified by inspection of the matrix shown in Table A1, scores were devised for each dimension. These scores each consisted of the number of complaints given by each person in response to the questions making up that dimension. Thus a respondent who complained about "closet space," "room," and "privacy" received a score of three on the Dwelling Unit Space Complaints Index. Six scores were computed for each respondent and used in the manner indicated in Chapters 3 and 5.

A "Combined Complaints Index" was then constructed according to the procedures outlined in Chapter 5. This procedure was essentially to count the number of complaints registered by each respondent in those dimensions which correlated significantly with moving desires.

NOTES

1. For a few dwelling unit aspects the "indifferent" responses ("it doesn't matter to me") reached rather high levels. The six highest indifference proportions were as follows:

Street noises	16%
Travel to work	10%
Kind of schools around here	41%
Kind of people around he	9%
Nearness to church	8%
Nearness to friends and relatives	15%

Especially significant is the large proportion of persons registering indifference to the quality of neighborhood schools, particularly in view of the emphasis placed on the elementary school as the integrating neighborhood institution in some planning philosophies.

2. The technically inclined reader is referred to the following publication for a more detailed account of this new technique: Stouffer, S.A., et al. *Studies in Social Psychology in World War II*, Volume 4, *Measurement and Prediction* Princeton, Princeton University Press, 1950, Chapters 9, 10 and 11.

3. The values (known as "cross-products") are defined as follows: A cross-product [i j] between complaint i and complaint j is

$$[i\,j] = P_{ij} - P_i P_j,$$

where P_{ij} is the proportion registering *both* complaints i and j; P_i is the proportion registering complaint i; and P_j is the proportion registering complaint j.

REFERENCES FOR
THE SECOND EDITION

ALBIG, W. (1933) "The mobility of urban populations." Social Forces 11.

BRADBURN, N. M., S. SUDMAN, and G. L. GOCKEL (1971) Side by Side: Integrated Neighborhoods in America. Skokie, IL: AVC.

BROWN, L. A., F. W. Horton, and R. I. WITTICK (1970) "On place utility and the normative allocation of intra-urban migrants." Demography 7: 175-183.

BROWN, L. A. and D. B. LONGBRAKE (1970) "Migration flows in intraurban space: place utility considerations." Annals of the Association of American Geographers 60: 368-384.

CAMPBELL, A., P. CONVERSE, and W. L. RODGERS (1976) The Quality of American Life. New York: Russell Sage Foundation.

CHUDACOFF, H. P. (1972) Mobile Americans: Residential and Social Mobility in Omaha 1880-1920. New York: Oxford University Press.

CLARK, W.A.V., J. O. HUFF, and J. E. BURT (1979) "Calibrating a model of the decision to move." Environment and Planning 11: 689-704.

CLARK, W.A.V. and E. G. MOORE [eds.] (1978) Population Mobility and Residential Change (Studies in Geography 25). Chicago: Northwestern University.

COLEMAN, J. S., S. P. KELLY, and J. MOORE (1974) Trends in School Segregation. Washington, DC: Urban Institute.

COLEMAN, R. D. and L. RAINWATER (1978) Social Standing in America. New York: Basic Books.

CRONIN, F. J. (1979) Low Income Households' Search for Housing: Preliminary Findings on Racial Differences. Washington, DC: Urban Institute.

DaVANZO, J. (1977) Why Families Move: A Model of the Geographic Mobility of Married Couples (U.S. Department of Labor, R & D Monograph 48). Washington, DC: Government Printing Office.

DUNCAN, G. and S. NEWMAN (1975) "People as planners: the fulfillment of residential mobility expectations," in J. N. Morgan and G. N. Duncan (eds.), Five Thousand American Families (vol. 3). Ann Arbor: University of Michigan, Institute for Social Research.

FARIS, R.E.L. and W. H. DUNHAM (1939) Mental Disorders in Urban Areas. Chicago: University of Chicago Press.

FOLLAIN, J. R. and S. MALPESSI (1979) Dissecting Housing Value and Rent: Estimates of Hedonic Indexes for Thirty Nine Large SMSAs. Washington, DC: Urban Institute.

FOOTE, N. N., J. ABU-LOGOD, M. M. FOLEY, and L. WINNICK (1960) Housing Choices and Housing Constraints. New York: McGraw-Hill.

FREDLAND, D. R. (1974) Residential Mobility and Home Purchase. Lexington, MA: Lexington.

GINSBURG, R. B. (1978) "Probability models of residence histories: analysis of times between moves," in W.A.V. Clark and E. G. Moore (eds.), Population Mobility and Residential Change (Studies in Geography 25). Chicago: Northwestern University.

GLICK, P. (1947) "The family cycle." American Sociological Review 12.

GOLDSTEIN, S. and K. MAYER (1963) Residential Mobility, Migration and Commuting in Rhode Island. Providence, RI: Development Council.

GOODMAN, J. (1974) "Local residential mobility and family housing adjustments," in J. N. Morgan (ed.), Five Thousand Families—Patterns of Economic Progress (vol 2). Ann Arbor: University of Michigan, Institute for Social Research.

GREEN, H. W. (1934) Movements of Families Within the Cleveland Metropolitan District (Report 3). Cleveland, OH: Real Property Inventory of Metropolitan Cleveland.

HENRY, A. F. and J. F. SHORT, Jr. (1954) Suicide and Homicide. New York: Macmillan.

HOLLINGSHEAD, A. B. (1949) Elmtown's Youth. New York: John Wiley.

HUFF, J. O. and W.A.V. CLARK (1978) "The role of stationarity in Markov and opportunity models of intraurban migration," in W.A.V. Clark and E. G. Moore (eds.), Population Mobility and Residential Change (Studies in Geography 25). Chicago: Northwestern University.

KAIN, J. F. and J. M. QUIGLEY (1975) Housing Markets and Racial Discrimination. New York: National Bureau of Economic Research.

LANSING, J. B. and L. KISH (1957) "Family life cycle as an independent variable." American Sociological Review.

LANSING, J. B. and E. MUELLER (1969) The Geographic Mobility of Labor. Ann Arbor: University of Michigan, Institute for Social Research.

MacMILLAN, J. (1978) Draft Report on Mobility in the Housing Allowance Demand Experiment. Cambridge, MA: Abt Associates.

McCARTHY, K. (1979) Housing Search and Mobility. Santa Monica, CA: Rand.

MICHELSON, W. (1977) Environmental Choice, Human Behavior and Residential Satisfaction. New York: Oxford University Press.

MOORE, E. G. (1978) "The impact of residential mobility on population characteristics at the neighborhood level," in W.A.V. Clark and E. G. Moore (eds.), Population Mobility and Residential Change (Studies in Geography 25). Chicago: Northwestern University.

——— (1971) "Comments on the use of ecological models in the study of residential mobility in the city." Economic Geography 47: 73-83.

MORGAN, J. [ed.] (1974-1975) Five Thousand American Families—Patterns of Economic Progress (vols. 1-3). Ann Arbor: University of Michigan, Institute for Social Research.

PACKARD, V. (1977) A Nation of Strangers. New York: David McKay.

PARK, R. E. (1967) "The city as social laboratory," in R. H. Turner (ed.), Robert E. Park on Social Control and Collective Behavior. Chicago: University of Chicago Press.

QUIGLEY, J. M. and D. H. WEINBERG (1977) "Intra-urban residential mobility: a review and synthesis." International Regional Science Review 2: 41-66.

Rand Corporation (1978) Fourth Annual Report of the Housing Assistance Supply Experiment. Santa Monica, CA: Author.

RIST, R. C. [ed.] (1976) The Desegregation Literature: A Critical Appraisal. Washington, DC: Government Printing Office.

ROSSI, P. H. and K. Lyall (1974) Reforming Public Welfare. New York: Russell Sage Foundation.

SHAW, C. R. and H. D. McKAY (1942) Juvenile Delinquency and Urban Areas. Chicago: University of Chicago Press.

SIMMEL, G. (1950) "The metropolis and urban life," in K. H. Wolf (trans.). The Sociology of Georg Simmel. New York: Macmillan.

SIMMONS, J. W. (1968) "Changing residence in the city: a review of intra-urban mobility." Geographical Review 58: 622-650.

SPEARE, A., S. GOLDSTEIN, and W. H. FREY (1974) Residential Mobility, Migration and Metropolitan Change. Cambridge, MA: Ballinger.

STOUFFER, S. A. (1940) "Intervening opportunities: a theory relating mobility and distance." American Sociological Review 5(December).

THOMAS, C. (1979) Mobility in the Seattle and Denver Income Maintenance Experiments. Denver, CO: Mathematics Police Research.

U.S. Bureau of the Census (1973-1976) Annual Housing Survey, Part D: Characteristics of Recent Movers. Washington, DC: Government Printing Office.

WARNER, W. L., M. MEEKER, and K. EELS (1949) Social Class in America. Chicago: Science Research Associates.

WEINBERG, D. H. (1975) "Intra-urban household mobility: a microeconomic study of San Francisco Bay Area Households." Ph.D. dissertation, Yale University.

——— J. FRIEDMAN, and S. K. MAYO (1979) A Disequilibrium Model of Housing Search and Residential Mobility. Cambridge, MA: Abt Associates.

WIRTH, L. (1964) "Urbanism as a way of life," in A. J. Reiss, Jr. (ed.), Louis Wirth on Cities and Social Life. Chicago: University of Chicago Press.

WOLPERT, J. (1965) "Behavioral aspects of the decision to migrate." Papers of the Regional Science Association 15.

ZIMMER, B. (1973) "Residential mobility and housing." Land Economics 43: 344-350.

ABOUT THE AUTHOR

PETER H. ROSSI is currently Professor of Sociology and Director of the Social and Demographic Research Center at the University of Massachusetts—Amherst. He has been on the faculties of Harvard University, Johns Hopkins University, and the University of Chicago, where he also served as Director of the National Opinion Research Center. He has been a consultant on research methods and evaluation to (among others) the National Science Foundation, National Institute of Mental Health, the Federal Trade Commission, and the Russell Sage Foundation. His research has largely been concerned with the application of social research methods to social issues and he is currently engaged in research on natural disasters and criminal justice. His most recent works include *EVALUATION: A Systematic Approach* (with H. E. Freeman and S. R. Wright), *EVALUATING SOCIAL PROGRAMS* (with W. Williams), *REFORMING PUBLIC WELFARE* (with K. Lyall), and *PRISON REFORM AND STATE ELITES* (with R. A. Berk). Professor Rossi is currently coeditor of *SOCIAL SCIENCE RESEARCH.* He is currently (1979-1980) serving as president of the American Sociological Association.